Math Starters!

Other Math Books by the Muschlas

The Algebra Teacher's Guide to Reteaching Essential Concepts and Skills: 150 Mini-Lessons for Correcting Common Mistakes

Algebra Teacher's Activities Kit: 150 Ready-to-Use Activities with Real-World Applications

Geometry Teacher's Activities Kit: Ready-to-Use Lessons & Worksheets for Grades 6–12

Hands-On Math Projects with Real-Life Applications, Grades 3–5

Hands-On Math Projects with Real-Life Applications, Grades 6–12, Second Edition

Math Games: 180 Reproducible Activities to Motivate, Excite, and Challenge Students, Grades 6–12

Math Smart! Over 220 Ready-to-Use Activities to Motivate & Challenge Students, Grades 6–12

The Math Teacher's Book of Lists, Second Edition

The Math Teacher's Problem-a-Day, Grades 4–8: Over 180 Reproducible Pages of Quick Skill Builders

Math Teacher's Survival Guide: Practical Strategies, Management Techniques, and Reproducibles for New and Experienced Teachers, Grades 5–12

Teaching the Common Core Math Standards with Hands-On Activities, Grades 6–8

Second Edition

Math Starters!

5- to 10-Minute Activities
Aligned with the Common Core
Math Standards, Grades 6-12

Judith A. Muschla, Gary Robert Muschla,
and Erin Muschla-Berry

JB JOSSEY-BASS™
A Wiley Brand

Cover image: © imagezoo/Getty
Cover design: JPuda

Published by Jossey-Bass
A Wiley Brand
One Montgomery Street, Suite 1200, San Francisco, CA 94104-4594—www.josseybass.com

Jossey-Bass books and products are available through most bookstores. To contact Jossey-Bass directly call our Customer Care Department within the U.S. at 800-956-7739, outside the U.S. at 317-572-3986, or fax 317-572-4002.

Wiley publishes in a variety of print and electronic formats and by print-on-demand. Some material included with standard print versions of this book may not be included in e-books or in print-on-demand. If this book refers to media such as a CD or DVD that is not included in the version you purchased, you may download this material at http://booksupport.wiley.com. For more information about Wiley products, visit www.wiley.com.

Library of Congress Cataloging-in-Publication Data

Muschla, Judith A.
   Math starters : 5- to 10-minute activities aligned with the common core math standards, grades 6-12. -- Second
  edition / Judith A. Muschla, Gary Robert Muschla, and Erin Muschla-Berry.
      pages cm
   Includes bibliographical references.
  ISBN 978-1-118-44979-0 (pbk.); ISBN 978-1-118-69064-2 (ebk.); ISBN 978-1-118-69074-1 (ebk.)
 1. Mathematics--Study and teaching (Elementary) 2. Mathematics--Study and teaching (Secondary)
I. Muschla, Gary Robert, author. II. Muschla-Berry, Erin, author. III. Title.
  QA135.6.M867 2013
  510.71′273--dc23

             2013020214

Printed in the United States of America
SECOND EDITION
PB Printing   10 9 8 7 6 5 4 3 2

CONTENTS

About the Authors

Judith A. Muschla received her BA in mathematics from Douglass College at Rutgers University and is certified to teach K–12. She taught mathematics in South River, New Jersey, for over twenty-five years at various levels at both South River High School and South River Middle School. As a team leader at the middle school, she wrote several math curriculums, coordinated interdisciplinary units, and conducted mathematics workshops for teachers and parents.

Together, Judith and Gary Muschla have coauthored a number of math books published by Jossey-Bass: *Hands-on Math Projects with Real-Life Applications, Grades 3–5* (2009); *The Math Teacher's Problem-a-Day, Grades 4–8* (2008); *Hands-On Math Projects with Real-Life Applications, Grades 6–12* (1996; second edition, 2006); *The Math Teacher's Book of Lists* (1995; second edition, 2005); *Math Games: 180 Reproducible Activities to Motivate, Excite, and Challenge Students, Grades 6–12* (2004); *Algebra Teacher's Activities Kit* (2003); *Math Smart! Over 220 Ready-to-Use Activities to Motivate and Challenge Students, Grades 6–12* (2002); *Geometry Teacher's Activities Kit* (2000); and *Math Starters! 5- to 10-Minute Activities to Make Kids Think, Grades 6–12* (1999).

Gary Robert Muschla received his BA and MAT from Trenton State College and taught in Spotswood, New Jersey, for more than twenty-five years at the elementary school level. In addition to math resources, he has written several resources for English and writing teachers, all published by Jossey-Bass; among them are *Writing Workshop Survival Kit* (1993; second edition, 2005); *The Writing Teacher's Book of Lists* (1991; second edition, 2004); *Ready-to Use Reading Proficiency Lessons and Activities, 10th Grade Level* (2003); *Ready-to-Use Reading Proficiency Lessons and Activities, 8th Grade Level* (2002); *Ready-to-Use Reading Proficiency Lessons and Activities, 4th Grade Level* (2002); *Reading Workshop Survival Kit* (1997); and *English Teacher's Great Books Activities Kit* (1994).

Erin Muschla-Berry received her BS and MEd from The College of New Jersey. She is certified to teach grades K–8 with mathematics specialization in grades 5–8. She currently teaches math at Monroe Township Middle School in Monroe, New Jersey, and has presented workshops for math teachers for the Association of Mathematics Teachers of New Jersey. She has coauthored four books with Judith and Gary Muschla for Jossey-Bass: *Teaching the Common Core Math Standards with Hands-On Activities, Grades 6–8* (2012); *The Algebra Teacher's Guide to Reteaching Essential Concepts and Skills* (2011); *Math Teacher's Survival Guide, Grades 5–12* (2010); and *The Elementary Teacher's Book of Lists* (2010).

Acknowledgments

For their support, we thank Jeff Corey Gorman, EdD, assistant superintendent of Monroe Township Public Schools, and these colleagues at the Monroe Township Middle School: Chari Chanley, principal; James Higgins, vice principal; and Scott Sidler, vice principal.

We also thank Kate Bradford, our editor at Jossey-Bass, for her guidance and suggestions on yet another book.

Special thanks to Diane Turso, our proofreader, for her efforts in putting the final polish on our work.

Our thanks to Geraldine Misiewicz, former math supervisor at South River High School, for her many helpful suggestions on the original edition of this book, which we have carried over to this new edition.

Thanks to Maria Steffero, EdD, for sharing her insights on math instruction and her continued support.

We also appreciate the support of our many colleagues who have encouraged us in our work over the years.

And, of course, we acknowledge the many students we have had the satisfaction of teaching.

About This Book

One of the most efficient and effective ways to start your math classes is with a starter problem. Math starters can help you get your students working from the moment they sit down in your classroom.

Math Starters! 5- to 10-Minute Activities Aligned with the Common Core Math Standards, Grades 6–12, Second Edition, is divided into two parts. Part 1, "Making Math Starters Part of Your Program," contains practical information that will help you implement and evaluate math starters in your classes. Part 2, "Math Starters," contains eight sections with a total of 662 problems. An answer key concludes the book.

Although this new edition follows the same general structure as the original edition did, we have thoroughly updated the material. Many problems have been revised, some have been retired, and new problems have been added. Because today's students are digital natives, some of the new problems incorporate the use of math websites, such as the National Library of Virtual Manipulatives at http://nlvm.usu.edu/en/nav /vlibrary.html. An important feature of this new edition is the identification of problems that support the Common Core State Math Standards for grades 6 to 12. Every standard is supported by at least one problem, and many are supported by two or more. Many other problems address prerequisite skills related to specific standards. The number and diversity of the problems throughout this book will help you meet the needs of the various abilities and learning styles of your students.

In part 1, we provide ideas for classroom management, tips on how to organize cooperative groups for math starters that are specifically designed for group work, and various methods for evaluation. We include in this part guidance that will support the efforts of your students as they work on the math starters in this book; for example, "Problem-Solving Strategies" and "Rules for Working in Teams on Math Starters." Overall, this part will help you implement math starters effectively. We recommend that you read through part 1 before using the problems with your students.

Part 2 is divided into eight sections.

Section 1, "Whole Numbers and Integers: Theory and Operations," has 80 problems that focus on topics such as whole numbers, place value, basic operations, division rules, multiples, factors, order of operations, expressions with exponents, the coordinate plane, absolute value, and operations with integers.

Section 2, "Rational Numbers: Fractions, Decimals, and Percents," contains 120 problems on topics including equivalent fractions, operations with fractions, place value with decimals, operations with decimals, ratios, proportional relationships, percents, complex fractions, operations with positive and negative fractions, operations with positive and negative decimals, and scientific notation.

Section 3, "Algebra and Beyond," contains 132 problems on topics such as expressions, equations, inequalities, square and cube roots, systems of equations, monomials, binomials, polynomials, factoring, rational expressions, and the quadratic formula.

Section 4, "Functions," contains 41 problems on topics such as domain, range, linear functions, graphs, exponential functions, inverses, and trigonometric functions.

Section 5, "Geometry," has 134 problems on topics including lines, segments, rays, angles, triangles, the Pythagorean theorem, rotations, reflections, translations, congruency, polygons, quadrilaterals, dilations, similarity, area, trigonometric ratios, circles, circumference, three-dimensional figures, volume, and surface area.

Section 6, "Statistics, Probability, and Data Analysis," has 65 problems on topics that include mean, median, mode, graphs, numerical data, probability, scatter plots, correlations, surveys, the permutations rule, the combinations rule, two-way frequency tables, and probability distribution.

Section 7, "Number and Quantity," contains 32 problems that focus on topics such as imaginary numbers, complex numbers, powers of i, the complex plane, vectors, and matrices.

Section 8, "Potpourri," contains 58 problems that include topics such as special kinds of numbers, measurement—customary and metric, time, temperature, palindromes, number ciphers, Roman numerals, figural analogies, figurate numbers, numerical patterns, symmetry, networks, and digraphs.

Each problem stands alone and is numbered according to section. For example, problem 2-61, "Order of Operations—Decimals," is the sixty-first problem in section 2; problem 3-83, "Generating Pythagorean Triples," is the eighty-third problem in section 3; and problem 6-19, "The Probability of Impossible and Certain Events," is the nineteenth problem in section 6. The titles of the problems focus on the topic, concept, or skill the problem addresses, making the Contents pages useful as a list of topics, concepts, and skills.

Problems are designated by one, two, or three stars: one star indicates a basic problem, two stars identify a more difficult problem, and three stars denote a challenging problem. Often several problems address a specific topic, concept, or skill with increasing degree of difficulty. Problems applicable to group work are marked with a **G**, and those that require use of the Internet are marked with a 💻 symbol.

Many of the problems support the Common Core State Math Standards; they are identified by the number of the standard they support. Because the topics, concepts, and skills in each section generally follow a sequence common to typical math curriculums and not the order of the standards of the Common Core (which is not to be interpreted as a curriculum), problems supporting the standards do not necessarily follow the numerical order of the standards. Moreover, because some standards address material that often requires multiple class periods of instruction, problems supporting these standards usually focus on an aspect of the particular standard. To make it easy to find problems that support specific standards, a Standards and Problems Chart is included.

A note on modeling: Modeling is an important area in mathematics and a topic of the high school standards. Because modeling is interpreted best in relation to other standards, many problems in this book incorporate modeling in conjunction with other skills.

We suggest that you select the problems that best contribute to your program. Beginning each class with a math starter will help you to make the most effective use of your class time.

Our best wishes to you for a successful and rewarding school year.

Judith A. Muschla
Gary Robert Muschla
Erin Muschla-Berry

Standards and Problems Chart

The following chart contains the standards and the problems that support them.

Standards	Problem Numbers
Sixth Grade	
6.RP.1	2-62, 2-63
6.RP.2	2-42
6.RP.3	2-53, 2-64, 2-76, 2-77, 2-78, 2-79, 2-81
6.NS.1	2-22, 2-23, 2-24, 2-25, 2-26, 2-27
6.NS.2	1-14, 1-15, 1-16
6.NS.3	2-43, 2-44, 2-45, 2-46, 2-47, 2-48, 2-49, 2-50, 2-51, 2-52, 2-59, 2-60, 2-61, 2-68, 2-69
6.NS.4	1-27, 1-30, 1-31, 1-32
6.NS.5	1-47, 1-48, 1-49
6.NS.6	1-50, 1-51, 1-58, 1-59
6.NS.7	1-52, 1-53, 1-56, 1-57
6.NS.8	1-60
6.EE.1	1-41, 1-42, 1-43, 1-44, 3-1, 3-2, 3-3
6.EE.2	3-4, 3-5, 3-6, 3-7, 3-8
6.EE.3	3-9, 3-10
6.EE.4	3-11, 3-12
6.EE.5	3-13, 3-14
6.EE.6	3-15, 3-16
6.EE.7	3-17, 3-18, 3-19, 3-20, 3-21, 3-22
6.EE.8	3-23, 3-24
6.EE.9	3-25
6.G.1	5-65, 5-87
6.G.2	5-121, 5-122
6.G.3	5-12
6.G.4	5-123
6.SP.1	6-1
6.SP.2	6-2
6.SP.3	6-8, 6-9
6.SP.4	6-10
6.SP.5	6-14

Seventh Grade	
7.RP.1	2-67
7.RP.2	2-65, 2-66, 2-80, 2-82, 2-84
7.RP.3	2-88, 2-89, 2-90, 2-91, 2-92
7.NS.1	1-61, 1-62, 1-63, 1-64, 1-65, 1-66, 2-93, 2-94, 2-95, 2-96, 2-97, 2-98, 2-99, 2-100, 2-104, 2-105
7.NS.2	1-67, 1-68, 1-69, 1-70, 1-71, 1-72, 2-37, 2-38, 2-75, 2-106, 2-107, 3-28
7.NS.3	1-73, 1-74, 1-75, 2-101, 2-102, 2-103, 2-108
7.EE.1	3-26
7.EE.2	2-86, 3-27
7.EE.3	1-17, 1-18, 1-19, 2-28, 2-29, 2-39, 2-40, 2-54, 2-55, 2-56, 2-57, 2-58
7.EE.4	3-29, 3-30
7.G.1	5-64
7.G.2	5-24
7.G.3	5-118
7.G.4	5-96, 5-97, 5-98, 5-99, 5-100
7.G.5	5-10
7.G.6	5-89, 5-90, 5-91, 5-92, 5-124, 5-125, 5-126
7.SP.1	6-15
7.SP.2	6-16
7.SP.3	6-17
7.SP.4	6-18
7.SP.5	6-19
7.SP.6	6-21, 6-22
7.SP.7	6-23, 6-24
7.SP.8	6-25
Eighth Grade	
8.NS.1	2-109, 2-110, 2-111
8.NS.2	2-112, 2-115
8.EE.1	2-113, 2-114
8.EE.2	2-115, 3-31
8.EE.3	1-77, 1-78, 2-116, 2-117
8.EE.4	1-79, 2-118
8.EE.5	3-32
8.EE.6	3-33
8.EE.7	3-41, 3-42, 3-43, 3-44
8.EE.8	3-45, 3-46, 3-47, 3-48, 3-49, 3-50
8.F.1	4-1, 4-2
8.F.2	4-3
8.F.3	4-4, 4-5

8.F.4	4-6
8.F.5	4-7, 4-8
8.G.1	5-35
8.G.2	5-36, 5-37, 5-38
8.G.3	5-55
8.G.4	5-56
8.G.5	5-9
8.G.6	5-26
8.G.7	5-25, 5-27
8.G.8	5-28
8.G.9	5-127, 5-128
8.SP.1	6-26
8.SP.2	6-27
8.SP.3	6-29
8.SP.4	6-30
High School— Algebra	
A-SSE.1	3-60
A-SSE.2	3-56, 3-69
A-SSE.3	3-70, 3-71, 3-72, 3-74, 3-76
A-SSE.4	3-79
A-APR.1	3-62, 3-63, 3-64, 3-65, 3-66, 3-67
A-APR.2	3-80
A-APR.3	3-81, 3-82
A-APR.4	3-83
A-APR.5	3-84
A-APR.6	3-85, 3-86, 3-87, 3-88
A-APR.7	3-89, 3-90, 3-91, 3-92, 3-93, 3-94
A-CED.1	3-129
A-CED.2	3-130
A-CED.3	3-131
A-CED.4	3-107, 3-114
A-REI.1	3-95, 3-96
A-REI.2	3-97, 3-98, 3-99, 3-101, 3-102, 3-103, 3-104, 3-105, 3-106
A-REI.3	3-108, 3.109
A-REI.4	3-68, 3-110, 3-112, 3-113, 3-115, 3-116, 3-117, 3-118, 3-119, 3-120
A-REI.5	3-121
A-REI.6	3-51
A-REI.7	3-122
A-REI.8	3-123

A-REI.9	3-124, 3-125
A-REI.10	3-126
A-REI.11	3-127
A-REI.12	3-128
High School — Functions	
F-IF.1	4-9
F-IF.2	4-10
F-IF.3	4-11
F-IF.4	4-12
F-IF.5	4-13
F-IF.6	4-14
F-IF.7	4-15, 4-16
F-IF.8	4-17, 4-18
F-IF.9	4-19
F-BF.1	4-20
F-BF.2	4-21
F-BF.3	4-22, 4-23
F-BF.4	4-24, 4-25
F-BF.5	4-26
F-LE.1	4-27
F-LE.2	4-28
F-LE.3	4-29
F-LE.4	4-30
F-LE.5	4-31
F-TF.1	4-32
F-TF.2	4-33
F-TF.3	4-34
F-TF.4	4-35
F-TF.5	4-36
F-TF.6	4-37
F-TF.7	4-38
F-TF.8	4-39
F-TF.9	4-40
High School — Geometry	
G-CO.1	5-39
G-CO.2	5-40, 5-41
G-CO.3	5-42
G-CO.4	5-43

G-CO.5	5-44
G-CO.6	5-45
G-CO.7	5-46
G-CO.8	5-49
G-CO.9	5-50
G-CO.10	5-51
G-CO.11	5-52
G-CO.12	5-53
G-CO.13	5-54
G-SRT.1	5-57
G-SRT.2	5-58
G-SRT.3	5-59
G-SRT.4	5-62
G-SRT.5	5-63
G-SRT.6	5-68
G-SRT.7	5-69
G-SRT.8	5-70
G-SRT.9	5-71
G-SRT.10	5-72
G-SRT.11	5-73, 5-74
G-C.1	5-101
G-C.2	5-103, 5-104, 5-106, 5-108
G-C.3	5-110
G-C.4	5-111
G-C.5	5-114
G-PE.1	5-115
G-PE.2	5-116
G-PE.3	5-117
G-PE.4	5-77
G-PE.5	5-81
G-PE.6	5-82
G-PE.7	5-93
G-GMD.1	5-130
G-GMD.2	5-131
G-GMD.3	5-129
G-GMD.4	5-119
G-MG.1	5-120
G-MG.2	5-132
G-MG.3	5-133

High School—Statistics and Probability	
S-ID.1	6-31
S-ID.2	6-32
S-ID.3	6-33
S-ID.4	6-34
S-ID.5	6-35
S-ID.6	6-36
S-ID.7	6-37
S-ID.8	6-38
S-ID.9	6-39
S-IC.1	6-40
S-IC.2	6-41
S-IC.3	6-42
S-IC.4	6-43
S-IC.5	6-44
S-IC.6	6-45
S-CP.1	6-46
S-CP.2	6-47, 6-48
S-CP.3	6-49
S-CP.4	6-50
S-CP.5	6-51
S-CP.6	6-52
S-CP.7	6-53
S-CP.8	6-54
S-CP.9	6-56, 6-57
S-MD.1	6-58
S-MD.2	6-59
S-MD.3	6-60
S-MD.4	6-61
S-MD.5	6-62
S-MD.6	6-63
S-MD.7	6-64
High School—Number and Quantity	
N-RN.1	7-1
N-RN.2	7-2
N-RN.3	7-3

N-Q.1	7-4
N-Q.2	7-5
N-Q.3	7-6
N-CN.1	7-7
N-CN.2	7-9
N-CN.3	7-10
N-CN.4	7-11
N-CN.5	7-12
N-CN.6	7-13
N-CN.7	7-14
N-CN.8	7-15
N-CN.9	7-16
N-VM.1	7-17
N-VM.2	7-18
N-VM.3	7-19
N-VM.4	7-20
N-VM.5	7-21
N-VM.6	7-22
N-VM.7	7-23
N-VM.8	7-24, 7-25
N-VM.9	7-26
N-VM.10	7-27
N-VM.11	7-29, 7-30
N-VM.12	7-31

Math Starters!

PART 1

Making
Math Starters
Part of Your Program

The first few minutes of all classes are critical. Classes in which students begin working from the moment they take their seats are usually more successful than those in which the first few minutes are lost as the students get settled. This is especially true of math classes, where there always seems to be too much to learn in too little time. For the typical class, losing just five minutes at the beginning of each day adds up to twenty-five minutes per week, or about a full period every two weeks. For the typical school year, that is a loss of twenty periods (or about twenty days of math instruction and learning). When cast in this context, losing "only" five minutes per day is significant. Math starters can help you regain this lost time.

THE VALUE OF MATH STARTERS

A math starter is a problem that students begin working on right after they step into your classroom. The problem is designed to take five to ten minutes, which includes reviewing the answer and conducting any follow-up discussion.

Math starters can be an important part of your program. By being presented with a problem on their arrival to class, students are encouraged to focus on math immediately. These math problems may be used to reinforce previously taught skills, supplement current instruction, or challenge students with new material. When used as a review, math starters can help keep students' skills sharp and give students a sense of success and achievement. When used to supplement current studies, the problems can provide different perspectives or applications of the skills and concepts students are learning. When used to introduce new material, the problems can challenge students by extending their learning horizons.

Using math starters at the beginning of class also supports classroom management. While students are working on the problem, you may take attendance, hand papers back, check homework, or circulate around the room observing your students as they work. These few minutes are valuable because they allow you to interact individually with your students. This is a time when you may note students' strengths and weaknesses; help them master a new skill; or offer encouragement, praise, or a helpful suggestion. Rather than being in front of the class, you become part of the class.

STARTING CLASS WITH A MATH STARTER

You and your students will benefit the most from the math starters in this book if you use the problems regularly at the beginning of class. On the first day of school, as you explain your goals, expectations, and the requirements of your class, tell students that they will be expected to complete a math starter on their arrival to class each day. (Of course, you may prefer not to use a math starter on days of quizzes, tests, or special projects or events.)

You may wish to begin this first class with a math starter, perhaps a review of skills students learned last year. This is a good way to demonstrate the idea and procedure for completing math starters. Be sure to explain the purpose of math starters, why they are valuable, and how you will assess your students' work. (See the "Evaluation" section at the end of this part.)

You may present starter problems using copies, an overhead projector, or a digital projector. Whichever method of delivery you choose, the problems should be readily available to begin the class.

If you prefer to use copies, you might put them on the corner of your desk or another accessible location so that students may take a copy of the problem as soon as they enter the classroom. Students should then go to their seats and start working. This method has several advantages. Students get their work on arriving at class; they are encouraged to sit down and begin working, thus reducing talking and fooling around; and class time is used efficiently. They may solve the problems right on the sheet, reducing the amount of paper the class uses, or you may prefer that they maintain a math-starter notebook for their work (See the next section, "Purpose and Value of a Math-Starter Notebook.")

Alternatively, instead of having students pick up the problems as they enter class, you may distribute them after all students have arrived. This method is ideal if you need to have everyone's attention before the class starts working. As you are handing out copies of the problems, you can give any directions, special instructions, or hints that you feel are necessary.

Using an overhead projector or a digital projector to present math starters eliminates the need for copies. Have the problem displayed on the screen as students enter the classroom and take their seats. While they may do their work on single sheets of paper, we recommend that students maintain a math-starter notebook, which will contain all of their work on math starters.

To ensure that your students fully benefit from working on math starters, set and maintain a classroom atmosphere that supports learning from the very beginning of class. Students should realize the importance of starting work as soon as they come to class, work in a serious manner, and take pride in their progress in learning math. The atmosphere that is established while they work on math starters will extend into the rest of the class.

PURPOSE AND VALUE OF A MATH-STARTER NOTEBOOK

An excellent way to emphasize the importance of math starters, as well as provide a place in which problems can be saved for future reference, is a math-starter notebook. This notebook will become a type of journal in which students work out starter problems, offer written explanations of solutions when necessary, and keep notes on the problems they solve. You may also encourage them to write down any thoughts, questions, concerns, or ponderings they may have about math. Using a math-starter notebook in this manner can eliminate the need for a separate math journal. In time, the notebook will become a storehouse of students' work and mathematical thinking, as well as cast light on their progress.

While spiral notebooks or composition books are best for a math-starter notebook, a section of a binder or even looseleaf pages stapled together may serve well. Instruct your students to put their names on their notebooks. If they fill one, they should number successive notebooks in order. Students should always date their work and include the number of the problem.

We recommend that you review the notebooks periodically. You may collect them every few weeks or check some from each class two to three times each week. Such a schedule makes your workload more manageable yet enables you to monitor the progress of your students. Although we do not recommend that you score each problem, you may wish to assign a point value for problems completed so that students realize they are accountable for their work (See the "Evaluation" section.) As you review your students' work, you may write notes, comments, or suggestions, encouraging them to respond. You will probably be surprised at how many students will write back and engage in a dialogue with you.

Since it is likely many of your students will not have had to maintain math-starter notebooks before, it is important that you explain how the notebooks will be used and what will be required. You might wish to distribute copies of "Math-Starter Notebook Guidelines" and review the information with your students.

Name _____ Date _____ Section _____

Math-Starter Notebook Guidelines

1. Use a standard spiral notebook or a composition book for your math-starter notebook.

2. Put your name and class number on your notebook. If you fill one notebook, number each additional notebook successively.

3. Bring your math-starter notebook to every math class.

4. Use your math-starter notebook only for math class. Do not use it for other subjects.

5. Start each problem on a new page. This will give you plenty of room for work.

6. Keep your work in order, and date and label it — for example — Nov. 2, 2014, problem 2-7.

7. Be aware that I will check your math-starter notebook periodically. I may offer comments and suggestions about your work. If you want, write brief notes to me in your notebook, and I will respond to you. We can carry on a dialogue about your progress in math.

8. While I will respect the privacy of your work and ideas, remember that if I read something in your notebook that I feel endangers you or someone else, I must report it.

9. Review your math-starter notebook from time to time and see how you are progressing.

10. Take some of your best work and share it with others. Discuss some of your ideas about math with others.

Math Starters! 5- to 10-Minute Activities Aligned with the Common Core Math Standards, Grades 6–12, 2nd Edition.

THE VALUE OF WRITTEN EXPLANATIONS

The importance of writing in math classes has been made clear through various studies and should be part of every math program. Writing offers students a way to analyze and share their thoughts about math in a formalized manner. Clear, effective writing requires students to think through their ideas, connect what they are learning to what they know about the real world, explain their reasoning, and communicate their conclusions to others. The math-starter notebook is a place where students may solve problems and provide written explanations of their work.

Whenever possible, encourage your students to share their ideas about math—its purpose, methods, applications, and value—through writing. Make writing an important and respected part of your program.

COOPERATIVE PROBLEM SOLVING USING MATH STARTERS

Many jobs require that people work together to solve problems. While projects, group reports, and other special activities focus on cooperation, you can offer your students a taste of cooperative problem solving with math starters designed for group work.

Working in groups offers many potential benefits to students. Along with fostering discussion and inquiry, cooperation provides a learning situation in which students can acquire considerable social skills. In small groups, where everyone has a role and must contribute, it is easier for students to take an active part in learning. As the group works together on the same problem, many students, even those who may feel intimidated speaking before the entire class, are more willing to share their thoughts. Moreover, ideas are usually debated quickly, resulting in fast feedback. As students work on solving a problem, they may engage in several tasks. They must consider various strategies that might lead to a solution, apply mathematics correctly, check solutions, and determine a method through which to share the group's results.

The math starters in this book designed for group work may require ten to fifteen minutes of class time: five to ten minutes to solve the problem and a few minutes for discussing the solution. Although the problems are not as complex as those you would find with major group projects, the math-starter cooperative problems promote critical thinking, foster cooperation, and build student confidence. Done periodically, they can provide a nice change to the class's routines yet still support your objectives and program.

ORGANIZING GROUPS FOR PROBLEM SOLVING

The best math groups are organized randomly. Groups of three to five work well for math starters that have been designed for cooperative problem solving. Fewer than three members becomes no group if someone is absent, and more than five will be unwieldy.

Because the time allotted for math starters is limited, you should design your groups so that members sit close to each other. For example, if the four members of group 1 sit in the first two seats of the first two rows, it is easy for them to come to class and push their desks together. This reduces the disruption of moving a lot of furniture or having students change seats.

Groups should be changed regularly, certainly after working together for three or four problems. Reorganizing your groups allows students to interact with many different personalities throughout the year, exposing them to varying viewpoints, dispositions, and abilities. They will be gaining experience for coping with the real world. When rearranging your groups, it is not necessary to change everyone. As long as you change half of the members of the group, you will have provided it with a new group personality. When changing groups, it is often best to change students' seats as well to keep the shuffle of furniture under control. (See "How to Set Up Groups for Cooperative Math Starters.")

To ensure that your groups work effectively, explain the purpose of group work, your expectations, and the procedures students should follow. Consider assigning members specific tasks, such as leader, recorder, time monitor, checker, and presenter. Distribute copies of "Rules for Working in Groups on Math Starters," and review the information with your students.

You will likely need to show your students the methods for working together effectively, model appropriate behavior, and sit in on your groups and remind them of the proper procedures often, particularly at the beginning of the year. As students gain experience, they will be able to assume more responsibility for the group's work and you will be able to fade to the background.

How to Set Up Groups for Cooperative Math Starters

Working together in cooperative groups offers students a stimulating way to learn math. The following suggestions can help you organize groups to solve challenging math starters:

- For solving math starters designed for cooperative groups, groups of three to five work best for middle and high school students.

- While you should organize your groups randomly, you should be sure to mix abilities, genders, personalities, and ethnicities.

- Always reserve the right to readjust groups. Some students, even when picked randomly, will not work well together. Other students should be kept apart. One disruptive group can disrupt the entire class.

- Set up groups so that group members sit close to each other. This reduces the need for moving desks, chairs, or students.

- Reorganize your groups regularly. This enables students to work with others and fosters cooperation with a variety of personalities.

- When you rearrange groups, change students' seats.

- Make sure students understand what is expected of them. Model appropriate behavior and remind students of the proper procedures.

- Consider assigning specific roles to promote the efficiency of the groups, such as these:

  ○ *Group leader:* Keeps the group focused on finding a solution to the problem

  ○ *Recorder:* Writes down the group's progress and solutions

  ○ *Monitor:* Keeps track of time and may also have the responsibility for any materials the group uses

  ○ *Checker:* Reviews the group's work, checking for accuracy

  ○ *Presenter:* Shares the group's solutions with the class

For small groups, students may assume multiple roles.

Name _____ Date _____ Section _____

Rules for Working in Groups on Math Starters

By following the suggestions below, you and your group will work more efficiently:

1. As soon as you come to class, organize your group and start work.

2. Be willing to work with other members of your group.

3. Be willing to share your ideas with others.

4. Carefully think about your ideas and construct your arguments before presenting them to others.

5. After you are done speaking, let others speak.

6. Listen carefully and politely when others are speaking.

7. Ask questions when you do not understand something or have not heard something clearly.

8. Remember to speak softly so as not to disturb other groups.

9. Strive to keep the discussion on finding the solution to the problem.

10. Remember that you are responsible for your behavior.

THE VALUE OF SHARING AND DISCUSSION

The importance of sharing and discussing the solutions to math problems cannot be overemphasized. After students have completed a math starter, the answer should be provided and explained. For problems that may have several solutions, the different solutions should be discussed and analyzed. Only when students understand how problems are solved can they fully master mathematical skills and concepts.

Whenever students present solutions to the class, encourage them to construct explanations of how they arrived at their answer. What operations did they use? What steps did they follow? What key words in the problem helped them to identify exactly what they needed to find? They should share successful strategies they used, as well as strategies they might have considered and then rejected. As they discuss the concepts, methods, and applications of math, students gain understanding and insight.

USING PROBLEM-SOLVING STRATEGIES

Many of the math starters in this resource require students to use problem-solving and critical-thinking skills along with computation. Since the types of skills needed to solve the problems vary, you should familiarize your students with various strategies they can use. Explain that strategies are simply methods or procedures that can be used individually or with other methods to solve problems. Note that some problems may be solved in many ways using different strategies and that the best strategy for solving a particular problem is often the one that works best for the person solving the problem.

To give students an idea of some of the more common problem-solving strategies, you may wish to distribute copies of "Problem-Solving Strategies." Review and discuss the strategies with your students, emphasizing that some strategies will work better than others for solving specific problems. Suggest that students keep this information in their binders or folders so that they may refer to it as needed.

Throughout the year as your students are working on problems, point out the use of various strategies and when they might be applied. Encourage your students to try different strategies and become proficient with them.

Problem-Solving Strategies

There are many ways to solve math problems. Before you can solve any problem, you must understand the problem and what you are asked to find. Use the first three steps below to clarify your understanding:

1. Read the problem carefully. If necessary, reread the problem several times so that you understand it.

2. Study the problem for hidden questions—for example, an unstated question you must answer in order to solve the main question the problem asks.

3. Identify the information you need to solve the problem. Because some problems contain more information than you need, eliminate unnecessary facts.

Now you are ready to formulate a plan to solve the problem. The following strategies may be helpful:

1. Carefully study any charts, tables, graphs, or illustrations included with the problem. It is essential that you understand them. For some problems, you may find it helpful to construct a table or chart of facts. This will help you to see your data clearly.

2. Look for connections, relationships, patterns, or causes and effects. Look for order and sequence.

3. Organize your facts. Writing information in the form of a list can show patterns, associations, and relationships you might otherwise miss.

4. Divide the problem into parts, working on one part at a time. Breaking down a big problem into smaller parts can make it easier to manage.

5. Use trial and error (also called guess and check). Try a strategy or method, and see if you can solve the problem. Keep trying different plans until one works.

6. Look at the problem in different ways. Assume you have found a solution; then work backward to try to see how you might have found it.

(continued)

Math Starters! 5- to 10-Minute Activities Aligned with the Common Core Math Standards, Grades 6–12, 2nd Edition.

Problem-Solving Strategies *(Continued)*

7. Estimate your way to a solution. Round off numbers. Working with whole numbers instead of fractions or decimals can make it easier to see relationships between numbers and help you to find a solution.

8. Draw a graph or sketch a model. This can help you to visualize a problem, which can lead to a solution.

9. Write an equation with a variable to model the problem.

10. Use the appropriate tools and materials — for example, pencil, paper, and calculator — to solve the problem.

When you feel you have found a solution, call on common sense. Some answers obviously cannot be right. Discard these. Double-check your work, be certain you have used all of the necessary facts, and check your calculations.

Notes

_____

_____

_____

_____

_____

_____

_____

EVALUATION

To ensure accountability, you should evaluate the work your students do on math starters. If students think that their work is not being evaluated, some will not put in the necessary effort that will enable them to benefit from the skills presented in the problems. There are several ways you can evaluate the progress of your students without burdening yourself with a significant increase to your workload. Some of the best methods through which to evaluate students' work for math starters are:

- Checklists
- Point systems
- Quizzes that include math starters
- Review math-starter notebooks
- Student participation
- Portfolios

Whichever method, or methods, you choose, be sure it is consistent with your school or department's grading policy. Also be sure to explain to your students how your evaluation of math starters will affect their grades. Only when students know what is required of them can they hope to satisfy your expectations.

Checklists

A checklist provides a relatively easy way to evaluate students' work. As students are working on a math starter, you may circulate around the room with a checklist that contains the names of the students, observing and noting their progress. An easy way to do this is to use a page in your record book. A check mark for acceptable work and a minus for unacceptable work may be used to record progress. You should determine what you want *acceptable* to mean. It may mean no more than that the student worked on the problem diligently, or it may require that the student found the correct answer. You must also decide what *unacceptable* means. Using checklists to chart daily progress will enable you to accumulate a record of your students' achievement throughout the marking period. The data on the checklist can become part of your students' classwork or class participation grade. The checklist is a simple but effective means of evaluation.

Point Systems

Some teachers prefer to use a point system for evaluation. To set up a point system, assign a specific value for the successful completion of a certain number of math starters.

For example, if you assign 30 starter problems during a marking period, students may earn 10 points toward their classwork grade by completing all 30 correctly. Completing 15 correctly may earn 5 points. Completing 5 may result in 2.5 points. (The rest of their grade may come from quizzes, tests, class participation, and homework.)

Quizzes That Include Math Starters

An easy way to monitor and evaluate your students' work on the math starters they have done is to include a few problems similar to the math starters on quizzes or tests that you give. This will help to ensure that they take the work they do on math starters seriously. An option here is to give students periodic quizzes that are based on the math starters that they have already completed. If you require students to maintain math-starter notebooks, they can use their notebooks to review or study prior to the quiz or test. This also encourages students to keep their math-starter notebooks accurate and up to date.

Review of Math-Starter Notebooks

If you require students to maintain math-starter notebooks, you may collect the notebooks periodically and review your students' work. You may wish to assign grades to the overall quality of the notebooks or assign point values that can be incorporated with students' classwork grades. An excellent notebook, for instance, might earn 10 points, an average one may earn 5 points, and one of poor quality may earn 2 points.

Student Participation

Some teachers prefer to evaluate the efforts of their students through participation. They may have students put solutions to problems on the board or a projector or explain their solutions to the class. While you should note students who consistently volunteer, you should also select students randomly to share their answers and solutions. Random selection helps to ensure that everyone does the work and is prepared to participate. The participation efforts of your students during work on math starters may be incorporated with their overall classroom participation grade.

Portfolios

If your students are required to maintain math portfolios, they may wish to include examples of the work they do on math starters with their portfolios. Selecting three to five problems each marking period that they feel best represents their work on math starters can be a nice addition to a general math portfolio. If the portfolios are used in evaluation, the math starters can be an important part of that assessment.

A FINAL WORD

Math starters offer practical and effective ways to begin your math classes. They help get your students working as soon as they enter the room, reducing the amount of time lost in getting prepared to work. Math starters encourage students to come to your class ready to work and help ensure that the greatest portion of class time is spent learning math.

PART 2

Math Starters

Whole Numbers and Integers: Theory and Operations

1-1   Natural Numbers ★

Natural numbers were likely the first numbers that ancient people used. They are represented by the set of numbers {1, 2, 3, 4, . . .}. The three dots, called ellipses, mean that the numbers continue in the same pattern without ending. Natural numbers are used in virtually all aspects of life.

Problem: Write at least three common or well-known phrases in which a natural number, or numbers, is used. Example: A cat has *nine* lives. Be ready to share your answers with the class.

1-2   Natural Numbers ★★

Natural numbers, also known as the counting numbers, are represented by the set of numbers {1, 2, 3, 4, . . .}.

Problem: Answer the questions below.

    (1) The sum of the first two natural numbers = _____.

    (2) The sum of the first three natural numbers = _____.

    (3) The sum of the first four natural numbers = _____.

    (4) The sum of the first five natural numbers = _____.

    (5) The sum of the first six natural numbers = _____.

Explain the pattern of the sums.

1-3   Whole Numbers ★

Whole numbers include the natural numbers and 0 and are represented by the set of numbers $\{0, 1, 2, 3, 4, \ldots\}$.

Problem: Sometimes a pattern that uses letters is actually a numerical pattern in disguise. Find the next three letters in the pattern below. (Hint: Think of the set of whole numbers.)

Z, O, T, T, F, F

1-4   Whole Numbers ★ G

Although 0 is a part of the set of whole numbers and is extremely important, ancient people had a lot of trouble with 0. For example, the ancient Romans conquered much of the known world, but they did not have a symbol for zero in their numeral system. In fact, a symbol for 0 did not come to Europe until around the twelfth century AD, when Europeans adopted the Arabic number system.

Problem: Speculate what would happen if we did not have 0 in our number system.

1-5   Place Value with Whole Numbers ★

Jackie Robinson was the first African American baseball player to appear in a National League game in 1947. Lawrence Eugene (Larry) Doby was the first African American baseball player to appear in an American League game.

Problem: To find out the year Larry Doby first played in the American League, use these clues:

- The year was in the twentieth century.
- The sum of the digits of this year is 21.
- The tens digit is 3 less than the units digit.

1-6   Place Value with Whole Numbers ★★

At a track meet on May 6 in Oxford, England, Roger Bannister was the first person to run the mile in less than 4 minutes. His time was 3:59.4.

Problem: Use the clues below to determine the year Bannister broke the 4-minute barrier for the mile:

>   The sum of the thousands and hundreds digit is 10.
>   The sum of the tens and units digit is one less than 10.
>   The units digit is one less than the tens digit.

1-7   Numerical Operations ★

The word *compute* comes from the Latin word *computare*, which means a "notched tally stick." Basic computation involves addition, subtraction, multiplication, and division. Computation requires an understanding of numerical facts, but it does not require creative thinking.

Problem: Explain why or why not the name *computer* is a fitting name for today's computers.

1-8   Numerical Operations ★ G

When you read a word problem in math, sometimes a key word, or words, suggests certain operations. For example, words such as *sum* and *combined* mean addition. Words like *minus* or *how much more than* mean subtraction.

Problem: Create a list of words or phrases that suggest mathematical operations.

1-9   Adding Whole Numbers ★

Although addition problems can be performed quickly with a calculator, calculators may not always be handy when numbers need to be added. Thus, the ability to add numbers remains an important skill.

Problem: Of the four problems below, which are correct? Correct those that are wrong.

(1)	4,659	(2)	1,863	(3)	1,359	(4)	58,614
	+4,979		+5,683		+4,055		+38,821
	9,738		7,546		5,314		97,435

1-10   Subtracting Whole Numbers ★

When people make mistakes in subtraction, more often than not, their mistakes are in regrouping (borrowing). Being careful to regroup reduces mistakes.

Problem: Imagine that you are explaining to a young student how to regroup. Write a step-by-step explanation of how regrouping is done. Include an example to clarify your explanation.

1-11   Subtracting Whole Numbers ★★

A solid understanding of subtraction is a basic math skill.

Problem: Find the missing digits to complete the problems below.

(1) $\square$,$\square$63
       $-3{,}9\square9$
       $\overline{2{,}83\square}$

(2)   71,$\square$4$\square$
       $-4{,}8\square6$
       $\overline{6\square{,}270}$

1-12   Multiplying Whole Numbers ★

The word *multiplication* comes from the Latin words *multi* and *plicare*. *Multi* means "many," and *plicare* means "fold." Multiplication therefore means repeated addition of numbers to obtain a solution. For example, rather than adding 318 twenty-nine times, you can simply multiply 318 × 29. The answer to a multiplication problem is called a *product*.

Problem: Multiply 318 × 29. Then write an explanation describing the steps you used to find the product.

1-13   Multiplying Whole Numbers ★★

Before multiplication was developed, people had a hard time calculating large numbers. Although calculators perform much of the multiplying we do now, a good understanding of multiplication facts is fundamental to computation.

Problem: Using the boxes below, one box for each of the numbers 1, 2, 3, 4, 5, write a multiplication problem that gives the largest product. You may use each number only once.

1-14   Dividing Whole Numbers ★ (6.NS.2)

Division is the mathematical operation of finding how many times a number, called the divisor, is contained in another number, the dividend. The answer to a division problem is called the quotient. Division is a basic skill in mathematics.

Problem: Which of the following quotients are correct? Correct the problems that are wrong.

(1)   49 R20 / 37)1,833   (2)   51 R7 / 49)2,506   (3)   88 R4 / 32)2,820   (4)   714 R40 / 53)3,803

1-15   Dividing Whole Numbers ★ (6.NS.2)

Division is much like learning to ride a bicycle. Once you master the steps, you will not forget them.

Problem: Explain the steps of long division.

1-16   Dividing Whole Numbers ★★ (6.NS.2)

Sports can be great fun for both players and spectators. Setting up teams and finding sponsors, however, may be a problem.

Problem: There are 112 students who signed up to play basketball in a recreation league. They have 14 sponsors. How many teams of 11 players each can be formed?

1-17   Whole Numbers — Multistep Problem ★★ (7.EE.3)

An old English children's rhyme goes like this:

> As I was going to St. Ives,
> I met a man with seven wives,
> Every wife had seven sacks,
> Every sack had seven cats,
> Every cat had seven kits.

Problem: How many people and animals were going to St. Ives?

1-18　　Whole Numbers — Multistep Problem ★★ G (7.EE.3)

In professional football, scoring is based on 6 points for a touchdown, 1 point for an extra point after a touchdown, 2 points for a two-point conversion after a touchdown, 2 points for a safety, and 3 points for a field goal.

Problem: List any number less than 50 that is impossible for a football team's final score.

1-19　　Estimation with Compatible Numbers ★ (7.EE.3)

Compatible numbers are numbers that are easy to compute mentally. They are often used to estimate answers.

Consider this example. The sophomore class made a profit of $572.70 at their annual car wash. They washed 185 cars. About how much profit did they make per car?

This answer could be easily estimated by using the compatible numbers of 600 (dollars) and 200 (cars). It is much easier to compute $600 \div 200 = 3$ than $\$572.70 \div 185$.

Problem: Make up a word problem in which compatible numbers could be used to estimate the answer. Exchange your problem with a classmate. Decide if the problems are correct. Correct them if they are incorrect.

1-20　　Rounding Whole Numbers ★

Attendance at many free events is often estimated because there is no accurate way of determining the exact number of people who show up.

Problem: A magazine article reported that 16,000 people attended a free concert in the park. What number, or numbers, below *cannot* be rounded to 16,000?

　　(1) 15,500　　　　**(2)** 15,400　　　　**(3)** 16,500　　　　**(4)** 16,499　　　　**(5)** 15,499

1-21   Divisibility by 2, 4, and 8 ★

Understanding divisibility is useful in several mathematical applications. The divisibility tests for 2, 4, and 8 are listed below:

A natural number is divisible by:

- 2 if the last digit is even.
- 4 if the number formed by the last two digits is divisible by 4.
- 8 if the number formed by the last three digits is divisible by 8.

Problem: Using the divisibility rules above, what numbers below are divisible by 2? By 4? By 8?

    (1) 1,326   **(2)** 3,174   **(3)** 7,368   **(4)** 17,208

1-22   Divisibility by 3, 6, 9, and 12 ★

Although a calculator can be used to test for divisibility, sometimes you may need to use old-fashioned divisibility tests. The divisibility tests for 3, 6, 9, and 12 are listed below.

A natural number is divisible by:

- 3 if the sum of the digits of the number is divisible by 3.
- 6 if the number is divisible by 2 and 3.
- 9 if the sum of the digits is divisible by 9.
- 12 if the number is divisible by 3 and 4.

Problem: Using the divisibility rules above, what numbers below are divisible by 3? By 6? By 9? By 12?

    (1) 102   **(2)** 153   **(3)** 1,755   **(4)** 4,644

1-23   Divisibility by 5 and 10 ★

The tests for divisibility for 5 and 10 only require you to look at the last digit of the number:

- A number is divisible by 5 if it ends in 5 or 0.
- A number is divisible by 10 if it ends in 0.

Problem: Complete the sentences below with the number 5 or 10.

If a number is divisible by _____, it is always divisible by _____. If a number is divisible by _____, it may be divisible by _____.

Give an example to show that your answers are correct.

1-24   Factors ★

Although our number system is based on 10, some items are grouped by 12, such as 12 eggs in a dozen. When it comes to pricing, 12 is a more practical number than 10 because it has more factors. The factors of 12 are 1, 2, 3, 4, 6, and 12, while the factors of 10 are 1, 2, 5, and 10. Because of this, commercial items are often counted in multiples of 12. For example:

- 12 items = 1 dozen
- 12 dozen = 1 gross
- 12 gross = 1 great gross

Problem: How many dozens are in a great gross? How many items are in a great gross?

1-25   Factors ★★

Mr. Thomas was thrilled when he received the list of students for his first-period math class. He likes to break his class into groups with an equal number of students in each group. When he saw the number of students, he knew he could have groups of 2, 3, 4, 6, 8, and 12.

Problem: How many students were in his class?

1-26   Greatest Common Factor ★ (6.NS.4)

The greatest common factor, GCF, of two numbers is the largest number that is a factor of both numbers. For example, the factors of 12 are $1, 2, 3, 4, 6,$ and 12. The factors of 32 are $1, 2, 4, 8, 16,$ and 32. The GCF of 12 and 32 is 4.

Problem: The greatest common factor of each pair of numbers below may or may not be correct. Find the incorrect greatest common factor or factors. Correct any that are wrong.

(1) 20 and 30   **(2)** 15 and 18   **(3)** 24 and 36   **(4)** 20 and 9
     GCF $= 5$ GCF $= 3$ GCF $= 12$ GCF $= 1$

1-27   Greatest Common Factor ★★ (6.NS.4)

Over 2,000 years ago, Euclid, a Greek mathematician, developed an algorithm, or method, that he used to find the greatest common factor, GCF, of two numbers. Euclid's algorithm is still used today.

Following are the steps of Euclid's algorithm:

1. Divide the larger number by the smaller.
2. Divide the divisor in step 1 by the remainder in step 1.
3. Repeat step 2 until there is no remainder.
4. The last divisor is the GCF of the original numbers.

Problem: Using Euclid's algorithm, find the GCF of 208 and 464.

1-28   Multiples ★

A multiple of a number is the product of the number and a natural number. For example, the multiples of 4 are $4, 8, 12, 16, 20, \ldots$

Problem: Write the first five multiples of $5, 9, 12,$ and 15.

1-29   Multiples ★★

The Great Wall of China, begun about 220 BC, was built over many centuries. One of the most extensive and best-preserved sections of the wall dates from the Ming dynasty (1368–1644).

Problem: Use the clues below to find the approximate length in miles of this part of the Great Wall:

The length is a four-digit number.

The tens digit and the units digit are 0.

The hundreds digit equals the thousands digit, and these digits are multiples of 5.

1-30   Least Common Multiple ★ (6.NS.4)

The least common multiple, or LCM, of two numbers is the smallest number that is a multiple of both numbers. For example:

The multiples of 6 are 6, 12, 18, 24, ...

The multiples of 8 are 8, 16, 24, 32, ...

The least common multiple of 6 and 8 is 24, because 24 is the smallest number that appears in both sets.

Problem: 12 is the least common multiple of one of the two pairs of numbers listed below. For which pair of numbers is 12 the least common multiple?

(1) 12 and 18   (2) 3 and 15   (3) 6 and 12   (4) 18 and 36

1-31   Least Common Multiple ★★ (6.NS.4)

A common way of finding the least common multiple of two numbers is to make lists of multiples and find the smallest number that appears in both lists. There is also a simple formula you can use:

$$LCM = Product \div GCF$$

In this equation, LCM stands for least common multiple, the Product is the result of the two numbers being multiplied together, and GCF stands for greatest common factor. Following is an example of how this equation works.

The LCM of 20 and 30 can be found by simplifying the expression $20 \times 30 \div 10$. (10 is the GCF of 20 and 30.) The LCM of 20 and 30 is 60.

Problem: Find the LCM of each pair of numbers by dividing the product of the numbers by their GCF.

     (1) 15 and 20   **(2)** 10 and 50   **(3)** 21 and 63   **(4)** 17 and 29

1-32   Multiples and the Distributive Property ★★ (6.NS.4)

Mika found an amazing way to write the sum of two whole numbers as a multiple of a sum of two numbers that have no common factor other than 1.

Following is Mika's method:

1. Choose any two numbers. Example: 20 and 50
2. Find the greatest common factor, GCF, of the numbers. The GCF of 20 and 50 is 10.
3. Divide both numbers by the GCF. $20 \div 10 = 2$ and $50 \div 10 = 5$
4. Add the quotients. $2 + 5$
5. Multiply the sum of the quotients by the GCF found in step 2. $10(2 + 5) = 70$
6. This is the same as the sum of the numbers in step 1. $10(2 + 5) = 20 + 50$

Problem: Choose any two numbers, and use Mika's method to write the sum as a multiple of a sum of two numbers that have no common factor other than 1. How do you know that the sum has no common factor other than 1?

1-33   Prime Numbers ★

A prime number is a number that has only two factors, 1 and the number.

Problem: List the prime numbers between 1 and 50.

1-34   Prime Numbers ★

Because prime numbers have only two factors, 1 and the number itself, understanding factors is helpful to understanding prime numbers.

Problem: Write an explanation of why 1 is *not* a prime number.

1-35   Composite Numbers ★

A composite number is a number that has more than two factors. 6 is a composite number because its factors are 1, 2, 3, and 6.

Problem: List the composite numbers that are greater than 9 and less than 21. Then state the number of factors of each composite number you listed.

1-36   Prime and Composite Numbers ★★ 🖳

Go to http://www.hbmeyer.de/eratosiv.htm. You will see a grid numbered from 1 to 400.

Here is what to do:

1. Click on the number 2, and all multiples of 2 will be removed from the grid.
2. Wait until all multiples of 2 have been removed.
3. Then click on the number 3 to remove all multiples of 3 from the grid.
4. Continue this process through the number 19.

Problem: Explain why after clicking on the number 19, all composite numbers have been removed and only prime numbers remain.

1-37   Perfect Squares ★

A perfect square is a product of a number multiplied by itself. An example of a perfect square is 16, the result of 4 × 4. Another is 25, the result of 5 × 5.

Problem: List the perfect squares starting with 1 and ending with 100.

1-38   Perfect Squares and Prime Numbers ★★

We see the American flag every day at school, sporting events, and buildings.

Problem: Use the clues below to determine numbers related to the flag:

The number of red stripes is the fourth prime number.
The number of white stripes is the sixth prime number minus the number of red stripes.
The total number of stars equals the square of the number of red stripes plus 1.

1-39   Order of Operations ★

When simplifying expressions, you must perform operations in a specific order:

1. Simplify expressions within grouping symbols. If more than one grouping symbol is used, simplify the innermost group first and continue simplifying to the outermost group.

2. Multiply and divide from left to right.

3. Add and subtract from left to right.

Problem: Four expressions are listed below. Which will have the same value if you use the order of operations to simplify them? What are the values of each expression?

(1) $8 + 4 \times 3 - 1$ **(2)** $(8 + 4) \times 3 - 1$ **(3)** $8 + (4 \times 3) - 1$ **(4)** $8 + 4 \times (3 - 1)$

1-40   Order of Operations ★★ G

Numbers may always be expressed in terms of other numbers. When simplifying expressions, the order of operations must always be followed.

Problem: Using the digits $1, 2, 3,$ and 4 and the order of operations, write expressions that equal the numbers from 1 to 10. You must use each digit only once per expression. The first number is done for you.

$$(2 \times 1) - (4 - 3) = 1$$

1-41   Powers of Numbers ★ (6.EE.1)

An exponent is the number written in the upper-right-hand corner of a number. In the expression 2^6, 6 is the exponent and 2 is the base. 2^6 is read as "2 to the sixth power" and means $2 \times 2 \times 2 \times 2 \times 2 \times 2$, which equals 64.

Problem: 64 can be written as a base raised to a power in four different ways. 2^6 is one of these ways. 64^1 is another. What are two other ways?

1-42   **Simplifying Expressions with Exponents ★ (6.EE.1)**

The order of operations must be followed to simplify expressions:

1. Simplify expressions within grouping symbols first. If several grouping symbols are used, simplify the innermost group and continue simplifying to the outermost group. As you do this, follow steps 2, 3, and 4.
2. Simplify powers.
3. Multiply and divide from left to right.
4. Add and subtract from left to right.

Problem: Place parentheses, if necessary, in each expression so that the result is 56.

(1) $7 \times 6 - 4 \times 4$ (2) $18 - 8 \times 5 + 6$
(3) $8^2 - 1 \times 2^3$ (4) $2^2 + 3 \times 9 - 1$

1-43   **Simplifying Expressions with Exponents ★★ (6.EE.1)**

The game of horseshoes is often played at picnics. For most players, it is a game of skill and a bit of luck. In a standard game of horseshoes, the stakes must be set a specific number of feet apart.

Problem: Simplify the expression below to find the distance in feet between stakes in a regulation game of horseshoes.

$$2 \times 3^2 + 3 \times 2^2 + 3^2 + 1^2$$

1-44   **Simplifying Expressions with Exponents ★★ (6.EE.1)**

Knowledge of numbers can increase your cultural literacy and provide you with insights in many areas. For this problem, knowing how to simplify expressions can even help you decipher the title of a classic book.

Problem: What is Fahrenheit $(7 + 8)^2 - (8 + 6)^2 + (9 + 10)^2 + 8^2 - 3$? What do you think the significance of this number is?

1-45   **Writing Numerical Expressions ★★**

A numerical expression names a number. $3 + 9$, $2^3 + 2^2$,   and $4(2 + 1)$ are examples of numerical expressions. All three of these expressions name the number 12.

Problem: Write a numerical expression for each phrase below. Find the number that each expression names.

(1) 4 squared   (2) 3 less than 2 squared
(3) The sum of 6 and 12   (4) 1 plus 5 squared
(5) 3 times 5 cubed   (6) 6 squared divided by 3 squared

1-46   **Identifying Parts of a Numerical Expression ★★**

The parts and value of an expression may be identified by using the correct mathematical terms. _Sum, difference, factor, product_, and _dividend_ are just some of the terms that relate to expressions.

Problem: Eight numerical expressions are listed below. Match each with a correct description. Some descriptions may describe more than one expression.

(1) $2 + 5$

(2) 2×5

(3) $12 \div 2$

(4) $3(5 + 2)$

(5) $3 \times 2 \times 6$

(6) $2 - 1$

(7) $12 \div 3$

(8) $9(3 + 1)$

Descriptions

(A) The product is 36.

(B) The sum is 7.

(C) The dividend is 12.

(D) The expression has two factors.

(E) A sum is one of the factors.

(F) The difference is 1.

1-47   Integers ★ (6.NS.5)

Integers are the set of the natural numbers, 0, and the opposites of the natural numbers. The set $\{\ldots -3, -2, -1, 0, 1, 2, 3, \ldots\}$ represents integers.

One of the many ways we use integers is for countdowns for space flights and satellite launchings. The negative numbers designate the seconds before blast-off, and the positive numbers represent the seconds after blast-off.

Problem: How many seconds elapse between T − 10 seconds and T + 10 seconds? On what number would blast-off occur?

1-48   Integers ★★ (6.NS.5)

Negative numbers troubled mathematicians well into the 1800s. Most mathematicians ignored them, calling them "inadequate" or "absurd," believing that negative numbers had no practical use or meaning.

This all changed with Leonhard Euler. In his *Complete Introduction to Algebra*, Euler stated that subtracting the opposite of a number is the same as adding the number. In Euler's words: "To cancel a debt signifies the same as giving a gift."

Problem: Explain Euler's words. Include an example with negative numbers to support your explanation.

1-49   Opposites ★ (6.NS.5)

Positive numbers and negative numbers are opposites. For example, gaining 3 pounds is the opposite of losing 3 pounds. In football, gaining 10 yards is the opposite of losing 10 yards.

Problem: Consider the following statement. If −10 °F is really cold, then 10 °F is really hot. Do you agree or disagree? Explain your answer.

1-50   The Number Line ★ (6.NS.6)

All numbers can be represented as points on a number line. The origin of a number line is 0. The numbers to the right of 0 are positive numbers, and the numbers to the left of 0 are negative numbers. The coordinate is the number paired with a point on the number line.

Problem: Use the number line to identify the coordinates described below.

(1) The origin

(2) The natural numbers

(3) The point halfway between D and H

(4) The point that is the same distance from the origin as H

1-51   The Number Line ★★ (6.NS.6)

The Smith family likes to take car trips. To help pass the time, Mrs. Smith, who does not like to rely on GPS, assumes the role of navigator and gives clues about the towns they will pass through.

Problem: Traveling south on an interstate highway, the Smiths will pass the cutoffs for three towns: Allenville, Browning, and Cooperton. The distance from Allenville to Browning is 16 miles, the distance from Browning to Cooperton is 8 miles, and the distance from Allenville to Cooperton is 24 miles. What town is between the other two? (Hint: To help you visualize the towns, sketch a number line.)

1-52   Absolute Value ★ (6.NS.7)

Absolute value is the distance of a number on the number line from 0. Note the following examples:

$$|3| = 3 \quad |7| = 7 \quad |15| = 15$$
$$|-3| = 3 \quad |-7| = 7 \quad |-15| = 15$$

Problem: From the examples above, Abby generalized that the absolute value of any number is a positive integer. Do you agree or disagree? Explain your answer.

1-53   Absolute Value ★★ G (6.NS.7)

Samantha borrowed $25 from her sister. Samantha described her debt as −$25. But her sister described the money Samantha owed her as $25 (without the negative sign).

Problem: Is each girl's description accurate? Support your answer in terms of absolute value.

1-54   Comparing Integers ★

Every integer can be paired with a point on the number line. The larger integers are always to the right of the smaller integers.

Problem: Each group of integers below is arranged from the least to the greatest or the greatest to the least, but one integer is out of order. Identify this integer, and rewrite the set correctly.

     (1) $\{-3, -2, 1, 0, 7\}$ **(2)** $\{0, -7, -6, -5, -4\}$
     (3) $\{-8, -9, -7, -6, -5\}$ **(4)** $\{-4, 2, 4, 8, 6\}$

1-55   Inequality Symbols ★

Symbols are often used in mathematics and real life. Two common symbols are < and >.

     < is read as "is less than."
     > is read as "is greater than."

Problem: Explain why the fast-forward symbol on a TV remote control resembles the greater-than symbol and the rewind resembles the less-than symbol.

1-56   Ordering Integers on a Number Line ★ (6.NS.7)

A number line is a line on which points correspond to numbers. Larger numbers are located to the right of smaller numbers. Conversely, smaller numbers are located to the left of larger numbers.

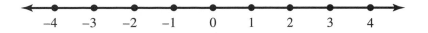

For example, because 4 is to the right of 1 on a number line, 4 > 1. Because 1 is to the left of 4, 1 < 4.

Problem: Write the correct inequality symbol for the numbers below. Refer to the number line above to confirm your results.

    (1) −2 is to the left of 2; therefore, −2 _____ 2.

    (2) −2 is to the right of −4; therefore, −2 _____ −4.

    (3) 1 is to the right of 0; therefore, 1 _____ 0.

    (4) −1 is to the left of 0; therefore, −1 _____ 0, or 0 _____ −1.

    (5) −3 is to the right of −4; therefore, −3 _____ −4, or −4 _____ −3.

1-57   Understanding Statements of Order ★★ (6.NS.7)

Sam's and Mike's math assignment was to make a map that shows the locations of their homes and their school. Sam lives 4 blocks to the east of the school, and Mike lives 4 blocks to the west. Mike said that this reminds him of a number line, where the school's location is the origin, Sam's house is paired with the number 4 on the number line, and Mike's house is paired with −4.

Because −4 is to the left of 0 and 0 is to the left of 4, Mike concluded that Sam's home is a greater distance from the school than his home. After all, −4 < 0 < 4.

Problem: Explain the error in Mike's reasoning.

1-58   **The Coordinate Plane ★★ (6.NS.6)**

The horizontal axis, called the x-axis, and the vertical axis, called the y-axis, divide the coordinate plane into four parts called quadrants. The point $(0, 0)$ is called the origin and is where the x-axis and y-axis intersect.

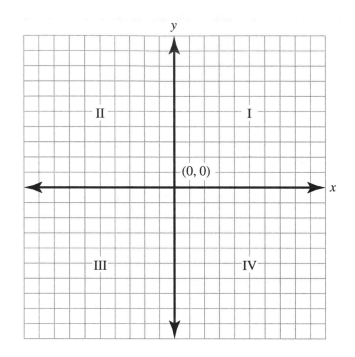

Problem: Of the four statements below, at least three are false. Identify the false statements, and rewrite them to make them true.

    (1) If the x-coordinate is greater than 0, the point is always in the first quadrant.

    (2) If the y-coordinate is 0, the point is always on the y-axis.

    (3) If the signs of the x- and y-coordinates are the same, then the point is always in the third quadrant.

    (4) If the signs of the x- and y-coordinates are different, then the point could be in the fourth quadrant.

1-59 Graphing Points in the Coordinate Plane ★ (6.NS.6)

When people attend a concert, major sporting event, or theater presentation, they find their seats by checking the row and seat number on their tickets. Without this information, they would likely have trouble finding their seats.

Problem: Explain how locating a seat in a theater or arena is similar to plotting points in a coordinate plane.

1-60 Solving Problems by Graphing Points in the Coordinate Plane ★★ (6.NS.8)

The coordinate plane is used not only for graphing points; it can also be used for graphing geometric figures. Because the horizontal and vertical lines are perpendicular, graphing rectangles is especially easy.

Problem: On graph paper, draw four rectangles in the coordinate plane that have the following characteristics:

- The points $(-3, -1)$ and $(1, -1)$ are the end points of one side of each rectangle.
- The longer side of each rectangle is twice as long as its shorter side.

List the vertices of these rectangles. Find the lengths of the sides to support your answer.

1-61 Adding Integers ★ (7.NS.1)

A magic square is a square in which all of the numbers in each row, column, and diagonal add up to the same number.

Problem: In the first magic square below, find the sum of each row, column, and diagonal. In the second magic square, each row, column, and diagonal add up to 3. Find the missing numbers.

(1)

-4	-9	-2
-3	-5	-7
-8	-1	-6

(2)

	5	0
		-1
2		

1-62   Adding Integers ★★ (7.NS.1)

Tom has trouble understanding how you can add certain integers and have an answer that is less than the number you started with. For instance, $8 + (-5) = 3$.

Problem: Write an explanation of why the equation above is correct. Provide an example from everyday life that supports your explanation.

1-63   Subtracting Integers ★ (7.NS.1)

To subtract integers correctly, you must pay close attention to the signs as well as the numbers.

Problem: Complete each equation by filling in the correct number.

(1) $7 - (\underline{\hspace{1cm}}) = 12$ (2) $\underline{\hspace{1cm}} - 5 = -13$
(3) $\underline{\hspace{1cm}} - (-16) = -23$ (4) $9 - (\underline{\hspace{1cm}}) = 16$

1-64   Subtracting Integers ★★ (7.NS.1)

When learning how to subtract integers for the first time, many students become confused because the answer may be greater than the numbers they started with. For example:

$$20 - (-5) = 25$$

Problem: Create a word problem that requires subtraction of integers in its solution. Exchange your problem for the problem of a classmate and solve each other's problem.

1-65   Adding and Subtracting Integers ★★ (7.NS.1)

Sometimes mathematicians are not interested in actual numbers but simply whether a number is positive. A good example is the stockholder who is concerned only with whether his or her stocks go up. Another is the racer who is interested in breaking a record (going faster).

Problem: Describe each situation below as positive, negative, zero, or cannot be determined.

   (1) The sum of two positive integers

   (2) The difference of two positive integers

   (3) The sum of an integer and its opposite

   (4) The sum of a negative integer and zero

   (5) The difference of two negative integers

1-66   Representing Addition and Subtraction on a Number Line ★★ (7.NS.1) 🖥

Go to http://www.funbrain.com/linejump/index.html to explore how the number line can be used to model addition and subtraction of integers.

Here is what to do:

   1. Click on "Really Hard" for the level of difficulty.

   2. You will be presented with a problem. There will be a number line below the problem.

   3. Click on the correct answer on the number line. You will be told if you are correct, and a number line that models the problem will be displayed.

   4. Try a few more practice problems by clicking on "Try Another One."

   5. After you have finished your practice session, complete the problem below.

Problem: Explain why $-1 - (-3) = 2$ is modeled by an arrow starting at -1 and extending 3 units to the right.

1-67   Multiplying Two Integers ★ (7.NS.2)

When multiplying positive and negative integers, you must determine whether your product is positive or negative. The rules for determining the sign of the product of two integers follow:

- If both integers have the same sign, the product is positive.
- If the integers have different signs, the product is negative.
- If one of the factors is 0, the product is 0.

Problem: Find the product of the integers below. Then arrange the products from least to greatest and explain the pattern.

(1) -8×2 (2) $8 \times (-1)$ (3) -10×0
(4) $-4 \times (-2)$ (5) $-8 \times (-2)$ (6) $-3 \times (-8)$

1-68   Multiplying More Than Two Integers ★★ (7.NS.2)

When multiplying integers, the order of the factors does not affect the product. There are several ways to multiply more than two integers. You should choose the way that is easiest for you.

- You may multiply the integers from left to right.
- You may multiply all the positive integers, multiply all the negative integers, and then find the product.
- You may look at the factors. If at least one of the factors is 0, the product is 0.
- You may count the number of negative integers. If this number is even, the product is positive. If this number is odd, the product is negative. (In either of the above cases, if one of the factors is 0, then the product is 0.) After finding whether the product will be positive or negative, multiply the absolute value of each number to find the product.

Problem: Write an explanation of which method of multiplying integers is easiest for you. Perhaps you use a combination of methods. If you do, explain which ones you use and why.

1-69   Multiplying More Than Two Integers ★★ (7.NS.2)

Multiplying integers correctly requires concentration and accuracy. Mistakes can be made in multiplication and using the correct sign with the product.

Problem: Of the four multiplication problems for each number below, one *does not* belong with the other three. Find which should be omitted, and explain your reasoning.

(1) (a) $-3 \times (-7) \times (-8)$ (b) $-8 \times 2 \times (-10) \times (-5)$
(c) $-6 \times (-3) \times (-2) \times (-7)$ (d) $-1 \times (-4) \times (-8)$

(2) (a) $-3 \times (-4) \times 0$ (b) $-6 \times (-6) \times 4$
(c) $8 \times (-1) \times (-2)$ (d) $-3 \times (-3) \times (-1)$

(3) (a) $-3 \times (-8) \times (-4)$ (b) $-1 \times 8 \times 7$
(c) $-6 \times (-8) \times 4$ (d) $-5 \times (-3) \times 9$

1-70   Dividing Two Integers ★ (7.NS.2)

The rules for dividing integers follow:

- If the signs of the divisor and the dividend are the same, the quotient is positive.

- If either the divisor or dividend is positive and the other is negative, the quotient is negative.

- If the dividend is 0, the quotient is 0.

- If the divisor is 0, the quotient is undefined because it is impossible to divide by 0.

Problem: Some of the problems below have errors. Identify which problems have errors and correct them.

(1) $15 \div (-5) = -3$ **(2)** $-21 \div (-7) = -3$ **(3)** $105 \div (-5) = -21$
(4) $-166 \div (-12) = 13$ **(5)** $-20 \div 0 = 0$ **(6)** $0 \div (-15) = 0$
(7) $-125 \div 5 = -25$ **(8)** $102 \div 17 = 6$ **(9)** $-35 \div 7 = -5$

1-71   Dividing Two Integers ★★ (7.NS.2)

A student said that if he uses the same numbers but different signs, he can make up two problems that have the same quotient. For example, $45 \div 5 = 9$ and $-45 \div (-5) = 9$.

Problem: Do you think this is true if the quotient is a negative number? Is it true if the quotient is 0? Explain your answers, and provide examples to support your reasoning.

1-72   Multiplying and Dividing Integers ★★ (7.NS.2)

Multiplication and division are inverse operations. This means that they are opposite operations. For example: $-12 \times 4 = -48$ is the inverse of $-48 \div 4 = -12$.

Problem: Fill in each blank with the correct number.

    (1) $-12 \times \underline{\hspace{1cm}} \div (-4) = -42$ **(2)** $\underline{\hspace{1cm}} \times (-15) \div 5 = -51$
    (3) $-144 \div \underline{\hspace{1cm}} \times 6 = 36$ **(4)** $8 \times \underline{\hspace{1cm}} \div (-4) = 20$

1-73   Four Operations with Integers ★★ (7.NS.3)

Only when you truly understand a topic are you able to apply your knowledge of it. This is as true for mathematics as it is for any other subject.

Problem: Create four problems that use integers: one for addition, one for subtraction, one for multiplication, and one for division. When you are done, exchange your problems with the problems of a partner and solve each other's integer problems. Remember to create an answer key for your problems.

1-74   Four Operations with Integers ★★ (7.NS.3)

Mrs. Wilson often gives quizzes with 10 problems. To discourage students from filling in just any answer, she devised this scoring method: students receive 1 point for each correct answer, no points for an unanswered question, and −1 point for an incorrect answer.

Alberto had 7 problems correct on his quiz, he left 1 problem unanswered, and he had 2 wrong answers. His score was 5, computed as $7 \times 1 + 0 + 2 \times (-1) = 5$.

Problem: Use Mrs. Wilson's grading system to answer these questions.

- **(1)** What is the highest possible score? What is the lowest?
- **(2)** How many ways could a student score an 8?
- **(3)** Annie's score was −5, and Jason's score was twice Annie's. What was Jason's score?
- **(4)** The scores of five students were $-5, -4, 3, 1$, and 0. Find the average of the scores.

1-75   Four Operations with Integers ★★★ (7.NS.3)

It is nice to have help for finding the solutions to some problems. This is one of those problems.

Problem: Use the numbers $20, 10, -4, -2$, and -1 and the signs $+, -, \times$, and $\div$ to obtain the highest and lowest numbers possible. All numbers and operations must be used once for each problem, and the answers must be integers. You may not use grouping symbols or exponents.

1-76   Using Positive Exponents with Integers ★

In the expression 2^3, 3 is the exponent and 2 is the base. The expression means that 2 is a factor three times, or $2 \times 2 \times 2 = 8$.

Whenever a number or group of numbers is written in parentheses with an exponent, the number or group of numbers is the base. For example, $(-3)^2 = -3 \times -3 = 9$, and $-3^2 = -(3 \times 3) = -9$. Here is another example: $(8+2)^3$ means 10^3 or $10 \times 10 \times 10 = 1,000$. This is not the same as $8 + 2^3$ which means $8 + 2 \times 2 \times 2 = 16$.

Problem: Simplify each expression.

(1) $(-5)^2$ (2) -5^2 (3) $5 + 2^4$
(4) $(5+2)^4$ (5) -5×3^3 (6) $(-5 \times 3)^3$

1-77   Using Scientific Notation to Express Large Numbers ★★ (8.EE.3)

A number is written in scientific notation when it is expressed as a product of a number greater than or equal to 1 but less than 10 with an integral power of 10. For example:

$$1,800,000 = 1.8 \times 10^6 \qquad 15,600 = 1.56 \times 10^4$$

Problem: A googol is the numeral 1 with 100 zeroes after it. A googolplex is the numeral 1 with a googol of zeroes after it. Write a googol and a googolplex in scientific notation.

1-78   Computing with Numbers Written in Scientific Notation ★★ (8.EE.3)

Scientific notation is often used to express very large numbers. We can use scientific notation to write the average distances of the planets from the sun:

Mercury: 5.79×10^7 km

Venus: 1.08×10^8 km

Earth: 1.50×10^8 km

Mars: 2.28×10^8 km

Jupiter: 7.78×10^8 km

Saturn: 1.43×10^9 km

Uranus: 2.87×10^9 km

Neptune: 4.50×10^9 km

Problem: Answer the following questions.

(1) Which planet is about 5 times the distance from the sun as Earth?

(2) Which planet is less than 2 times as far from the sun as Earth?

(3) Which planet is over 30 times as far from the sun as Earth?

(4) Which planet is about 13 times as far from the sun as Mars?

1-79   Changing Numbers in Scientific Notation to Standard Form ★★ (8.EE.4)

Any number written in scientific notation can be written in standard form. Since whole numbers and integers written in scientific notation will always be expressed as a positive power of 10, move the decimal point to the right the same number of places as the exponent. Following are two examples:

- Our solar system is about 4.6×10^9 years old. To write this number in standard form, move the decimal point 9 places to the right. 4.6×10^9 years = 4,600,000,000 years.

- The product of 1,600,000 and 6,000,000 will be displayed on a calculator as 9.6 E12. This is the same as 9.6×10^{12}, or 9,600,000,000,000. The decimal point is moved 12 places to the right.

Problem: Express each number in standard form.

(1) The diameter of the sun: 1.392×10^6 miles

(2) The distance of a light-year: 9.461×10^{12} km

(3) The calculator display: 5.46 E11

(4) The calculator display: 4.326 E15

1-80   A Quotation Applicable to Mathematics ★

Hypathia of Alexandria (370–415) was the first woman mathematician about whom we know many details. Along with her pursuits in mathematics, Hypathia was also a writer, teacher, scientist, and astronomer at a period in history when it was unusual for women to receive an education. By all counts, she was a remarkable person and a true trendsetter of her time.

Hypathia received much of her passion for learning from her father, Theon, a noted writer and thinker. Although at the time Christians believed that math and science were heresy, Theon is credited with helping to keep mathematical and scientific thought alive through tireless inquiry and discussion.

Problem: Explain these words that Theon said to Hypathia: "Reserve your right to think, for even to think wrongly is better than not to think at all." How might they be applied to mathematics?

Rational Numbers: Fractions, Decimals, and Percents

2-1   Equivalent Fractions ★

When a whole number is multiplied by 1, the product is the original number. Sometimes when a fraction is multiplied by 1, the product is equal to the fraction but it may be expressed in a different form.

Here is an example:

$$\frac{5}{6} \times 1 = \frac{5}{6} \qquad \frac{4}{4} = 1$$

$$\frac{5}{6} \times \frac{4}{4} = \frac{20}{24}, \text{ which is equivalent to } \frac{5}{6}.$$

Problem: Find the missing numerator or denominator by writing equivalent fractions for the problems below.

(1) $\dfrac{5}{8} = \dfrac{}{24}$ 　　　 (2) $\dfrac{3}{4} = \dfrac{27}{}$ 　　　 (3) $\dfrac{2}{3} = \dfrac{8}{}$ 　　　 (4) $\dfrac{7}{22} = \dfrac{}{132}$

2-2   Simplifying Fractions ★

Simplifying a fraction often makes the fraction easier to work with. A large numerator or denominator sometimes "hides" the value of a fraction.

Problem: Of the fractions listed below, which are simplified? Simplify the others.

$$\frac{21}{49} \qquad \frac{13}{14} \qquad \frac{29}{37} \qquad \frac{15}{21} \qquad \frac{19}{38} \qquad \frac{47}{63} \qquad \frac{12}{18} \qquad \frac{2}{9} \qquad \frac{10}{45}$$

2-3   Simplifying Fractions ★★

A Venn diagram consists of two or more circles that overlap and may be used to show the way certain groups of numbers are related. The numbers in the portion that overlaps are in both groups.

Problem: Place each fraction below in the appropriate part of the Venn diagram.

$$\frac{20}{21} \qquad \frac{63}{81} \qquad \frac{21}{27} \qquad \frac{9}{11} \qquad \frac{3}{14} \qquad \frac{7}{9} \qquad \frac{77}{99}$$

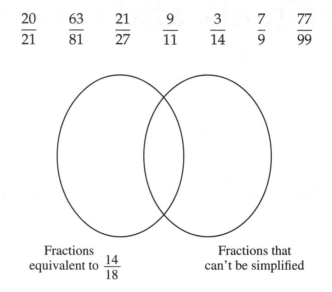

Fractions equivalent to $\frac{14}{18}$

Fractions that can't be simplified

2-4   Writing Improper Fractions as Mixed Numbers ★

An improper fraction is a fraction in which the numerator is equal to or greater than the denominator. All improper fractions can be expressed as a mixed number or a whole number. Simply divide the numerator by the denominator and write the remainder (if there is one) over the denominator.

Problem: Which of the following fractions are expressed correctly as a mixed number? Correct any incorrectly expressed fractions. Simplify, if necessary.

(1) $\dfrac{32}{7} = 4\dfrac{3}{7}$ **(2)** $\dfrac{76}{8} = 9\dfrac{1}{2}$ **(3)** $\dfrac{367}{100} = 3\dfrac{67}{100}$ **(4)** $\dfrac{41}{9} = 4\dfrac{5}{9}$

2-5   Writing Mixed Numbers as Improper Fractions ★

To convert a mixed number to a fraction, multiply the denominator by the whole number, add the numerator, and write the sum over the denominator. For example, $7\frac{3}{4} = \frac{31}{4}$.

Problem: Write the numerator in each fraction below.

(1) $9\frac{1}{4} = \frac{}{4}$ (2) $13\frac{2}{5} = \frac{}{5}$ (3) $5\frac{7}{8} = \frac{}{8}$ (4) $6\frac{4}{9} = \frac{}{9}$

2-6   Comparing Fractions ★★ 💻

Go to http://nlvm.usu.edu.

Here is what to do:

1. Click on "Number & Operations, 6–8."

2. Scroll down to "Fractions—Comparing" and click. You will see two models and two fractions.

3. Move the up/down arrows to change the number of equal parts on the models so that the models have the same number of equal parts and the fractions have the same denominator. Then write two pairs of equivalent fractions in the boxes.

4. Click on "Check" to see if you are correct.

5. Then click on the number line to show where the fractions are graphed.

6. Click on "New Fractions" for more practice, then complete the problem below.

Problem: Describe the locations of fractions on the number line.

2-7   Ordering Fractions ★★

You must compare fractions before putting them in order. Remember to first find common denominators, if necessary.

Problem: Write the following fractions in order from least to greatest. Write equivalent fractions to support your answer.

$$\frac{2}{3}, \ \frac{3}{5}, \ \frac{2}{5}, \ \frac{21}{25}, \ \frac{33}{75}$$

2-8   Adding Fractions ★

When adding fractions with like denominators, you must add the numerators and simplify, if necessary. When adding fractions with unlike denominators, you must find common denominators first, write equivalent fractions, and then add the numerators and simplify.

Problem: Complete the addition problems.

(1)
$$\frac{3}{7} = \frac{}{35}$$
$$+\frac{4}{5} = \frac{28}{}$$
$$\overline{}$$
$$\frac{}{35} = 1\frac{}{35}$$

(2)
$$\frac{5}{6} = \frac{10}{}$$
$$+\frac{3}{4} = \frac{9}{}$$
$$\overline{}$$
$$\frac{19}{} =$$

2-9   Adding Fractions ★

In some communities, special routes are designed for people who wish to walk or jog. On many of these routes, distances are marked for those who like to keep track of how far they have gone.

Problem: José is starting a running program. He plans to alternate walking and running for 2 miles today. As his endurance increases, he hopes to gradually walk less and run more. If he walks $\frac{1}{2}$ mile, runs $\frac{1}{4}$ mile, walks $\frac{3}{4}$ mile, runs $\frac{1}{4}$ mile, and walks $\frac{1}{8}$ mile, what is his total distance?

2-10   Adding Mixed Numbers ★

Adding mixed numbers requires several steps. You must find the least common denominator, write equivalent fractions, add, and simplify, if necessary. Since it is possible to make a mistake in any of these steps, accuracy is very important.

Problem: Find the sums.

(1) $8\frac{7}{12}$ (2) $7\frac{5}{6}$

$+6\frac{3}{4}$ $+2\frac{1}{9}$

2-11   Adding Mixed Numbers ★★

When double-checking your work, go through the problem step by step. Otherwise you might overlook an error.

Problem: Which of the four problems below are correct? Correct the ones that are wrong.

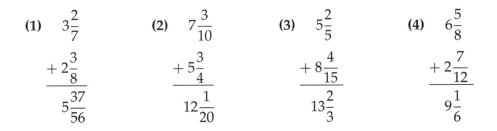

(1) $3\frac{2}{7}$ (2) $7\frac{3}{10}$ (3) $5\frac{2}{5}$ (4) $6\frac{5}{8}$

$+2\frac{3}{8}$ $+5\frac{3}{4}$ $+8\frac{4}{15}$ $+2\frac{7}{12}$

$5\frac{37}{56}$ $12\frac{1}{20}$ $13\frac{2}{3}$ $9\frac{1}{6}$

2-12   Subtracting Fractions ★

Finding the least common denominator is the first step to subtract fractions with unlike denominators. You must then write equivalent fractions, subtract, and simplify, if necessary.

Problem: Find the differences.

(1) $\frac{2}{9}$ (2) $\frac{4}{5}$ (3) $\frac{2}{3}$ (4) $\frac{7}{8}$

$-\frac{1}{6}$ $-\frac{2}{3}$ $-\frac{4}{7}$ $-\frac{9}{20}$

2-13   Subtracting Fractions ★★

Good cooks follow recipes carefully. Since many recipes call for fractional portions of ingredients, a solid understanding of fractions is helpful in cooking.

Problem: 4 tablespoons of butter equal $\frac{1}{4}$ cup. $5\frac{1}{3}$ tablespoons equal $\frac{1}{3}$ cup. How much larger is $5\frac{1}{3}$ tablespoons of butter than 4 tablespoons? Express your answer in terms of cups.

2-14   Subtracting Mixed Numbers ★

To subtract mixed numbers with unlike denominators, find common denominators, write equivalent fractions, subtract the fractions, subtract the mixed numbers, and simplify, if necessary.

Problem: Which of the following are correct? Correct the problems that are wrong.

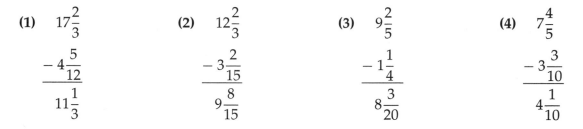

$$(1)\quad \begin{array}{r} 17\frac{2}{3} \\ -\ 4\frac{5}{12} \\ \hline 11\frac{1}{3} \end{array} \qquad (2)\quad \begin{array}{r} 12\frac{2}{3} \\ -\ 3\frac{2}{15} \\ \hline 9\frac{8}{15} \end{array} \qquad (3)\quad \begin{array}{r} 9\frac{2}{5} \\ -\ 1\frac{1}{4} \\ \hline 8\frac{3}{20} \end{array} \qquad (4)\quad \begin{array}{r} 7\frac{4}{5} \\ -\ 3\frac{3}{10} \\ \hline 4\frac{1}{10} \end{array}$$

2-15   Subtracting Mixed Numbers ★★

Regrouping is necessary for subtracting some mixed numbers from others.

Problem: Write an explanation of the process for regrouping when subtracting mixed numbers. Provide an example to clarify your explanation.

2-16   Subtracting Mixed Numbers ★★

A solid understanding of fractions is useful in many real-life problems.

Problem: Eddie is helping his father panel the family room. As they are working with the trim, Eddie's father notes that the final piece of trim is $6\frac{1}{2}$ feet long. The last section of wall they need to trim is $4\frac{3}{4}$ feet. There are also a few other small sections where they could use any trim that is left over. How much trim will they have left after completing the last section of wall?

2-17   Multiplying Fractions ★

Gardening and planting provide enjoyment and relaxation for many people. Sometimes a sound understanding of fractions comes in handy.

Problem: Erica needs $\frac{1}{4}$ pound of peat moss for each shrub she plants. How many pounds of peat moss are required for 20 shrubs?

2-18   Multiplying Fractions ★★

At Elmville Middle School, students take a unit test at the end of each math unit. Three tests are taken each quarter, and the test average counts $\frac{1}{3}$ of a student's quarterly average. There is no midterm or final exams.

Problem: One test is what part of the quarterly grade? One test is what part of the end-of-the-year average?

2-19   Multiplying Fractions and Mixed Numbers ★

Multiplying fractions and mixed numbers is a basic skill in mathematics.

Problem: Which of the following problems have the correct answer? Correct any problems that are wrong.

(1) $\dfrac{4}{9} \times \dfrac{3}{8} = \dfrac{1}{18}$ 　　　 **(2)** $20 \times \dfrac{1}{8} = 2\dfrac{1}{2}$ 　　　 **(3)** $\dfrac{5}{3} \times 3\dfrac{3}{10} = 1\dfrac{17}{18}$

2-20   Multiplying Mixed Numbers ★

Being able to solve problems quickly and efficiently is an advantage when taking tests. You can improve your problem-solving speed and efficiency through practice.

Problem: Which of the following problems equals 12? What are the answers to the other problems?

(1) $2\dfrac{1}{4} \times 5\dfrac{1}{3}$ 　　 **(2)** $2\dfrac{3}{7} \times 4\dfrac{2}{3}$ 　　 **(3)** $1\dfrac{5}{6} \times 6\dfrac{3}{4}$ 　　 **(4)** $3\dfrac{1}{3} \times 4\dfrac{1}{5}$

2-21   Estimating and Multiplying Mixed Numbers ★★

Estimation is an important skill when working with fractions, just as it is with whole numbers.

Problem: Estimate the answer to the problem below. Explain how you arrived at your answer.

$$2\dfrac{3}{4} \times 4\dfrac{1}{3}$$

2-22   Dividing Fractions ★ (6.NS.1)

Using a model often proves helpful when solving a problem. Models can help you to recognize relationships you might otherwise overlook.

Problem: Sam's mother bought 2 dozen eggs. She decorated $\frac{3}{4}$ of them. She kept $\frac{1}{2}$ of the decorated eggs for her family and gave the remaining decorated eggs to her friends and neighbors. How many decorated eggs did she give away? Explain how the model below can be used to solve the problem.

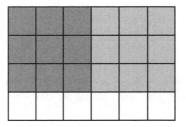

2-23   Dividing Fractions ★ (6.NS.1)

For the holidays, some people prepare special family recipes and give the food as gifts.

Problem: Sue plans to use a recipe that yields 15 pounds of fudge. She intends to wrap the fudge she makes in $\frac{3}{4}$-pound boxes and give one box to each of her friends and relatives for gifts. How many gifts will she have?

2-24   Dividing Fractions ★★ G (6.NS.1)

When dividing fractions, you must rewrite the problem by changing the division sign to a multiplication sign and using the reciprocal of the divisor. For example, $\frac{3}{4} \div \frac{1}{5} = \frac{3}{4} \times \frac{5}{1} = \frac{15}{4} = 3\frac{3}{4}$.

Problem: Using the digits 2, 7, 9, and 11, write a division problem for fractions that results in the smallest quotient. (Hint: More than one problem results in the smallest quotient. Try to find all of them.)

2-25   Dividing Fractions and Mixed Numbers ★ (6.NS.1)

When you divide mixed numbers, remember to convert the mixed numbers to improper fractions, change the division sign to a multiplication sign, write the reciprocal of the divisor, multiply, and simplify, if necessary.

Problem: Which of the following problems are correct? Correct those that are wrong.

$$\textbf{(1)} \quad 4\frac{1}{3} \div \frac{5}{6} = 3\frac{11}{18} \qquad\qquad \textbf{(2)} \quad 4 \div 1\frac{1}{7} = 3\frac{1}{2} \qquad\qquad \textbf{(3)} \quad 3\frac{3}{4} \div 1\frac{2}{3} = 3\frac{3}{4}$$

2-26   Dividing Mixed Numbers ★ (6.NS.1)

Ribbons often come in spools of different lengths. For example, a spool of ribbon might contain 10 yards, 15 yards, 20 yards, or more.

Problem: Mariana is making goodie bags for her little brother's birthday party. She has a partially used spool of ribbon that has $15\frac{1}{2}$ feet of ribbon left. She needs $1\frac{1}{4}$ feet of ribbon to tie each goodie bag with a nice bow. How many goodie bags can she tie using the ribbon left on this spool?

2-27   Dividing Mixed Numbers ★★ (6.NS.1)

Most operations in mathematics require that you follow specific steps. Once you understand the steps, you can easily perform the operation.

Problem: Find the quotient of the problem below. Then list all the steps you followed.

$$6\frac{2}{3} \div 5\frac{1}{3}$$

2-28   **Fractions — Multistep Problem ★★ (7.EE.3)**

Fractions are especially important in building, whether it is a new structure, a renovation, or a simple installation.

Problem: Will is installing a shelf to hold some items in his room. Brackets that are $\frac{1}{4}$-inch thick are to be fastened through a $\frac{1}{2}$-inch sheetrock wall and extend at least $1\frac{1}{2}$ inches into wooden studs behind the wall. He has only 2-inch nails for securing the brackets. Are the nails long enough? What are the shortest nails that he can use?

2-29   **Fractions — Multistep Problem ★★ (7.EE.3)**

Taxi fares depend on the distance that is traveled. Fares may also vary according to the city and number of passengers.

Problem: Tony's Taxi charges $2.50 for entering and $0.40 for each $\frac{1}{5}$ mile traveled. If the taxi ride is $5\frac{1}{5}$ miles, what is the fare?

2-30   **Decimals ★**

Simon Stevin (1548–1620), a Flemish mathematician, first used decimals in his book *La Disme,* which was published in 1585. He used a circle to represent a decimal point instead of the period used today. The word *dime* is taken from the title of Stevin's book.

Problem: Write an explanation of how the word *dime* could be taken from a work dealing with decimals.

2-31   Ordering Decimals ★

The first person to swim across the English Channel was Matthew Webb in 1875. Webb's time was 21.25 hours. The second, third, and fourth people and their times were Thomas Burgess, 22.583 hours; Henry Sullivan, 26.83 hours; and Enrico Tiraboschi, 16.55 hours.

Problem: Arrange the times of these four people in order from the greatest to the least.

2-32   Ordering Decimals ★

To write decimals in order, you must pay close attention to place value. Decimals may be ordered least to greatest or greatest to least.

Problem: Of the four sets of decimals below, only one set is correct. Find the correct set, and correct the other three.

(1) Least to greatest: 0.01, 0.12, 0.0638, 2.03, 5.1

(2) Least to greatest: 0.35, 0.4, 0.828, 1.1, 4

(3) Greatest to least: 10.21, 6.04, 0.75, 101.2, 0.468

(4) Greatest to least: 0.103, 0.92, 1, 2.5, 0.565

2-33   Place Value with Decimals ★★

The Great Pyramid in Giza, Egypt, was constructed about 2580 BC.

Problem: To find the height of the Great Pyramid in meters, use the following clues:

The tenths digit is 4 more than the hundreds digit.

The tenths digit is the only prime number in this decimal.

The tens digit is 4 times the hundreds digit.

The units digit is 1 more than the tenths digit.

2-34   Writing Fractions as Decimals ★

Every fraction can be written as a decimal. For example, $\frac{2}{5} = 0.4$ in decimal notation, and $\frac{3}{4} = 0.75$.

Problem: List three fractions, and express them as decimals.

2-35   Writing Decimals as Fractions ★

Reading decimals using place value can help you to write the decimals as fractions. Following are some examples:

- 0.1 is read as "one-tenth" or $\frac{1}{10}$.

- 0.25 is read as "twenty-five hundredths" or $\frac{25}{100}$ or $\frac{1}{4}$.

- 3.61 is read as "three and sixty-one hundredths" or $3\frac{61}{100}$.

Problem: Express each decimal below as a fraction or mixed number. Simplify, if necessary.

    (1) 2.6   **(2)** 0.75   **(3)** 14.95   **(4)** 1.004

2-36   Writing Decimals as Fractions ★★

Decimals such as $0.3\frac{1}{3}$, $0.87\frac{1}{2}$, and $0.66\frac{2}{3}$ can be expressed as fractions.

To express such decimals as a fraction, look at the number to the right of the decimal point. If there is one digit to the right, multiply the number by $\frac{1}{10}$; if there are two digits to the right, multiply the number by $\frac{1}{100}$, and so on. For example: $0.3\frac{1}{3} = 3\frac{1}{3} \times \frac{1}{10} = \frac{10}{3} \times \frac{1}{10} = \frac{1}{3}$.

Problem: Each decimal on the left can be written as one of the fractions on the right. Match each decimal with its equivalent fraction.

$$0.1\frac{1}{9} \qquad\qquad \frac{1}{3}$$

$$0.6\frac{1}{3} \qquad\qquad \frac{1}{9}$$

$$0.7\frac{1}{7} \qquad\qquad \frac{5}{6}$$

$$0.33\frac{1}{3} \qquad\qquad \frac{5}{7}$$

$$0.83\frac{1}{3} \qquad\qquad \frac{19}{30}$$

2-37   Repeating Decimals ★ (7.NS.2)

Repeating decimals are nonterminating decimals in which a number or a group of numbers repeats infinitely. A bar is placed over the number or group of numbers that repeats. For example: $\frac{1}{3} = 0.\overline{3}$ and $\frac{1}{6} = 0.1\overline{6}$.

Problem: Listed below are some fractions whose numerators are 1. These are called unit fractions. Some unit fractions repeat; some do not. Which fractions below are repeating decimals? Express these fractions as repeating decimals.

$$\frac{1}{2}, \ \frac{1}{4}, \ \frac{1}{5}, \ \frac{1}{7}, \ \frac{1}{8}, \ \frac{1}{9}$$

2-38   Repeating Decimals ★★ (7.NS.2)

Repeating decimals do not end. Instead, a number or group of numbers repeats.

Problem: The fractions $\frac{1}{3}$, $\frac{5}{6}$, $\frac{2}{9}$, $\frac{7}{11}$, and $\frac{13}{15}$ are fractions whose decimal equivalents, also called decimal expansions, repeat. Write each of these as a repeating decimal.

2-39   Comparing Fractions and Decimals ★★ (7.EE.3)

Drill bits are used to drill a hole in wood or other solid materials. The sizes of drill bits are often measured in fractions, using increments of 64ths of an inch.

Problem: Joe wants to drill a hole that is large enough to allow a 0.425-inch diameter wire to pass through as tightly as possible. Which of the following drill bits should he use? (The diameters of the bits are given in inches.)

(1) $\frac{13}{32}$ (2) $\frac{7}{16}$ (3) $\frac{15}{32}$ (4) $\frac{3}{8}$

2-40   Estimating with Decimals ★ (7.EE.3)

Estimation may be used to find an approximate answer or to see if an answer is reasonable.

Problem: Maria is ordering lunch at a fast-food restaurant. She estimates her bill as she is ordering. (All costs include sales tax.) Following are her estimates for lunch:

Low-fat milk, $1.29, estimate, $1.00

Chicken salad, $2.59, estimate, $3.00

Cup of fruity yogurt, $1.29, estimate, $1.00

Maria has $5.00. Does she have enough money according to her estimate? Does she have enough according to the actual full amount? Write an explanation of your answer.

2-41   Rounding Decimals ★

Rounding decimals is useful when you wish to be reasonably accurate but not exact. Following are some examples:

- 4.802 rounded to the nearest hundredth is 4.80
- 1.76 rounded to the nearest tenth is 1.8
- 7.86851 rounded to the nearest thousandth is 7.869

Problem: Make a chart, and round each of the numbers below to the nearest whole number, tenth, hundredth, and thousandth.

    (1) 0.9375   **(2)** 2.7638   **(3)** 3.05882   **(4)** 0.4444

2-42   Rounding Decimals and Unit Pricing ★ (6.RP.2)

Merchants and store owners are reluctant to round down prices. As a result, in pricing, the rules for rounding are changed slightly.

If an item is priced 3 for \$1.00, the price of one item is \$0.333 . . . If you follow the rules for rounding, the price would be \$0.33. However, because there is a digit (other than 0) to the right of the hundredths place, you would actually pay \$0.34. Rather than rounding down, the price is rounded up.

Problem: Determine how much you would pay for one item if the prices were the following.

    (1) 2 for \$1.99   **(2)** 3 for \$4.00   **(3)** 9 for \$10.00   **(4)** 7 for \$1.99

2-43   Adding Decimals ★ (6.NS.3)

When adding decimals, it is necessary to line up the decimal points in the numbers that are added. This will help you to keep each digit in its proper place.

Problem: Find the sums.

    (1) $27.3 + 5.65$ **(2)** $52.0 + 1.345 + 0.54$

    (3) $0.657 + 2.3 + 86.389$ **(4)** $5.678 + 3 + 19.4$

2-44   Adding Decimals ★ (6.NS.3)

Cash registers in most supermarkets are actually computer terminals. As a cashier scans an order, the information is entered in the store's computer, which instantly records the information on an itemized cash register receipt.

Problem: Thomas purchased the following items:

     1 bag of pretzels for $3.29
     1 loaf of bread for $3.19
     1 carton of orange juice for $2.29
     1 jar of peanut butter for $2.99
     1 carton of milk for $2.99

How much did Thomas have to pay for these items?

2-45   Subtracting Decimals ★ (6.NS.3)

To subtract decimals accurately, you must first line up decimal points so that digits are in their correct places. (Remember to regroup when necessary.)

Problem: Subtract the following.

      (1) $1.867 - 0.947$ **(2)** $356.2 - 4.7826$

      (3) $6 - 2.49$ **(4)** $0.09348 - 0.058$

2-46   Subtracting Decimals ★ (6.NS.3)

Although computers calculate the change a customer is to receive after making a cash purchase, the wise shopper always counts the change she or he receives. The items purchased might have been priced incorrectly, or the cashier might make a mistake in providing the change. Even in this day of superfast computers, being able to quickly count change remains a valuable skill.

Problem: Find the change in the fewest bills and coins as in this example:

Purchase price, $13.95

Amount paid, $15.00

Change, $1.05 (one dollar bill, one nickel)

Purchase Price	Amount Paid	Change
(1) $15.89	$20.00	
(2) $2.59	$5.00	
(3) $23.35	$30.35	
(4) $47.63	$60.03	

2-47   Multiplying Decimals ★ (6.NS.3)

It is easy to overlook a decimal point when multiplying decimals, but decimal points can make a big difference in your answer. Would you rather have $1,000.00 or $10.00?

Problem: The numbers in each product below are correct, but a decimal point is missing in one or both factors. Write the decimal points in the correct place in the factors. (Hint: You may need to add placeholders.) Is there more than one way to write the decimal points in the factors? Explain.

(1) $36 \times 54 = 194.4$ (2) $78 \times 21 = 0.1638$

(3) $324 \times 65 = 2,106$ (4) $7 \times 3 = 0.00021$

2-48   Multiplying Decimals ★ (6.NS.3)

When multiplying decimals, pay close attention to your multiplication facts as well as decimal points.

Problem: Which of the problems below are correct? Correct those that are wrong.

(1)	0.256	(2)	0.54	(3)	7.024	(4)	34.7
	×0.56		×2.4		×0.86		×6.7
	0.14386		0.1296		6.0464		232.49

2-49   Dividing a Decimal by a Whole Number ★ (6.NS.3)

When dividing a decimal by a whole number, remember to write the decimal point in the quotient directly above the decimal point in the dividend.

Problem: The admission cost to the planetarium for Jacob's class of 25 students was $181.25. (Jacob's teacher and two chaperones paid for their own admissions.) What was the cost of admission for each student?

2-50   Dividing Decimals ★★ (6.NS.3)

When dividing by a decimal, it is often necessary to multiply a divisor by 10, 100, 1,000, and so on to express the divisor as a whole number.

Problem: Solve the problem below. Then write an explanation of how you found the quotient.

$$0.31\overline{)210.8}$$

2-51   Dividing Decimals ★★ (6.NS.3)

Dividing decimals correctly requires careful work.

Problem: Which, if any, of the problems below are correct? Correct the problems that are wrong.

(1) $0.91\overline{)6.825}$ gives 7.8

(2) $7.6\overline{)0.56468}$ gives 0.743

(3) $0.006\overline{)0.5154}$ gives 8.59

(4) $0.36\overline{)0.00306}$ gives 0.085

2-52   Decimals — Multistep Problem ★★ (6.NS.3)

Everyone's body is different, and the average of this uniqueness leads to some interesting facts.

The average lengths of the six longest bones in the human body are listed below:

Femur (upper leg), 19.88 inches
Tibia (inner lower leg), 16.94 inches
Fibula (outer lower leg), 15.94 inches
Humerus (upper arm), 14.35 inches
Ulna (inner lower arm), 11.10 inches
Radius (outer lower arm), 10.4 inches

Problem: Find the average length of the human arm and the average length of the human leg. Which is longer, the average length of the human leg or arm? (Hint: Pay close attention to the bones you will use to find these averages.)

2-53   Decimals — Multistep Problem ★★★ (6.RP.3)

A unit price (or unit rate) is the amount charged per unit. A unit may be a single item, a measurement such as an ounce or pint, or some other quantity, depending on the product.

You can compare the cost of similar items by comparing unit prices. A lower unit price is the better buy.

Problem: Julia likes Toasted Flakes cereal. At her local supermarket, she can buy a 12-ounce box on sale for $3.00. Her brother told her that she could buy six 18-ounce boxes from an online store for $22.00. But she would have to pay a shipping and handling charge of $6.00. Her brother says that buying the cereal from the online store will be cheaper. Which is the better buy? Explain your answer.

2-54   Decimals — Multistep Problem ★★ (7.EE.3)

Some companies pay employees time and a half for overtime. Usually overtime refers to time worked after 8 hours per day or the time worked after 40 hours per week. Time and a half means 1.5 times the hourly wage.

Problem: A local store pays cashiers $10.40 per hour and time and a half for overtime. (This store pays overtime for the number of hours worked after 40 hours.) Casey worked 43.5 hours last week. How much money did Casey earn?

2-55   Decimals — Multistep Problem ★★ (7.EE.3)

Many people use coupons to save money when they shop. Most coupons may be used only for a specific brand or size of products.

Problem: Eat Rite Supermarket is having a "buy one, get one free" sale on bags of sandwich rolls (8 rolls per bag). One bag sells for $2.79. Samantha has a coupon that is worth $1.25 off one bag of the same rolls. But the coupon cannot be used with any other promotion or sale. Which is the better buy? Explain your answer.

2-56   Decimals — Multistep Problem ★★ (7.EE.3)

Most people like pizza. Plain pies usually come with cheese and tomato sauce, but most pizza shops let you order extra toppings—for an additional cost.

Problem: Vinny's Pizza sells his famous pizza for $14.49. The plain pie comes with tomato sauce and cheese. A special combination of any three additional toppings is $2.50 extra. If a fourth, fifth, or sixth topping is selected, the cost is $0.49 per topping. What is the cost of a pizza with anchovies, onions, pepper, and pepperoni?

2-57   Decimals — Multistep Problem ★★ (7.EE.3)

Electricians often charge a set amount for each hour they work, plus a service charge. The service charge does not vary and is charged regardless of how long a job takes.

Problem: How much will an electrician charge for doing 4.5 hours of work if the rate is $50 per hour, plus a service charge of $95?

2-58   Decimals — Multistep Problem ★★ (7.EE.3)

An odometer records the number of miles a car has traveled. Some people like to record the distance they travel, especially on long trips.

Problem: When the Santos family left for Florida, the odometer on their car read 8,765.2 miles. When they arrived in Florida, the odometer read 9,382.7 miles. While they were in Florida, they drove 18.6 miles. They returned home on the same roads they used for driving to Florida. What did the odometer of their car read when they returned home?

2-59   Order of Operations — Decimals ★ (6.NS.3)

An expression is a group of numbers and operations. To simplify an expression means to find its value.

Mathematicians agree on steps for simplifying expressions with more than one operation.

1. Perform all multiplication and division from left to right.
2. Perform all addition and subtraction from left to right.

Problem: Simplify the expression below.

$$3.8 + 6.4 \div 0.2 - 1.8 \times 2.6 - 3.2 \div 0.8$$

2-60   Order of Operations — Decimals ★★ (6.NS.3)

Sometimes groups of numbers and operations are enclosed within grouping symbols such as parentheses. The steps for simplifying these expressions are listed below:

1. Compute the numbers in parentheses first.
2. Multiply or divide in order from left to right.
3. Add or subtract from left to right.

Problem: Simplify the expression.

$$6.2 \times 0.03 + (4.6 + 5.6) \div (2 + 3.1) - 2.06$$

2-61   Order of Operations — Decimals ★★★ (6.NS.3)

The word *parentheses* is taken from the Greek word *parentithenai*, which means "putting in beside." In mathematics, parentheses permit you to put a number, or numbers, beside other numbers. In equations, any operations within parentheses are always computed first.

Problem: Place the decimals 1.7, 2.4, 3.8, 5.2, and 13.68 in the blanks below to complete the equation.

$$\underline{\hspace{1cm}} \div \underline{\hspace{1cm}} + \underline{\hspace{1cm}} \times (\underline{\hspace{1cm}} - \underline{\hspace{1cm}}) = 7.24$$

2-62   Ratio ★ (6.RP.1)

A ratio is a comparison of two numbers. A ratio that compares the number 4 to the number 5 can be written in three ways:

- As a fraction: $\dfrac{4}{5}$
- With the word *to*:   4 to 5
- With a colon: 4:5

Problem: Use three different ways to express the ratio of the number of days that school is in session this month to the number of days in the month.

2-63   Ratio ★★ (6.RP.1)

The Statue of Liberty in New York Harbor was a welcome sight for many immigrants. Being one of the largest statues in the world, its size makes it an impressive object from quite some distance away.

Following are some measurements of the Statue of Liberty:

- The statue is 151 feet, 1 inch from the bottom of the pedestal to the tip of the torch.
- The length of the right arm is 42 feet.
- The length of the hand is 16 feet, 5 inches.
- The length of the index finger is 8 feet.

Problem: Answer the questions.

(1) What is the ratio of the Statue of Liberty's height to the length of the right arm?

(2) What is the ratio of the length of the Statue's right arm to the length of the hand?

(3) What is the ratio of the length of the Statue's hand to its index finger?

You may round off the lengths to the nearest foot.

2-64 Ratio Reasoning ★★ (6.RP.3)

Sometimes scores on tests or quizzes may be expressed as a fraction, comparing the number of problems correct to the number of problems on the test or quiz.

Problem: Manuel had two math quizzes this marking period. On the first quiz, he got 24 out of 30 questions correct. On the next quiz, he got 15 out of 20 correct. On which quiz did he receive the higher score? Explain your answer.

2-65 Proportional Relationships ★ (7.RP.2)

A proportion is a statement that two ratios are equal. Cross products are used to determine which statements are proportions. If the cross products are equal, then the statement is a proportion.

For example, $\frac{3}{5} = \frac{12}{20}$ is a proportion because each cross product, 3×20 and 5×12, equals 60.

Problem: Identify the number of the statements that are *not* proportions. Rewrite them by changing one number so that the statement is a proportion.

(1) $\frac{2}{3} = \frac{14}{21}$ (2) $\frac{5}{7} = \frac{25}{49}$ (3) $\frac{3}{8} = \frac{24}{64}$ (4) $\frac{10}{9} = \frac{30}{3}$

2-66 Proportional Relationships ★★ (7.RP.2)

Since a proportion is a statement about the equality of ratios, some surprising patterns may emerge with certain sets of proportions.

Problem: Find the missing value in each proportion. Then explain the pattern.

(1) $\frac{6}{-} = \frac{2}{7}$ (2) $\frac{6}{-} = \frac{3}{7}$ (3) $\frac{6}{-} = \frac{6}{7}$ (4) $\frac{6}{-} = \frac{12}{7}$

2-67   Proportional Relationships and Scale ★★★ (7.RP.1)

Road maps always contain a scale. Cities, towns, and places of interest are located on the map, and the scale can be used to determine the actual distance between different sites.

Problem: The scale on a map is $\frac{1}{2}$ inch $= 15$ miles. If two towns, Jackson and Lincoln, are 50 miles apart, how far apart are they on the map? Washington is 20 miles from Jackson. According to the scale, how far is Washington from Lincoln? Write an explanation of your answer.

2-68   Ratio and Rate Reasoning ★★ (6.RP.3)

Along with nutritional information, a serving size is carefully defined on a food product's label. Many people believe that a serving is a quantity, or helping, that can be eaten in one sitting. If a person asks for seconds, these people feel that this is a second serving. Depending on the amount of the serving size, it may actually be a third, fourth, or more.

Problem: According to the label on a box of pretzels, a serving is about 1 ounce, or 12 pretzels. Each serving contains 110 calories. Use this information to complete the table.

	Number of Servings	Weight (in ounces)	Number of Pretzels	Number of Calories
1.	1			
2.			36	
3.		6		
4.				1,100

2-69   Equivalent Ratios and the Coordinate Plane ★ (6.RP.3)

By completing tables and plotting pairs of values, you can use the coordinate plane to solve problems.

Problem: Tickets to a small museum cost $2.00 per student. Complete the table, and plot the first three pairs of values in the coordinate plane. What do you notice about the ratio of the total cost to the number of students for each pair of values in the table? What do you notice about the ratio of y to x for each point plotted in the coordinate plane?

	Number of Students	Total Cost
1.	1	
2.	2	
3.		$10
4.	16	
5.		$50

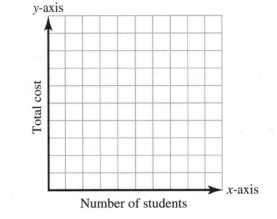

2-70   Percents ★

The word *percent* means the number of parts out of a hundred, which represents a whole: 100% means 1 whole, 200% means 2 wholes, 300% means 3 wholes, and so on.

Problem: Ms. Smith's first-period class had 100% attendance on the day she planned to show an exciting math movie. Before the movie began, Ms. Smith had 200% attendance in her classroom. How could this be?

2-71   Percents ★★

Fred's Fix-It is having a sale on various auto services:

    20% off tune-ups
    50% off oil changes
    20% off the cost of rotating tires
    20% off the cost of wheel alignments

Wanting to attract a lot of customers, Fred displayed the following sign: "110% Off Auto Services."

Problem: Fred may know how to repair cars, but he does not know his math. What must Fred fix on his sign? Explain your answer.

2-72   Equivalencies — Fractions, Decimals, and Percents ★

Fractions, decimals, and percents can be expressed as each other. Charts are an easy way to do this.

Problem: Express each word in the following chart as a fraction, decimal, and percent.

Word	Fraction	Decimal	Percent
one-tenth			
three-fourths			
one-half			
one-eighth			
two-fifths			
one			

2-73   Equivalencies — Fractions, Decimals, and Percents ★

Fractions, decimals, and percents are related and may be expressed in various ways.

Problem: Complete the chart and explain the pattern. The first one has been done for you.

Fraction	Decimal	Percent
$\frac{1}{8}$	0.125	12.5%
$\frac{2}{8} = \frac{1}{4}$		
$\frac{3}{8}$		
$\frac{4}{8} = \frac{1}{2}$		
$\frac{5}{8}$		
$\frac{6}{8} = \frac{3}{4}$		
$\frac{7}{8}$		

2-74   Equivalencies — Fractions, Decimals, and Percents ★★

Fraction, decimal, and percent equivalencies are often expressed in a table that has equivalent values written on the same line.

Problem: In the table, one value on each line is incorrect. Find the incorrect value and correct it.

Fraction	Decimal	Percent
$\dfrac{2}{3}$	$0.\overline{6}$	66%
$\dfrac{3}{27}$	0.375	37.5%
$\dfrac{1}{10}$	0.1	1%
$\dfrac{3}{8}$	$0.83\dfrac{1}{3}$	$83.\overline{3}$%
$\dfrac{5}{9}$	0.55	$55\dfrac{5}{9}$%

2-75   Equivalencies — Repeating Decimals ★★★ (7.NS.2)

Fractions such as $\dfrac{1}{3}, \dfrac{1}{6}, \dfrac{1}{9}$, and $\dfrac{1}{12}$ can be expressed as repeating decimals. If they are written as a percent, the percent is a mixed number.

Problem: Do you think all fractions whose denominators are multiples of 3 are repeating decimals? Explain your answer. Give examples (or counterexamples) of the fraction, decimal, and percent equivalencies.

2-76   **Finding the Percent of a Number ★ (6.RP.3)**

Here is an easy way for finding the percent of a number. Simply change the percent to an equivalent decimal and multiply. For example, 65% of $354 = 0.65 \times 354 = 230.1$.

Problem: Which of the problems below are correct? Correct those that have wrong answers.

(1) 78% of $6,284 = 4,801.52$ (2) 39% of $756 = 294.04$

(3) 230% of $348 = 80.04$ (4) 68.5% of $125 = 85.625$

2-77   **Finding the Percent of a Number ★ (6.RP.3)**

Items are often grouped together. A group of 20 items is called a score.

Problem: Calculate 60% of the number of items in a score. Your answer will be a number that is a common grouping today. What is the grouping?

2-78   **Finding the Percent of a Number ★★ (6.RP.3)**

You have probably already learned that it is easier to spend money than it is to acquire it. To help themselves plan how to spend their money, many people set up a budget.

Problem: Assume that you have developed the following monthly budget to help you spend and save your money. You have decided that the money you receive for your allowance and earn from chores will be divided in the following ways:

25% will go to savings.

20% may be spent on recreation and entertainment.

15% may be spent on extras for lunch.

30% may be spent on clothing.

10% will be set aside for miscellaneous expenses.

Assuming that you had $96.50 last month from your allowance and chores, how much money would you put in each category? Round the money to the nearest dollar.

2-79   Finding the Percent of a Number ★★ (6.RP.3)

When Mary and her friend Liz had to find the percent of numbers for homework, the first problem was 84% of 540. Mary multiplied 0.84 × 540 and found the answer, 453.6. She did not think it could be right, because her answer was less than 540. She called Liz for help. Liz told her the answer was correct, but Mary wondered how, after multiplying, a product could be less than the number she started with.

Problem: How would you explain to Mary that she was right?

2-80   Using Proportional Relationships to Find the Percent of a Number ★ (7.RP.2)

The proportion below may be used to find the percent of numbers:

$$\frac{\text{Part}}{\text{Whole}} = \frac{\text{Percent}}{100}$$

For example, in the expression 20% of 80, the Part is n (which is the number to be found), the Whole (which is always after the word "of") is 80, and 20% is written as 20 over 100.

$$\frac{n}{80} = \frac{20}{100}$$

Problem: Solve each problem using proportions.

    (1) What is 40% of 238?   **(2)** What is 34% of 240?

    (3) What is 110% of 150?   **(4)** What is 68% of 100?

2-81   Finding a Number When a Percent of It Is Known ★★ (6.RP.3)

Tennis is a game that may be played with singles or doubles. To accommodate four players (doubles), the size of the court is widened. A singles tennis court is 75% as wide as a doubles tennis court.

Problem: A singles tennis court is 27 feet wide. How wide is the doubles court?

2-82 Using Proportional Relationships to Find a Number When a Percent of It Is Known ★★ (7.RP.2)

$\dfrac{\text{Part}}{\text{Whole}} = \dfrac{\text{Percent}}{100}$ is a proportion that is useful for solving percent problems such as the following: 12% of what number is 15? In this proportion, 15 is the Part, the Whole is n since we do not know this number, and 12, as the percent, is written over 100.

The proportion is set up like this: $\dfrac{15}{n} = \dfrac{12}{100}$. You then solve for n.

Problem: Each problem below is written with two proportions. Choose the correct proportion, and solve it.

(1) 24 is 30% of what number? $\quad \dfrac{24}{n} = \dfrac{30}{100} \qquad \dfrac{n}{24} = \dfrac{30}{100}$

(2) 5% of what number is 6? $\quad \dfrac{6}{100} = \dfrac{5}{n} \qquad \dfrac{6}{n} = \dfrac{5}{100}$

(3) 42 is 150% of what number? $\quad \dfrac{42}{n} = \dfrac{150}{100} \qquad \dfrac{n}{42} = \dfrac{150}{100}$

2-83 Finding What Percent a Number Is of Another Number ★

Test scores are calculated by the ratio of correct answers to the total number of questions on the test. This ratio is usually expressed as a percent.

Problem: Raphael had 5 math tests this marking period. The ratios of correct answers to the total number of questions are listed below. Express each ratio as a percent to find his score on each test.

(1) $\dfrac{8}{10}$ (2) $\dfrac{12}{15}$ (3) $\dfrac{21}{24}$ (4) $\dfrac{20}{25}$ (5) $\dfrac{18}{25}$

2-84   **Using Proportional Relationships to Find What Percent a Number Is of Another Number** ★★ **(7.RP.2)**

To find what percent a number is of another, you may use the proportion $\dfrac{\text{Part}}{\text{Whole}} = \dfrac{\text{Percent}}{100}$.

For example, to find what percent of 125 is 60, set up your proportion as shown below and solve for n.

$$\frac{60}{125} = \frac{n}{100}$$

$$125n = 6{,}000$$

$$n = 48$$

The number sentence is then written as 48% of 125 is 60.

Problem: Solve each proportion below, and then translate it into a number sentence.

(1) $\dfrac{28}{70} = \dfrac{n}{100}$ (2) $\dfrac{22}{60} = \dfrac{n}{100}$ (3) $\dfrac{14}{7} = \dfrac{n}{100}$ (4) $\dfrac{9}{1{,}800} = \dfrac{n}{100}$

2-85   The Three Types of Percentage Problems ★★ 🖳

Go to http://nlvm.usu.edu.

Here is what to do:

1. Click on "Number & Operations, 6 − 8."

2. Scroll down to "Percentages" and click. You will see a Percent Gauge on the left.

3. Read and follow the directions on the right-hand side of the page.

4. Use the Percent Gauge to solve the problems presented on the website. (Click on "Reset" to clear the Gauge.)

5. After you have finished the practice problems, complete the problem below.

Problem: Answer the questions.

(1) Sue typed 56 pages. Seven pages were double-spaced, and the rest were single-spaced. What percent of the pages were single-spaced?

(2) Of the 56 students in the algebra classes, 7% have an A average for the marking period. About how many students is this?

(3) The PTA at MacArthur School has 56 members, which is only 7% of the total number of members the PTA wishes to enroll. What is the enrollment goal?

2-86   Percents and Sales Tax — Multistep Problem ★ (7.EE.2)

At a Dollar Day Sale, everything in the designated section of the store is priced at a dollar or in multiples of a dollar.

Mary and José went shopping at a store holding a Dollar Day Sale. The cost of the items they decided to buy was $5. They had to pay sales tax of 6%.

Problem: José figured that he could multiply $5 by 0.06 to get $0.30, then add this to the $5 to get the total cost. Mary said to multiply $5 by 1.06 to arrive at the total cost. Who is correct? What do you think is the better way to solve the problem?

2-87 Percents and Discounts ★★

Many stores run discount ads that say 10%, 20%, 30%, or 50% off the regular price.

Problem: Why are these the most common discounts? Why do you think stores sometimes run discounts of $33\frac{1}{3}$% off? Explain your answer.

2-88 Percents and Discounts — Multistep Problem ★★ (7.RP.3)

A successive discount is a discount after a previous discount has been made. Successive discounts can lead to big savings.

Problem: The price of a jacket is reduced 40%. For one day only, the reduced price is reduced another 10%. Is this the same as a 50% discount? Provide an example to support your answer.

2-89 Percents and Sales Price — Multistep Problem ★★ (7.RP.3)

Buying things on sale is a great way to save money. It is important that you watch circulars and commercials to be aware of bargains.

Problem: A DVD is marked 30% off the original price. The sale price is $12.60. Assuming there is no sales tax, find the original price of the DVD.

2-90   **Percents and Tips — Multistep Problem ★★★ (7.RP.3)**

A tip is a gratuity, or a payment, for good service. People commonly tip waiters and waitresses, hairdressers, bellhops, and cab drivers. In most cases, a tip of 15% is acceptable.

Problem: Four friends went to lunch together. The bill came to $36.40, plus a 5% sales tax. They decided to leave a 15% tip on the entire cost of the lunch (including the tax) and divide the cost equally, each paying the same amount. How much should each person pay for lunch, including the tip? (Round answers to the nearest cent, if necessary.) Do you think this is a reasonable amount for each person to leave for the tip, or might they choose to pay a slightly different amount? Explain your answer.

2-91   **Percent of Increase ★★ (7.RP.3)**

Memorabilia are the kinds of things that everybody once had but are scarce years later. Because they are hard to find, such items may become worth much more money than they originally cost.

For example, past issues of *TV Guide* of the 1950s and 1960s sold for as little as $0.15 per copy. Today these copies may fetch as much as $25 to $30 each from collectors.

Problem: Assuming an issue of *TV Guide* that once sold for $0.15 now sells for $28, what is the percent of increase? Round your answer to the nearest percent.

2-92   **Percent of Decrease ★★ (7.RP.3)**

Henry Ford worked to produce an inexpensive, universal car. When introduced in 1908, his Model T retailed for $850, but by 1924, because of mass production, it was selling for $290.

Problem: Find the percent of decrease. Round your answer to the nearest percent.

2-93 **Adding Positive and Negative Fractions ★★ (7.NS.1)**

When you add fractions with unlike signs, the sign applies to the quantity. For example, in the mixed number $-2\frac{3}{4}$, both 2 and $\frac{3}{4}$ are negative.

Problem: Identify fractions that complete each problem. Choose your answers from the fractions below the problems. Not all of the numbers will be used.

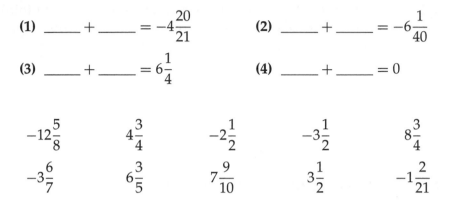

(1) _____ + _____ $= -4\frac{20}{21}$

(2) _____ + _____ $= -6\frac{1}{40}$

(3) _____ + _____ $= 6\frac{1}{4}$

(4) _____ + _____ $= 0$

$$-12\frac{5}{8} \qquad 4\frac{3}{4} \qquad -2\frac{1}{2} \qquad -3\frac{1}{2} \qquad 8\frac{3}{4}$$

$$-3\frac{6}{7} \qquad 6\frac{3}{5} \qquad 7\frac{9}{10} \qquad 3\frac{1}{2} \qquad -1\frac{2}{21}$$

2-94 **Adding Positive and Negative Fractions ★★★ (7.NS.1)**

When adding positive and negative fractions, you must pay close attention to computation as well as the signs of the numbers.

Problem: Use the numbers 6, 9, 1, 3, 7, and −8 to write an addition problem containing mixed numbers that equals $-2\frac{4}{9}$. (Hint: Make one whole number 6, one numerator 7, and one denominator 3.)

2-95   Subtracting Positive and Negative Fractions ★★ (7.NS.1)

Subtracting positive and negative fractions is the same as adding the opposite of the second number: $x - y = x + (-y)$.

Problem: Which of the following four problems are correct? Correct those that are wrong.

$$\text{(1)} \quad \frac{5}{8} - \frac{7}{8} = -\frac{1}{4} \qquad\qquad \text{(2)} \quad -7\frac{5}{6} - 1\frac{2}{3} = -6\frac{2}{3}$$

$$\text{(3)} \quad 6\frac{7}{12} - \left(-9\frac{1}{6}\right) = 15\frac{3}{4} \qquad\qquad \text{(4)} \quad -2\frac{1}{2} - \left(-3\frac{3}{4}\right) = -6\frac{1}{4}$$

2-96   Subtracting Positive and Negative Fractions ★★ (7.NS.1)

Some students find subtracting negative numbers to be confusing. After all, you are "taking away" a quantity that is less than zero, resulting in an answer that is larger than the first number.

Problem: Are the following two problems correct? If yes, explain why. If they are incorrect, correct them.

$$-7\frac{3}{5} + 2\frac{1}{5} = -5\frac{2}{5} \qquad\qquad -7\frac{3}{5} - \left(-2\frac{1}{5}\right) = -5\frac{2}{5}$$

2-97   Multiplying Positive and Negative Fractions ★ (7.NS.2)

When multiplying positive and negative fractions, you must multiply numerator times numerator and denominator times denominator. You must also write the correct sign in your product.

Problem: Using the digits 2, 3, −5, and −7, write two fractions that have the largest product.

2-98   Multiplying Positive and Negative Fractions ★★ G (7.NS.2)

Usually students are asked to solve problems and find answers. In the problem below, you are asked to write a problem that results in a specific answer.

Problem: Create a problem in which two mixed numbers multiplied together equal $-7\frac{2}{3}$. Explain the strategy you used to create your problem.

2-99   Dividing Positive and Negative Fractions ★★ (7.NS.2)

When solving problems, working accurately reduces the chances for making mistakes. Correcting mistakes can often be more challenging than solving the problem in the first place.

Problem: Find and correct the error in each problem so that the quotient is correct.

$$\text{(1)} \quad -5\frac{5}{6} \div 3\frac{2}{3} = -1\frac{3}{4} \qquad\qquad \text{(2)} \quad -3 \div \left(-\frac{3}{4}\right) = -4$$

$$\text{(3)} \quad 7\frac{1}{3} \div \left(-2\frac{1}{5}\right) = 3\frac{1}{3} \qquad\qquad \text{(4)} \quad -10\frac{1}{4} \div \left(-1\frac{4}{5}\right) = 6\frac{1}{4}$$

2-100   Dividing Positive and Negative Fractions ★★ G (7.NS.2)

Sometimes the best way to solve a problem is to work backward. Working backward from a solution can help you to understand the process that results in the solution.

Problem: Complete the problem by filling in the missing numbers. (Hint: Remember to use the reciprocal of the divisor and change the division sign to a multiplication sign before multiplying.)

$$8\frac{1}{4} \div \left(-\underline{\quad}\frac{1}{2}\right) = -2\frac{1}{2}$$

2-101   **Four Operations with Positive and Negative Fractions**
            ★★★ (7.NS.3)

When solving problems with positive and negative fractions and more than one operation, you must follow the order of operations.

Problem: Use the numbers $-\dfrac{3}{4}, -\dfrac{1}{4}, \dfrac{1}{2}, \dfrac{3}{8},$ and $\dfrac{3}{4}$. Place one number in each blank so that the equation equals 0. Each number must be used once.

$$\underline{\quad\quad} \times \underline{\quad\quad} \div \underline{\quad\quad} + \underline{\quad\quad} - \underline{\quad\quad} = 0$$

2-102   **Simplifying Complex Fractions ★★ (7.NS.3)**

Any fraction is the quotient of two quantities. A complex fraction has a fraction in the numerator, the denominator, or both the numerator and denominator.

Problem: Phil often rushes to complete his homework, and sometimes he copies homework problems from the board incorrectly. This time he copied $\dfrac{\frac{5}{7}}{\frac{4}{}}$ and found that it was equal to $2\dfrac{6}{7}$.

He double-checked his work and was sure that he was correct. When he got to school the next day, his teacher said that the answer was $\dfrac{5}{28}$. As soon as he heard her explanation, Phil found his error. What did Phil do wrong?

2-103   **Simplifying Complex Fractions ★★★ (7.NS.3)**

Simplifying complex fractions has four steps:

1. Write the numerator as a fraction or whole number.
2. Write the denominator as a fraction or whole number.
3. Divide the fraction (or whole number) in step 1 by the fraction (or whole number) in step 2.
4. Simplify if necessary.

Problem: Which of the following complex fractions have the same value?

$$(1)\ \dfrac{\frac{2}{5}+1}{\frac{2}{5}} \qquad (2)\ \dfrac{1+\frac{2}{3}}{\frac{1}{4}+\frac{1}{4}} \qquad (3)\ \dfrac{2+\frac{1}{2}}{\frac{1}{2}+\frac{1}{4}} \qquad (4)\ \dfrac{\frac{4}{5}+\frac{3}{5}}{\frac{1}{5}+\frac{1}{5}}$$

2-104   **Adding Positive and Negative Decimals ★ (7.NS.1)**

When adding positive and negative decimals, you must add each digit according to place value and then follow the rules for adding integers.

Problem: Find the sums.

(1) $-3.048 + 4.67$ 　　　　　　　**(2)** $67.5 + (-346.87)$

(3) $16 + (-0.54) + 8.6$ 　　　　　**(4)** $-0.75 + (-6.79) + 2.008 + 3$

2-105   Subtracting Positive and Negative Decimals ★ (7.NS.1)

When subtracting positive and negative decimals, you must add the opposite of the second number, then follow the rules for adding integers. Remember to add the digits according to place value.

Problem: Which of the problems equals −1.612? What are the answers to the other problems?

(1) −7.05 − 6.673	**(2)** −39 − (−37.388)
(3) 107.4 − 105.788	**(4)** −25.04 − (−23.428)

2-106   Multiplying Positive and Negative Decimals ★ (7.NS.2)

Some problems in math may be solved by using various strategies. In multiplication, some products can be the result of numerous factors.

Problem: Using decimals, create a multiplication problem that results in the product of −97.52. Explain how you arrived at your answer.

2-107   Dividing Positive and Negative Decimals ★ (7.NS.2)

To divide positive and negative decimals, follow the steps for dividing decimals, and write the correct sign in the quotient.

Problem: Match each problem with its quotient.

(1) 0.0384 ÷ (−0.64)	(A) −6
(2) −2.406 ÷ (−4.01)	(B) −0.006
(3) −18.72 ÷ 3.12	(C) −0.06
(4) 0.0138 ÷ (−2.3)	(D) 0.6

2-108   Four Operations with Positive and Negative Decimals ★★ G (7.NS.3)

Sums, differences, products, and quotients may be positive, negative, or zero, depending on the numbers.

Problem: Using the numbers -1.4, 2.8, and -0.8, choose the two numbers that:

(1) Have the largest sum   (3) Have the smallest product

(2) Have the smallest difference   (4) Have the largest quotient

2-109   Classifying Numbers as Rational or Irrational ★★ (8.NS.1)

Rational numbers can be expressed as a fraction. Examples of rational numbers and the way they can be expressed as fractions include $-3 = -\dfrac{3}{1}$, $3\dfrac{1}{2} = \dfrac{7}{2}$, $0.4 = \dfrac{4}{10}$, and $-6.9 = -6\dfrac{9}{10} = -\dfrac{69}{10}$. Irrational numbers cannot be expressed as fractions. Examples include $\sqrt{2}$ and π.

Problem: Alicia was asked to classify the following numbers as rational or irrational: 1, -0.38, 4.7, -5, -10.1, and $\sqrt{4}$. She said that all were rational numbers except $\sqrt{4}$ because all square roots are irrational numbers. Do you agree? Explain your answer.

2-110   Changing Repeating Decimals to Rational Numbers ★★ G (8.NS.1)

Danielle always looks for short-cuts when doing math. She recently made this conjecture about how to change repeating decimals to fractions: If there is only one digit to the right of the decimal point and that digit repeats, place the digit over 9 and simplify the fraction. For example, $0.\overline{2} = \dfrac{2}{9}$. She also noted that if there are two digits to the right of the decimal point and those two digits repeat, place the two digits over 99 and simplify the fraction. For example, $0.\overline{42} = \dfrac{42}{99} = \dfrac{14}{33}$.

Problem: Is Danielle's conjecture correct? Explain your reasoning.

2-111   Changing Repeating Decimals to Rational Numbers ★★★ (8.NS.1)

A decimal expansion may be expressed in various ways. For example, $0.8\overline{3}$ may be expressed as $0.83\overline{3}$ or $0.833\overline{3}$ and so on.

Problem: Shane is having trouble expressing $0.41\overline{6}$ as a rational number. Here is what he did. He let $n = 0.41\overline{6}$. Because one digit repeats, he said that $10n = 4.1\overline{6}$, but he was unable to find n, as his math below shows. What was his mistake?

$$10n = 4.1\overline{6}$$
$$-n = 0.41\overline{6}$$
$$\overline{}$$
$$9n =$$

2-112   Rational Approximations of Irrational Numbers ★★ (8.NS.2)

Irrational numbers have a decimal expansion that neither terminates nor repeats. Although irrational numbers cannot be expressed as a fraction, it is possible to find two rational numbers that an irrational number is between when graphed on a number line.

Problem: Use your calculator to find the decimal expansion of $\sqrt{2}, \sqrt{3}, \sqrt{5}, \sqrt{6}, \sqrt{7},$ and $\sqrt{8}$. Then answer the questions. (Hint: You may find it useful to sketch a number line to help you visualize the locations of the irrational numbers.)

(1) What numbers are between 2 and 3?

(2) What numbers are between 1.74 and 2.50?

(3) What numbers are between 1.5 and 2.5?

(4) What numbers are between 1.41 and 1.72?

2-113   Integer Exponents ★ (8.EE.1)

Some properties of exponents are summarized below:

- Any nonzero number raised to the 0 power is equal to 1.
- Any number raised to a negative power is the reciprocal of the number raised to a positive power.
- To multiply numbers with the same bases, add the exponents.
- To divide numbers with the same bases, subtract the exponent of the base in the denominator from the exponent of the base in the numerator.

Problem: Fill in each blank with a missing value so that the equation is true.

(1) $5^{-3} \times 5^2 = $ _____ or _____

(2) $2^3 \div 2^5 = $ _____ or _____ or _____

(3) $-2^3 \div 8 = $ _____ or _____

(4) $5^{-4} = $ _____ or _____

2-114   Integer Exponents ★★ (8.EE.1)

Knowing how to use the properties of exponents allows you to write equivalent expressions correctly and find their values.

Problem: One expression in each row of the following chart is not equivalent to the other three. Identify this expression and find its value. Then find the values of the other expressions in the row.

1.	$(2^3)^2$	8^2	2^6	2^5
2.	$3^4 \times 3^{-1}$	3^3	$\dfrac{3^4}{3^{-1}}$	$\dfrac{3^4}{3^1}$
3.	$\dfrac{1}{5^{-1}}$	$5^3 \times 5^{-4}$	$\dfrac{1}{5}$	5^{-1}
4.	$\dfrac{1}{4^0}$	$\dfrac{1}{2^2}$	2^{-2}	$\dfrac{1}{4}$

2-115   Square and Cube Roots ★★ (8.EE.2)

A perfect square is an integer that is raised to the second power. $3^2 = 9$ because $3 \times 3 = 9$. The square root of a number is a number that when multiplied by itself equals the original number. $\sqrt{9} = 3$ because $9 = 3^2 = 3 \times 3$.

A perfect cube is an integer that is raised to the third power. $3^3 = 27$ because $3 \times 3 \times 3 = 27$. The cube root of a number is a number that when multiplied as a factor three times equals the original number. $\sqrt[3]{27} = 3$ because $27 = 3^3 = 3 \times 3 \times 3$.

Problem: Find the numbers described below.

(1) It is the square root of 16 and the cube root of 64.

(2) The square root of this number is equal to 2^3.

(3) The cube root of this number is equal to 3^2.

(4) The cube root of this number is equal to the square root of 100.

2-116   Using Scientific Notation to Express Small Numbers ★★ (8.EE.3)

Extremely small numbers such as a milligram, which is a thousandth of a gram, and a picogram, which is a trillionth of a gram, are difficult to imagine as well as write. Recopying so many zeroes is tedious and may lead to errors. It is also easy to forget the place value names. Scientific notation eliminates these problems. Unlike large numbers that are written with a positive exponent, small numbers are written with a negative exponent. For example:

1 milligram $= 0.001$ gram $= 1 \times 10^{-3}$ gram

1 picogram $= 0.000000000001$ gram $= 1 \times 10^{-12}$ gram

23 milligrams $= 0.023$ gram $= 2.3 \times 10^{-2}$ gram

781 micrograms $= 0.000781$ gram $= 7.81 \times 10^{-4}$ gram

Problem: Pretend that you are explaining how to express 0.000081 in scientific notation. Write your explanation.

2-117 Using Scientific Notation to Express Large and Small Numbers ★★ (8.EE.3)

A number is written in scientific notation when it is expressed as a product of a number greater than or equal to 1 but less than 10, and a power of 10 in exponential form.

Problem: Express the following in scientific notation.

(1) The nearest star, other than our sun, is about 25,000,000,000,000 miles from Earth.

(2) The diameter of Earth is about 12,700,000 meters.

(3) The mass of an electron is 0.0000000000000000000000000009 grams.

(4) The diameter of a cell is about 0.000025 centimeters.

2-118 Performing Operations with Numbers Expressed in Scientific Notation ★★ (8.EE.4)

When adding, subtracting, multiplying, or dividing numbers written in scientific notation, your answers should also be written in scientific notation.

Problem: Using the numbers 1.6×10^3, 4.8×10^2, 1.6×10^2, and 3.2×10^{-2}, find two numbers whose:

(1) Sum is 6.4×10^2

(2) Difference is 3.2×10^2

(3) Product is 5.12×10^1

(4) Quotient is 5×10^4

2-119   Expressing Large and Small Numbers in Standard Form ★★

Numbers written in scientific notation can easily be written in standard form by "moving" the decimal point.

- If the exponent is positive, move the decimal point to the right the same number of places as the exponent. For example, if the exponent is 7, move the decimal point 7 places to the right.

- If the exponent is negative, move the decimal point to the left the same number of places as the exponent. For example, if the exponent is −7, move the decimal point 7 places to the left.

Problem: Express each number in standard form.

(1) The average adult human has about 1×10^5 hairs on his or her head.

(2) The mass of a carbon atom is 2×10^{-23} gram.

(3) Neptune, the outermost planet, is about 4.5×10^9 kilometers from the sun.

(4) The diameter of an oxygen molecule is 3.19×10^{-8} centimeter.

2-120   A Quotation about Mathematics ★★

Albert Einstein (1879–1955) was a brilliant German physicist who fit the stereotype of an absent-minded professor. Although it was said that he could not remember his phone number—he explained that if he needed it, he could always look it up—he developed the theory of relativity, which has led to profound discoveries about our universe.

Problem: Explain these words of Albert Einstein: "Do not worry about your difficulties in mathematics. I assure you mine are still greater."

Algebra and Beyond

3-1 Simplifying Numerical Expressions with Exponents
★ (6.EE.1)

A symphony orchestra typically has a set number of instruments.

Problem: Simplify the expression below to find the number of instruments in a typical symphony orchestra. How does this number compare to the number of instruments in the band at your school?

$$(4^4 \div 2) - 7 \times 4$$

3-2 Simplifying Numerical Expressions with Exponents
★★ (6.EE.1)

Of Thomas Edison's many inventions, the phonograph is one of his best known. The first words he recorded were "Mary had a little lamb." Although Edison had, without question, an "inventive" mind, he was not very original with his first recording.

Problem: To find the year this message was recorded, simplify this expression.

$$9(3^2 + 2^2)^2 + 89 \times 2^2$$

3-3   Simplifying Numerical Expressions with Exponents
★★★ (6.EE.1)

Imagine if you had a penny. The next day you double it to two pennies. The third day you double the two pennies to four pennies and then continue doubling for a total of 15 days.

Problem: Simplify the expression to find out how much money in dollars you would have at the end of 15 days.

$$1 \times 10^2 + 6 \times 10^1 + 3 \times 10^0 + 8 \times \frac{1}{10} + 4 \times \frac{1}{10^2}$$

3-4   Words and Phrases as Mathematical Expressions
★ G (6.EE.2)

Expressing words as mathematical symbols can be difficult but is necessary to solve equations.

Problem: Compile a list of words or phrases that may be expressed as mathematical symbols. Include the symbol for each phrase. (One example is addition, +. Another is *pi*, π.)

3-5   Writing Phrases as Algebraic Expressions ★ (6.EE.2)

An algebraic expression can be compared to a phrase. Translating a phrase into an algebraic expression is easier if you think about the meanings of the words.

Problem: Match each description with its algebraic expression. (Some expressions are not used.)

(1) 5 times a number	(A) $n - 5$
(2) 5 more than a number	(B) $5n$
(3) A number divided by 5	(C) $5 - n$
(4) 5 less than a number	(D) $5 + n$
	(E) $\dfrac{n}{5}$
	(F) $\dfrac{5}{n}$

3-6   Evaluating Expressions without Exponents ★ (6.EE.2)

In 1897 Sears, Roebuck and Company published its first catalogue, offering a variety of goods, including clothing, jewelry, toys, and farm equipment.

Problem: If $a = 3$, $b = 10$, and $c = 20$, find the cost in cents of each item in 1897 by evaluating the expression. You may be surprised at the prices of these items back then. Why were they so inexpensive compared to prices today?

(1) One pair of steel blade ice skates: $ac + 2$

(2) A baseball: $\dfrac{abc + 4ab}{b}$

(3) A catcher's mitt: $2(a + b) - 2a$

(4) A deck of playing cards: $a + b$

3-7   Evaluating Expressions with Exponents ★ (6.EE.2)

The toy company Mattel produced the Barbie doll and soon afterward introduced Ken, Barbie's boyfriend; Midge, her friend; and Skipper, Barbie's younger sister. By 1980, Barbie was so popular that top fashion designers created clothes for her.

Problem: Evaluate the expression $a^2b + cd$, if $a = 12$, $b = 13$, $c = 43$, and $d = 2$, to find the year the Barbie doll was first produced.

3-8   Evaluating Expressions with Exponents ★★ (6.EE.2)

Many of the numbers in astronomy are, well, "astronomical." For example, distances are so big that they are often expressed in light-years rather than miles. A light-year is the distance light travels in one year. Light travels at a speed of about 186,000 miles per second.

Problem: Let $a = 2$, $b = 3$, and $c = 5$ to evaluate the following expressions.

(1) The approximate rate at which Earth travels around the sun (in miles per second): $ac + b^a$

(2) The approximate rate at which our sun is orbiting around the Milky Way Galaxy (in miles per second): $c(a + b)^a$

(3) The approximate number of years for the Milky Way Galaxy to complete one full rotation (in millions of years): $a(ac)^a$

(4) The approximate distance from Earth to Polaris, the North Star (in light-years): $4(ac)^2 + abc$

3-9   Generating Equivalent Expressions ★ (6.EE.3)

The distributive property states that if a, b, and c are real numbers, then $a(b + c) = ab + ac$ and $ab + ac = a(b + c)$. The a is distributed and multiplied by b, and a is distributed and multiplied by c. The products are then added.

Problem: One or more terms are missing below. Use the distributive property to fill in the blanks.

(1) $4(11 - x) = 44 - $ _____

(2) $2(3x + 1) = $ _____ $+ 2$

(3) $21x - 28y = $ _____ $(3x - $ _____ $)$

(4) _____ $+$ _____ $+ x + x = 4x$

3-10   Generating Equivalent Expressions ★★ (6.EE.3)

If an expression has a common term, an equivalent expression can be written by dividing each term by a common factor and rewriting the expression using the distributive property, $ab + ac = a(b + c)$.

Problem: Nikki rewrote $20x - 100$ as $2(10x - 50)$. There are four other ways to rewrite this expression using the distributive property. What are they?

3-11   Identifying Equivalent Expressions ★ (6.EE.4)

Expressions that look very different may in fact be equivalent. Careful analysis is necessary to identify these expressions.

Problem: Several expressions are written below. Match each expression with an equivalent expression. Be careful—in one case, three expressions are equivalent.

$$16x - 24 \qquad 16x - 40 \qquad 3x + 2x \qquad 8(2x - 5) \qquad 5x$$
$$5(x - 8) \qquad 8(2x - 3) \qquad 5x - 40 \qquad 8x - 3x$$

3-12   Identifying Equivalent Expressions ★★ (6.EE.4)

Two expressions are equivalent if they have the same value. This is true no matter what value is substituted for the variable.

Problem: Tara said that $20x - 4x$ and $4x(5x - 1)$ are equivalent expressions. She explained that she substituted 0 for x in both expressions and found that both expressions were equal to 0. Is Tara correct? Explain your reasoning.

3-13   Identifying the Solution of an Equation ★ (6.EE.5)

An equation may be true or false depending on the value of the variable. A value that makes the equation true is the solution of the equation.

Problem: Three solutions are $x = \dfrac{1}{3}$, $x = 0$, and $x = 3$. Match the solutions with their equations. Some solutions will match two equations. State which equation does not have a solution and explain why.

(1) $3x = 1$	**(2)** $3x = 0$	**(3)** $\dfrac{1}{3}x = 1$
(4) $5x = 15$	**(5)** $x + 3 = 3$	**(6)** $x \div 0 = 0$

3-14   Identifying the Solutions of an Inequality ★ (6.EE.5)

To determine if a number is a solution to an inequality, substitute the value for the variable in the inequality. If the statement is true, the value is a solution of the inequality.

Problem: Sarah wants to see if 0, 1, 3, and 9 are solutions to these inequalities: $3x - 1 \geq 8$ and $x + 4 \leq 5$. She said that of these numbers, 9 is a solution to $3x - 1 \geq 8$ and 0 is the only solution to $x + 4 \leq 5$. Her teacher said that Sarah misunderstood one concept. What do you think Sarah misunderstood?

3-15   Variables ★ (6.EE.6)

Not all stars shine with constant brightness. Some, called variable stars, change in brightness.

Problem: Using your experience with variables in your math classes, do you think "variable stars" is an appropriate name for stars that change in brightness? Explain your answer.

3-16   Using Variables to Represent Numbers ★ (6.EE.6)

An expression is a group of symbols such as numbers, operation signs, variables, or grouping symbols that can be used to solve a real-world mathematical problem.

Problem: Joaquin is in charge of the student council dance at his school. Because he does not know the exact number of students who will attend the dance, he said: "Let $s =$ the number of students attending." Using the variable s, write the expressions described below.

(1) The total amount of money collected if each student who attends pays $6.

(2) The number of chaperones needed if the school requires 1 chaperone per 20 students.

(3) The number of tables required if 4 students sit at each table.

(4) The number of balloons needed if there are to be 2 balloons per table.

3-17   Solving One-Step Equations — Addition ★ (6.EE.7)

Solving an equation is like using a balance. If you add a number to one side of the equation, you must add the same number to the other side.

Problem: Write a word problem that can be solved by using the equation $x - 7 = 8$. Then use addition to solve the problem. Be sure to show all the steps.

3-18   Solving One-Step Equations — Subtraction ★ (6.EE.7)

Solving an equation by subtraction involves "taking" the same amount from both sides of the equation. Think of it like this. Suppose two of your friends have the same amount of money in their wallets. If each pays $12 for a movie admission, they will still have an equal amount of money.

Problem: Which problems below can be solved by subtraction? Use subtraction to solve these equations. Can any other problem, or problems, be solved by another method? If yes, what method?

(1) $x + 15 = 20$ (2) $x + 11 = 12$ (3) $x + 15 = 60$
(4) $x + 14 = 14$ (5) $x - 13 = 13$ (6) $x + 10 = 25$

3-19   Solving One-Step Equations — Addition and Subtraction ★★ (6.EE.7)

Equivalent equations are two or more equations that have the same solution. To solve an equation, try to write it as an equivalent equation. Addition and subtraction are two ways this might be done.

Problem: State which problems can be solved by adding 8 to both sides. Show those that can be solved by subtracting 8 from both sides. Then solve each equation.

(1) $x - 8 = 15$ (2) $x + 8 = 27$ (3) $x + 8 = 10$
(4) $x + 8 = 24$ (5) $x - 8 = 10$ (6) $x + 8 = 16$

3-20   **Solving One-Step Equations — Multiplication ★ (6.EE.7)**

If each side of an equation is multiplied by the same nonzero number, the resulting equation has the same solution as the original equation.

Problem: Imagine that you are a teacher. Explain how you would teach your math class to solve $\frac{1}{4}x = 20$ using multiplication. Then solve the problem.

3-21   **Solving One-Step Equations — Division ★ (6.EE.7)**

Dividing both sides of an equation by the same nonzero number results in a second equation that will have the same solution as the original equation.

Problem: Solve for x.

    (1) $3x = 48$ **(2)** $6x = 48$ **(3)** $12x = 48$

    (4) $\frac{1}{4}x = 48$ **(5)** $\frac{1}{2}x = 48$ **(6)** $\frac{3}{8}x = 48$

3-22   **Solving One-Step Equations — Multiplication and Division ★★ (6.EE.7)**

Multiplication and division are inverse (or opposite) operations. For example, dividing a number by 2 is the same as multiplying the number by $\frac{1}{2}$. Some equations may be solved by multiplication and by division depending on what numbers are used.

Problem: Each equation can be solved in two ways. Fill in the blanks; then solve each equation.

    (1) $3x = 15$ can be solved by dividing each side by _____ or multiplying each side
        by _____. $x =$ _____

    (2) $\frac{1}{3}x = 15$ can be solved by dividing each side by _____ or by multiplying each
        side by _____. $x =$ _____

3-23   Writing Inequalities ★ (6.EE.8)

An inequality is a mathematical statement that shows that two quantities are not equal. One quantity may be < (less than), ≤ (less than or equal to), > (greater than), ≥ (greater than or equal to), or ≠ (not equal to) another quantity.

Problem: Write an inequality to describe each situation.

> **(1)** n = the number of people. At least 4 people are needed to play a game.
>
> **(2)** t = today's temperature. The temperature today exceeded the record high of 96°F.
>
> **(3)** e = Michelle's earnings. Yesterday Michelle earned more than $30 babysitting.
>
> **(4)** h = height of children able to ride the kiddie bumper cars. If you are over 4 feet tall, you cannot ride the kiddie bumper cars.

3-24   Solving Inequalities ★★ (7.EE.4)

When solving inequalities, it is important to determine if the answer makes sense. The answer to an inequality may be mathematically correct but may not apply to a real-world situation.

Problem: Marco wants to do well in math class. He has taken one test and received a score of 80. There is only one more test this marking period, and he wants to achieve at least a 95 test average. His brother said that this is impossible, but Marco wrote an inequality to show that it is possible. What inequality might Marco have written? Is Marco's mathematical conclusion reasonable? Explain.

3-25   Representing Relationships between Dependent and Independent Variables ★★ G (6.EE.9)

Stores often have sales where the sale price is a fraction of the regular price. The sale price of an item, of course, depends on the item's regular price.

Problem: Discount Dan's Sporting Goods Shop is having a huge sale. Everything is $\frac{1}{4}$ off the regular price. Complete the table where r = the regular price and s = the sale price. Then write an equation to show how the sale price is related to the regular price.

	r	s
1.	$50	
2.	$100	
3.	$75	
4.	$30	

3-26   Generating Equivalent Expressions ★★ (7.EE.1)

A variable expression is a group of numbers, variables, and operation symbols. An equivalent expression is an expression that has the same value as another expression. For example, $3a + 2b + 6a + 5b$ is equivalent to $9a + 7b$.

Problem: Mrs. Sanchez, who is in charge of the testing program at Wilson Middle School, must have enough test booklets and teachers' manuals for every teacher participating in the school's testing program. Write a variable expression that represents each situation. Then write an equivalent expression.

(1) Mrs. Sanchez has a stack of 58 test booklets and 1 teacher's manual and another stack of 42 test booklets and 3 teachers' manuals on her desk.

(2) Mrs. Sanchez gave Mr. Ellis 10 test booklets and 1 teacher's manual.

(3) Show, by factoring, that there are enough booklets and teachers' manuals left to distribute evenly for 3 classes of 30 students each and 1 teacher each.

3-27   **Rewriting Expressions in Different Forms ★★ (7.EE.2)**

When solving problems that contain expressions, rewriting the expressions can make computation easier. This is a good problem-solving strategy.

Problem: Trisha lives in a state that has a 7% sales tax. When she goes out to eat with friends, she multiplies the amount of the sales tax by 2 rather than figure out 15% of the bill to estimate the tip for the meal. Trisha says that the result is a close approximation of what the tip should be. Write two expressions to show how the tip is related to the sales tax.

3-28   **Solving Two-Step Equations ★★ (7.EE.3)**

Two-step equations are equations that require two steps to solve. If each side of an equation is in simplest form, follow the steps below:

1. Add the same number to each side of the equation, or subtract the same number from each side of the equation.

2. Multiply or divide each side of the equation by the same nonzero number.

Problem: Of the four problems listed below, which have the same solution?

    (1) $3a + 4 = -2$ **(2)** $2a + 14 = 0$
    (3) $11 = 7 - 2a$ **(4)** $-3a + 18 = 39$

3-29   **Solving Two-Step Equations ★★ G (7.EE.4)**

Creating word problems is sometimes more difficult than solving them.

Problem: Write a word problem. The solution to your problem should require writing an equation that can be solved by adding or subtracting the same number from both sides, and then multiplying or dividing both sides by the same nonzero number. Then write an explanation of how you created the problem.

3-30　Solving Two-Step Equations ★★ (7.EE.4)

Using equations to solve problems is an important problem-solving skill. It is sometimes possible to write two different equations to solve the same problem.

Problem: Joe and Joanna were given the following problem to solve: "The perimeter of a rectangle is 132 inches, and the rectangle's width is 30 inches. Find the rectangle's length."

Joe wrote the equation $132 = 2(l + 30)$, where $l =$ the length of the rectangle. Joanna wrote the equation $132 = 2l + 60$. Both found the length to be 36 inches. Which one of the equations is correct? Or are both correct? Explain your answer.

3-31　Square Roots, Cube Roots, and Equations ★★ (8.EE.2)

Solving the equation $s^2 = A$ can be thought of as finding the length of a side of a square, given its area. For example, if the area of a square is 36 square units, solve the equation $s^2 = 36$, where s is the length of a side. Therefore, $s = \sqrt{36} = 36$ units. Another solution to the equation is $s = -6$, but this has no meaning in an area problem because the lengths of the sides must be positive.

Similarly, the solution to $s^2 = 7$ is $s = \sqrt{7}$, which is an irrational number because no rational number raised to the second power is equal to 7. Another solution is $s = -\sqrt{7}$, which is also irrational.

Solving the equation $e^3 = V$ can be thought of as finding the length of a side of a cube given the volume. For example, if the volume of a cube is 125 cubic units, $e^3 = 125$, where e is the length of an edge. $e = \sqrt[3]{125} = 5$. Likewise, if $e^3 = 10$, the solution is $e = \sqrt[3]{10}$, which is irrational because no rational number raised to the third power equals 10.

Problem: Solve each equation. State whether each solution is rational or irrational.

(1) $s^2 = 100$	**(2)** $e^3 = 216$	**(3)** $s^2 = 8$
(4) $e^3 = 8$	**(5)** $e^3 = 1,000$	**(6)** $s^2 = 1$

3-32   **Interpreting the Unit Rate ★★ G (8.EE.5)**

Talia's mother is eating healthier food and is very interested in the number of calories per serving for the foods she eats. By reading the labels on bags or cans of vegetables, she can find the number of calories per serving. On a recent shopping trip she noted the following:

- Beans (no salt): 20 calories per serving
- Vegetables in butter sauce: 90 calories per serving
- Veggie medley: 60 calories per serving
- Mixed vegetables: 45 calories per serving

Problem: Write an equation that relates the total number of calories to the number of servings for each vegetable. (Let $C =$ the total number of calories and $s =$ the number of servings.) Sketch the graph of the vegetable that has the most calories per serving.

3-33   **Using Similar Triangles to Explain Slope ★★★ (8.EE.6)**

$\triangle ABC \sim \triangle ADE$ because corresponding sides are proportional.

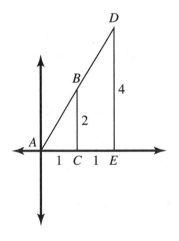

Problem: Use the fact that the triangles above are similar to show that the slope of $\overline{AB}$ is the same as the slope of $\overline{AD}$. Explain why the slope between any two points on a nonvertical line in the coordinate plane is the same.

3-34   Finding the Slope of a Line ★★

The coordinates of pairs of points can be used to find the slope of a line. If two points are on a line, the slope of the line between the points is always the same regardless of which points you select.

To calculate the slope, m, of a line, use any two points (x_1, y_1) and (x_2, y_2) and substitute them into the formula: slope $= \dfrac{y_2 - y_1}{x_2 - x_1}$ where $(x_1 \neq x_2)$. Note, if $x_1 = x_2$, then the slope of the line is undefined because division by 0 is undefined.

Problem: The slope of each line below is given. Find the point that is not on the line.

    (1) $m = -2$: $(-1, 8), (-2, 10), (-3, 12), (-5, 15)$

    (2) $m = 1$: $(0, 1), (3, 3), (4, 4), (7, 7)$

    (3) $m = -1$: $(0, 4), (2, 2), (6, -1), (8, -4)$

3-35   Slopes of Horizontal and Vertical Lines ★

$m = \dfrac{y_2 - y_1}{x_2 - x_1}$ is the formula for finding the slope of a line through two points having the coordinates (x_1, y_1) and (x_2, y_2), provided that $x_1 \neq x_2$.

Problem: Write an explanation of why a horizontal line has a slope of 0. Then write an explanation of why the slope of a vertical line is undefined.

3-36   Application of Finding the Slope ★★

Slopes are used in planning and constructing roofs of buildings. The slope of a roof is called the *pitch*. You can find the pitch of a roof by using this formula:

$$\text{pitch} = \text{rise of the roof} \div \frac{1}{2} \text{ the span of the roof}$$

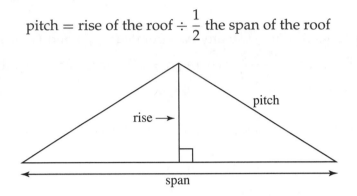

Problem: If the rise of a roof is 10 feet and the span is 24 feet, find the pitch. Compare the pitch of a roof to the slope of a line, using the formula: $\text{slope} = \dfrac{\text{rise}}{\text{run}}$.

3-37   Identifying Like Terms ★

The word *coefficient* comes from two Latin words, *co* and *efficiens*, which mean "to effect together."

A coefficient, or a numerical coefficient, is the number directly in front of a variable. For example:

   $3x$ means 3 times x; 3 is the coefficient.

   x means 1 times x; 1 is the coefficient.

A coefficient is an important part of the definition of like terms, which states that like terms are the same except for their numerical coefficients.

Problem: Two pairs of numbers below are like terms. Name them, and then rewrite the pairs of numbers that are not like terms so that they are like terms.

   (1) $3x, 4x$ **(2)** $7x^2, 4x^3$ **(3)** $8y, 8y^2$ **(4)** $-x, x$

3-38 Simplifying Expressions ★

An expression can be compared to a phrase. To simplify an expression, you must combine like terms and numbers so that the expression has the fewest possible terms. Then you add, subtract, multiply, or divide the other numbers.

Problem: Simplify the following expressions. If you simplified correctly, you will find a relationship between some of the answers. Describe this relationship.

(1) $3x - 4y - (-6x) + 4y + 7y + 6x$

(2) $3 + x - 2y + 7 + 3x + 4y - 5y$

(3) $x - (-3y) + 4x - x - 6y + 8 + 2$

(4) $7y - 4x - 10x + 21x - 2x$

(5) $8x - 3y + 4y - 9x + 10$

3-39 Simplifying Expressions ★★

Simplifying an expression involves combining similar terms and combining numbers.

Problem: Fill in the missing terms to complete the equations.

(1) $9a + \underline{\hspace{1cm}} + \underline{\hspace{1cm}} + 10 = 7a + 13$

(2) $2a - 4b - \underline{\hspace{1cm}} + \underline{\hspace{1cm}} - 3 + \underline{\hspace{1cm}} = -2a + 16b + 3$

(3) $-a - (-b) + c - \underline{\hspace{1cm}} + \underline{\hspace{1cm}} - \underline{\hspace{1cm}} = -2a - b + 2c$

(4) $3a + 2a + 6b - 4b + 10 - \underline{\hspace{1cm}} - \underline{\hspace{1cm}} = 2b + 2$

3-40   Simplifying and Evaluating Expressions ★

Whereas simplifying an expression results in an expression with fewer terms, evaluating an expression results in a number.

Problem: Simplify each of the following expressions. Then evaluate the expression if $a = -2$, $b = 3$, and $c = 5$. What do you notice about the values of the expressions?

(1) $-15 - 6c + 3b - 6c + 9 + 2a$

(2) $3a - 4a + 6a - 9b + 4c - 10$

(3) $b - 3c + 2a - c - 4b - 6a$

(4) $3c - 5a + 9b + a - b + 10$

3-41   Solving Equations involving Several Steps with Variables on the Same Side ★ (8.EE.7)

The following steps will help you solve equations in which all of the variables are on the same side:

1. Simplify each side of the equation. This may involve using the distributive property and/or combining like terms and numbers.

2. Add or subtract the same number from each side of the equation.

3. Multiply or divide each side of the equation by the same nonzero number.

Problem: Fill in the blanks in each step below.

$$-10 + 4(3a + 10) = 18$$

$$-10 + 12a + \underline{\qquad} = 18$$

$$12a + \underline{\qquad} = 18$$

$$12a = \underline{\qquad}$$

$$a = \underline{\qquad}$$

3-42   **Solving Equations involving Several Steps with Variables on the Same Side ★★ (8.EE.7)**

Solving equations is a skill that has a great potential for errors in solving the problem and checking the solution.

Problem: The two equations below have been solved. Are they correct? If a solution is incorrect, find the correct solution.

(1) $a - (1 - 2a) + (a - 3) = -4; a = 0$ (2) $-9 - 3(2a - 1) = -18; a = 2$

3-43   **Solving Equations involving Several Steps with Variables on Both Sides ★★ (8.EE.7)**

Sometimes equations have variables on both sides of the equal sign. If this is the case, you may add the variable expression to both sides of the equation or subtract the variable expression from both sides of the equation.

Problem: Which solutions to the problems below are even numbers? What are these solutions?

(1) $9n = 7n + 16$ (2) $12n - 84 = 5n$
(3) $5(2 + n) = 3(n + 6)$ (4) $5(n + 3) - (1 + 2n) = 4n - 1$

3-44   **Solving Equations involving Several Steps with Variables on Both Sides ★★ (8.EE.7)**

Sometimes the final step to the solution of an equation is equivalent to a false statement, such as $3 = 8$ or $-6 = 15$. These equations have no solution.

If the final step is equivalent to a statement that is always true, such as $x = x$ or $3 = 3$, then the equation is called an identity and is true for all real numbers.

Problem: Which equations below have no solution? Which are true for all real numbers?

(1) $3n = 2n + n$ (2) $4c = c$
(3) $a + 4 = 1 + a$ (4) $2n - 7 = 7 + 2n$
(5) $3(n + 5) - 6 = 3(n + 3)$ (6) $6a - 2(2 - a) = 4(2a - 1)$

3-45   **Points of Intersection of Linear Equations ★ (8.EE.8)**

Carrie graphed $y = 2x + 1$ and $y = x + 4$ in the coordinate plane. She found that the point of intersection was (3, 7) and said that this was the solution of both equations.

Problem: Is Carrie correct? Explain your reasoning.

3-46   **Estimating Solutions to Systems of Linear Equations by Graphing ★★ (8.EE.8)**

The graphing method of solving systems of linear equations works well if the numbers are small and the equations intersect at a point where the grid lines on the plane intersect. If the lines do not intersect there, you must estimate the solution.

Problem: Graph $y = \dfrac{1}{2}x - \dfrac{1}{2}$ and $y = 3x + 5$ in the coordinate plane, and estimate the solution.

3-47   **Using the Graphing Method to Solve Systems of Linear Equations ★ (8.EE.8)**

A system of equations is two or more equations with the same variables. To use the graphing method, graph each equation in the same coordinate plane.

- If the lines intersect, the point of intersection is the solution to both equations.
- If the lines are parallel, there is no solution.
- If the lines coincide—meaning the graphs are the same—there are an infinite number of solutions.

Problem: Graph each system of equations. State whether the lines intersect, are parallel, or coincide. If the lines intersect, find the solution. You may have to estimate.

(1) $y = x$
$\quad\ y = 3x + 5$

(2) $y = \dfrac{1}{2}x + 5$
$\quad\ 2y - x = 4$

(3) $y = 2x - 1$
$\quad\ y - 2x + 1 = 0$

(4) $y = \dfrac{1}{2}x - 1$
$\quad\ y - 3x - 5 = 0$

3-48   Using the Substitution Method to Solve Systems of Linear Equations ★★ (8.EE.8)

The substitution method is one of the many algebraic methods for solving a system of equations. It is best to use this method when the coefficient of one of the variables is 1 or −1.

A list of steps used to solve equations with the substitution method follows:

1. Solve one equation for one of the variables whose coefficient is 1.

2. Substitute this expression in the equation you have not used. This results in an equation in one variable. Solve this equation.

3. Substitute this expression in the equation you used in step 1 and solve it.

4. Check your answers in both original equations.

Problem: Each system of equations can be solved by using the substitution method. Identify the variables for which the substitution method could be used. Solve each system by using the substitution method.

(1) $y - 5x = 0$ **(2)** $3x + 4y = 19$ **(3)** $5x - y = -17$

$\quad\;\; x + y = 12$ $\quad\;\; 4x = y + 19$ $\quad\;\; 3x = 4y$

3-49 **Using the Addition-or-Subtraction Method to Solve Systems of Linear Equations ★★ (8.EE.8)**

If the coefficients of one of the variables are the same or if the coefficients are opposites, the addition-or-subtraction method can be used to solve a system of linear equations. The method is described below:

1. Add or subtract the equations to eliminate one variable. Add the equations if the coefficients of one of the variables are opposites. Subtract the equations if the coefficients of one of the variables are the same.

2. Solve the equation that results from step 1.

3. Substitute this value in either of the original equations.

4. Check your answer in both of the original equations.

Problem: Manuel received a score of 75% on his quiz on solving systems of linear equations using the addition-or-subtraction method. His work is shown below. Explain how you think his teacher graded the quiz.

(1) $4x - y = 0$
$x + y = 10$
$5x = 10$
$x = 2$
$y = 8$

(2) $3y - x = 0$
$5y - x = 18$
$-2y = -18$
$y = 9$

(3) $2x - 3y = 17$
$2x + 3y = -1$
$4x = 16$
$x = 4$
$y = -3$

(4) $2x - 5y = 14$
$2x + 3y = 10$
$-8y = 4$
$y = -\dfrac{1}{2}$
$x = 16\dfrac{1}{2}$

3-50   Using Multiplication with the Addition-or-Subtraction Method to Solve Systems of Linear Equations ★★ (8.EE.8)

To use the multiplication method to solve systems of linear equations, multiply one or both equations so that the coefficients of one of the variables will be the same or the opposite. Then use the addition-or-subtraction method.

The multiplication method is usually used with the following conditions:

- To clear equations of fractions
- If the coefficients of a variable are relatively prime (have a greatest common factor of 1)
- If one of the coefficients of a variable is a factor (other than 1) of the other

Problem: There are two ways to solve the following system of linear equations.

$$5x - 9y = 51$$
$$4x + 3y = -17$$

John said to multiply the second equation by 3 and then use the addition method. Maria said to multiply the first equation by 4, the second equation by 5, and use the subtraction method. Explain which method you like better and why. Use the method you chose to solve the system of equations.

3-51   Choosing Methods and Solving Systems of Linear Equations ★★ (A-REI.6)

There are several ways to solve a system of linear equations: graphing, substitution, addition-or-subtraction, and multiplication with addition-or-subtraction.

Problem: Solve each system of linear equations. Use the method you prefer.

(1) $2x + y = 0$

$y = \dfrac{1}{3}x$

(2) $x + y = 2$

$3x - 2y = -9$

(3) $\dfrac{x}{3} - \dfrac{y}{2} = 6$

$\dfrac{x}{2} + \dfrac{y}{8} = 2$

(4) $x - y = 1$

$-2x + y = -3$

3-52   **Multiplying Monomials** ★

To multiply monomials, first multiply the numerical coefficients. Then use the rule of exponents, which states $a^m \cdot a^n = a^{m+n}$ where m and n are natural numbers.

Problem: There are seven errors in the equations below. Find and correct them.

     (1) $(3a^3)(5a^5) = 8a^5$ **(2)** $(6x^3)(3x^3) = 18x^9$

     (3) $(2c)(3c) = 5c$ **(4)** $(a^4)(a^3) = a^7$

     (5) $(4c^2)(-2c^3) = 8c^5$ **(6)** $(5r^3s^2)(-3s)(2r^3s^4) = -30r^6s^6$

3-53   **Multiplying Monomials** ★★ G

Geometry and algebra are connected. Geometry includes the study of angles and polygons, but the length of the sides of the figures may be algebraic expressions rather than numbers.

Problem: Show that the volume of the cylinder equals the volume of the sphere plus the volume of the cone. The radius of each figure is r. The height of the cylinder and cone is $2r$.

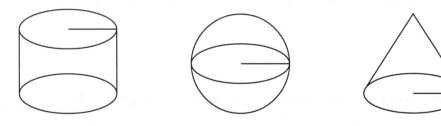

3-54   Powers of Monomials ★★

Rules of exponents are very specific for multiplying powers of monomials:

- The rule of exponents for a power of a power is $(a^m)^n = a^{mn}$ where m and n are positive integers.
- The rule of exponents for a power of a product is $(ab)^m = a^m b^m$ where m is a positive integer.

Problem: In each row, one expression does not belong because it is not equivalent to the others. Identify these expressions.

(1) $a^2 \cdot a^2 \cdot a^2$	$(a^2)^3$	a^5	a^6
(2) $16a^{12}$	$(4a^6)(4a^6)$	$(2a^3)^4$	$8a^7$
(3) $9a^2$	$-9a^2$	$-(3a)^2$	$-3a^2 \cdot 3$
(4) $2a^6b^8$	$4a^6b^8$	$2(a^3b^4)^2$	$2a^3b^4 \cdot a^3b^4$

3-55   Powers of Monomials ★★

The volume of a cube is found by raising the length of a side to the third power.

Problem: One cube has a side with the length of $2x$. Another cube has a side with the length of $6x$. How does the volume of the larger cube compare with the volume of the smaller cube?

3-56   Rewriting Monomials ★★ (A-SSE.2)

A perfect square is a number or monomial raised to the second power. A perfect cube is a number or monomial raised to the third power.

Problem: Which of the following expressions can be rewritten as a monomial raised to the second power? Which can be rewritten as a monomial raised to third power? Rewrite each monomial.

(1) $8x^3$	**(2)** $4x^6$	**(3)** $25x^8$	**(4)** $16x^{12}$
(5) $27x^6$	**(6)** $81x^{10}$	**(7)** $125x^3$	**(8)** $36x^4$

3-57   Dytextbf{Dividing Monomials} ★

The rule of exponents for division states: If m and n are integers and a is not equal to 0, then $\frac{a^m}{a^n} = a^{m-n}$.

Problem: Write an explanation of the rule of exponents for division. Use the examples below to help you.

$$\frac{a^5}{a^2} \qquad \frac{a^8}{a^9} \qquad \frac{a^3}{a^3}$$

3-58   **Dividing Monomials** ★

The word *billion* comes from two French words, *bi*, which means "two," and *million*, which means "million." A billion may be represented as 10^9. A million may be represented as 10^6.

Problem: How many times greater is 1 billion than 1 million?

3-59   **Dividing Monomials** ★★

Division of monomials can be checked the same way as division of whole numbers. For example, $12 \div 4 = 3$ can be checked by multiplying 3×4, which equals 12. Likewise, $\frac{12a^6}{3a^4} = 4a^2$ can be checked by multiplying $4a^2 \times 3a^4$, which equals $12a^6$.

In each case, the quotient is multiplied by the divisor.

Problem: Check the problems below to make sure they are correct. Find the correct quotient for any incorrect problems. Assume no denominator equals 0.

(1) $\dfrac{a^9}{a^2} = a^7$ (2) $\dfrac{a^8 b^3}{a^6 b^4} = \dfrac{a^2}{b}$ (3) $\dfrac{24a^6 b^3}{8a^2 b^3} = 3a^3$ (4) $\dfrac{5a^2 b^5}{25a^3 b} = \dfrac{b^4}{5a}$

3-60   Interpreting Algebraic Expressions ★ (A-SSE.1)

Sometimes even simple expressions may have several parts. Identifying and interpreting their parts will help you to solve difficult equations.

Problem: Consider the expressions $4s$, $2(l+w)$, and $2a+b$. $4s$ is commonly used to find the perimeter of a square, $2(l+w)$ is used to find the perimeter of a rectangle, and $2a+b$ is used to find the perimeter of an isosceles triangle. Use this information to answer the following questions.

(1) Which expressions have two factors?

(2) Which expressions (or part of expressions) are sums?

(3) Which expressions (or part of expressions) have two terms?

(4) Which expression can be rewritten so that each variable has a numerical coefficient?

3-61   Finding the Greatest Common Factor (GCF) of Monomials ★

The greatest common factor (GCF) of two or more monomials is the common factor that has the greatest coefficient and the greatest degree in each variable.

Follow the steps below to find the GCF of two or more monomials:

1. Find the GCF of the numerical coefficients.
2. Find the smaller power of each variable that appears in both monomials.

For example, the greatest common factor of $20x^2y$ and $15x^3$ is $5x^2$.

Problem: Match the pairs of monomials with their greatest common factor.

(1) $8x, 2xy$ (A) 1

(2) $14x^3y^2, 21x^3y^3$ (B) $2x^2y^7$

(3) $2x^2, 3y$ (C) xy

(4) $4x^2y^7, 6x^5y^{10}$ (D) $2x$

(5) $15x^2y^3, 10x^2y^3$ (E) $5x^2y^3$

(6) $12x^3y^2, 5xy$ (F) $7x^3y^2$

3-62   Polynomials ★ G (A-APR.1)

A polynomial is an algebraic expression that has more than one term. Polynomials have many uses. For example, they may be used to determine an individual's or team's score in basketball. The following formula may be used:

$S = 3t + 2g + f$, where S is the total score, t is the number of three-point goals, g is the number of two-point goals, and f is the number of free throws.

Problem: Find the total score for a basketball player who scored two three-point goals, 10 two-point goals, and seven free throws. Write a polynomial to determine the score in another sport.

3-63   Adding and Subtracting Polynomials ★ (A-APR.1)

Binomials and trinomials are special types of polynomials. Whereas a polynomial is an algebraic expression that has more than one term, a binomial has two terms, and a trinomial has three terms.

To add or subtract polynomials, you must first combine like terms. A polynomial is simplified if there are no like terms.

Problem: Polynomials are either added or subtracted to obtain the sum or difference. Find the missing polynomials.

(1) $(3a - 2) + (\underline{}) = 8a + 7$

(2) $5n + 3 - (\underline{}) = 3n - 4$

(3) $(7x^2 - 3xy + 4y^2) + (\underline{}) = 9x^2 - 4xy + 3y^2$

(4) $(3a - 5) - (\underline{}) = 2a - 7$

3-64   Multiplying a Monomial by a Binomial ★ (A-APR.1)

The distributive property can be helpful in multiplying a monomial by a binomial. Just remember to "distribute" the monomial to each term of the polynomial.

Problem: Which problems below are correct? Correct those that are incorrect.

(1) $2(x - 5) = 2x - 10$

(2) $4x(x + 7) = 4x^2 + 28$

(3) $-3a(6a^2 - 4b) = -18a^3 - 12ab$

(4) $3x(x - 5) + 2x(4x + 3) = 11x^2 - 9x$

3-65   **Dividing a Polynomial by a Monomial ★ (A-APR.1)**

To divide a polynomial by a monomial, divide each term of the polynomial by the monomial; then add the quotients.

Problem: There is at least one error in each problem below. Correct the problems.

(1) $\dfrac{18a - 24}{6} = 3a - 18$

(2) $\dfrac{27b^2 - 18b - 9}{-9} = -3b^2 - 2b - 1$

(3) $\dfrac{42s^2t^4 - 49st^2}{7st^2} = 6st^2 - 1$

(4) $\dfrac{45r^4s^2 - 75r^3s + 30r^2}{-15r^2} = 3r^2s^2 - 5s - 2$

3-66   **Multiplying Binomials ★ (A-APR.1)**

FOIL is an acronym for **First, Outer, Inner, Last.** Remembering FOIL can help you to multiply binomials:

1. Multiply the *first* term of each binomial.

2. Multiply the *outer* terms (the first term of the first binomial by the last term of the second binomial).

3. Multiply the *inner* terms (the second term of the first binomial by the first term of the second binomial).

4. Multiply the *last* terms of each binomial.

5. Simplify.

Problem: Match each binomial with its product.

(1) $(x + 7)(x + 2)$ (A) $x^2 - 5x - 14$
(2) $(3x - 1)(3x + 1)$ (B) $9x^2 - 1$
(3) $(9x + 5)(x - 4)$ (C) $x^2 + 9x + 14$
(4) $(x - 7)(x + 2)$ (D) $9x^2 - 31x - 20$

3-67   Multiplying Binomials ★ (A-APR.1)

If the length and width of a rectangle are binomials, the area of the rectangle is the product of the binomials.

Problem: Find the area of each rectangle in terms of x.

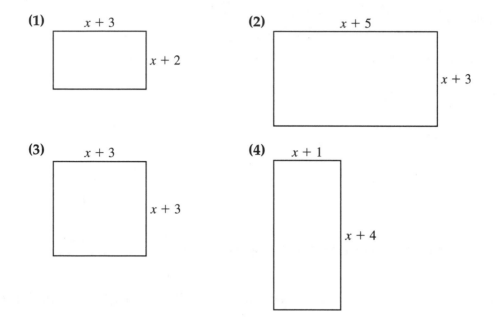

(1) $x + 3$, $x + 2$

(2) $x + 5$, $x + 3$

(3) $x + 3$, $x + 3$

(4) $x + 1$, $x + 4$

3-68   Cubes of Binomials ★★ (A-APR.4)

Cubing a binomial means using the binomial as a factor three times. For example:

$$(a + b)^3 = a^3 + 3a^2b + 3ab^2 + b^3$$
$$(a - b)^3 = a^3 - 3a^2b + 3ab^2 - b^3$$

Problem: Substitute 4 for a and 6 for b to show that each equation above is true for these values. Multiply $(a + b)(a + b)(a + b)$ to verify the first equation; then multiply $(a - b)(a - b)(a - b)$ to verify the second equation.

3-69   Rewriting Differences of Squares ★★ (A-SSE.2)

A perfect square is a number (or a monomial) multiplied by itself. The difference of squares can be written in factored form.

Following are some examples:

$$a^2 - b^2 = (a - b)(a + b)$$
$$a^2 - 9 = (a - 3)(a + 3)$$
$$4a^2 - 25b^2 = (2a - 5b)(2a + 5b)$$

Problem: How could you factor $9a^6 - 25b^8$?

3-70   Factoring Squares of Binomials ★★ (A-SSE.3)

Squaring a binomial can be compared to finding the area of a square. Multiply the length of the side by itself. Following are two examples:

$$(a + b)^2 = a^2 + 2ab + b^2$$
$$(a - b)^2 = a^2 + 2ab - b^2$$

Problem: The areas of four squares are listed below. Find the length of each side.

(1) $a^2 + 8a + 16$ **(2)** $a^2 - 10a + 25$

(3) $49a^2 - 56a + 16$ **(4)** $36a^4 - 12a^2b^3 + b^6$

3-71   **Factoring Trinomials of the Form $x^2 + bx + c$ Where $c > 0$**
          ★★ (A-SSE.3)

Being able to identify patterns is an important skill in factoring binomials. Following are two examples:

- $x^2 + 7x + 10 = (x+5)(x+2)$.   Note that 7, the coefficient of x, on the left side of the equation is equal to the sum of 5 and 2 on the right side.   10 on the left side is equal to the product of 5 and 2 on the right side.
- $x^2 - 11x + 10 = (x-10)(x-1)$.   Note that -11, the coefficient of x, on the left side of the equation is equal to the sum of -10 and -1 on the right side.   10 on the left side is equal to the product of -10 and -1 on the right.

Problem: Fill in the blanks to complete the equations.

(1) $x^2 + 6x + 5 = (x + \underline{\quad})(x + \underline{\quad})$

(2) $x^2 - 13x + 42 = (x - \underline{\quad})(x - \underline{\quad})$

(3) $x^2 + 9x + \underline{\quad} = (x + 6)(x + \underline{\quad})$

(4) $x^2 - \underline{\quad} + 45 = (x - 9)(x - \underline{\quad})$

3-72   **Factoring Trinomials of the Form $x^2 + bx + c$ Where $c < 0$**
          ★★ (A-SSE.3)

The product of a positive number and a negative number is always negative. The sum of a positive number and a negative number may be positive, negative, or zero, depending on the numbers. These facts are important when factoring trinomials. Following are two examples.

- $x^2 - x - 12 = (x-4)(x+3)$.   Note that -1, the coefficient of x, on the left side of the equation, is equal to the sum of -4 and 3 on the right side. -12 on the left side is the product of -4 and 3 on the right side.
- $x^2 + 2x - 15 = (x+5)(x-3)$.   Note that 2, the coefficient of x, on the left side of the equation, is equal to the sum of -3 and 5 on the right side. -15 on the left side is equal to the product of 5 and -3 on the right.

Problem: Consider $x^2 + \underline{\quad}x - 10$. The coefficient of x is missing. List all of the coefficients of x that could be used so that the polynomial could be factored. Then factor the polynomial.

3-73 Factoring Polynomials of the Form $ax^2 + bx + c$ Where a Is an Integer > 1 ★★★

Following is a method for using guess and check to factor polynomials:

1. List the factors of a.
2. List the factors of c.
3. Test the possibilities to see which produces the correct coefficient of x.

Problem: The area of a rectangle is $6x^2 - 7x + 2$. How does the perimeter of this rectangle compare with a rectangle whose area is $5x^2 - x - 4$? Assume $x > 0$.

3-74 Factoring by Grouping ★★★ (A-SSE.3)

The distributive property, $ab + ac = a(b + c)$, is true if a is a number, a monomial, or a polynomial.

For example, if a is replaced by $(x - 6)$ in the equation above, then $(x - 6)b + (x - 6)c = (x - 6)(b + c)$.

Remember that multiplying a polynomial by -1 results in a product that is the opposite of the polynomial.

When factoring polynomials, try to group terms in ways that can be factored. Then factor out the common polynomials.

Problem: Find the missing binomials.

(1) $2(x + y) - y(x + y) = ($ _____ $)(x + y)$

(2) $(x + 3y) - a(3y + x) = ($ _____ $)(x + 3y)$

(3) $6a - 3ax + 7x - 14 = 3a($ _____ $) - 7($ _____ $) = (3a - 7)($ _____ $)$

(4) $4y^2 + 8xy - y - 2x = y($ _____ $) + 2x($ _____ $) = (y + 2x)($ _____ $)$

3-75   Sums and Differences of Cubes ★★★

Patterns often become apparent in factoring the sums or differences of cubes. Following are two examples:

$$a^3 + b^3 = (a+b)(a^2 - ab + b^2)$$
$$a^3 - b^3 = (a-b)(a^2 + ab + b^2)$$

Problem: The formula, $V = Bh$, where V is the volume, B is the area of the base, and h is the height, can be used to find the volume of a rectangular prism. Solve for V, B, or h in terms of the variable in each problem.

(1) $B = m^2 + 3m + 9$ **(2)** $B =$ **(3)** $B =$
     $h = m - 3$ $h =$ $h =$
     $V =$ $V = z^3 + 1$ $V = 8x^3 - y^3$

3-76   Completing the Square ★★ (A-SSE.3)

The equation $y = x^2 + bx + c$ can be rewritten as $y - k = (x - h)^2$ by completing the square. The graph of the equation $y - k = (x - h)^2$ is a parabola whose vertex is (h, k).

For example, $y = x^2 - 6x + 11$ can be rewritten as $y - 11 = x^2 - 6x$. Complete the square by identifying the coefficient of x (which is -6), take half of the coefficient to find -3, square -3, and add the result (which is 9) to both sides of the equation:

$$y - 11 + 9 = x^2 - 6x + 9$$
$$y - 2 = (x - 3)^2$$

The vertex is (3, 2).

Problem: Complete the square to find the vertex of each parabola.

(1) $y = x^2 - 4x + 1$ **(2)** $y = x^2 - x + 3$ **(3)** $y = x^2 + 4x - 1$

3-77   **Arithmetic and Geometric Sequences** ★

A sequence is a group of numbers (called terms) arranged in a pattern.

Each term of an arithmetic sequence is formed by adding a constant to the preceding term.

Each term of a geometric sequence is formed by multiplying the preceding term by a constant.

Problem: Consider the following sequences and terms. Match each term with the sequence to which it belongs. Some terms belong to more than one sequence.

Sequences	Terms
(1) 1, 6, 11, . . .	(A) 16
(2) 4, 8, 12, . . .	(B) 36
(3) 256, 128, 64, . . .	(C) 20
	(D) 1
	(E) 32

3-78   **Finding the Partial Sums of Infinite Series** ★★

A series is the sum of the terms of a sequence. If a sequence is infinite, the series is infinite because you cannot find the sum of an infinite number of terms. You can, however, find the partial sums of the first n terms, S_n.

Problem: Find the partial sums, S_{10}, for each series.

(1) $3 + 6 + 9 + \ldots$

(2) $12 + 9 + 6 + \ldots$

(3) $1 + 2 + 4 + 8 + \ldots$

(4) $\dfrac{1}{3} + \dfrac{2}{3} + 1 + \ldots$

3-79 Deriving the Formula for Finding the Sums of a Geometric Series ★★★ G (A-SSE.4)

On April 1, Ethan's teacher posed this problem: Suppose you received $1 today, $2 on April 2, $4 on April 3, $8 on April 4, $16 on April 5, and so on throughout the month of April. If you did not spend any of the money you received, how much money would you have on May 1?

Ethan identified this problem as a geometric series with $a_1 = 1$ and $r = 2$. (a_1 is the first term and the common ratio is 2.).

$$a_1 = 1, \ a_2 = 2a_1, \ a_3 = 2^2 a_1, \ a_4 = 2^3 a_1, \text{ and } a_5 = 2^4 a_1$$

He said that S_5, the sum of the first five terms, is $1 + 2 + 2^2 + 2^3 + 2^4 = 31$.

Ethan multiplied S_5 by the common ratio, 2. $\quad 2S_5 = 2 + 2^2 + 2^3 + 2^4 + 2^5$

Then he subtracted. $\quad S_5 - 2S_5 = 1 - 2^5$

By factoring $S_5 - 2S_5 = 1 - 2^5$, he found $S_5(1 - 2) = 1 - 2^5$.

He divided both sides by -1 to find $S_5 = \dfrac{(1 - 2^5)}{-1} = 31$.

After completing this work, Ethan was unable to generalize to find S_n.

Problem: Use Ethan's reasoning to derive the formula for finding S_n. Then use the formula to find S_{30}.

3-80   Using the Remainder Theorem and the Factor Theorem ★★ (A-APR.2)

The remainder theorem states that if polynomial $P(x)$ is divided by $(x - a)$, then $P(a)$ is equal to the remainder.

The factor theorem states that if $P(a) = 0$, then $(x - a)$ is a factor of the polynomial and if $(x - a)$ is a factor of the polynomial, then $P(a) = 0$.

Problem: Roxanne divided $P(x) = x^2 - 7x + 10$ by $(x - 5)$ and found that the remainder was equal to 70. She concluded that $P(5) = 70$. But she knows that $(x - 5)(x - 2) = x^2 - 7x + 10$, which means that $(x - 5)$ is a factor of the polynomial and $P(5)$ must equal 0. Find and explain her error.

3-81   Identifying Zeros of Polynomials ★ (A-APR.3)

The zeros of a polynomial $P(x)$ are the values for which $P(x) = 0$.

Problem: Identify the zeros of each polynomial.

(1) $f(x) = x^2 - 1$ **(2)** $g(x) = x^3$ **(3)** $h(x) = (x - 2)(x - 3)(x + 1)$

3-82   Using Zeros to Sketch Graphs of Functions Defined by Polynomials ★★ (A-APR.3)

Represented graphically, the zeros of a polynomial $P(x)$ are the values for which $P(x) = 0$, and therefore the zeros are the x-intercepts of the graph. They can be used to sketch the graph of a function defined by a polynomial.

Problem: Ella knows that the zeros of $P(x) = x^3 - x^2 - 2x$ are -1, 0, and 2. She graphed these points on the x-axis. She did not know whether the left-hand side of the graph should rise or fall. How would you explain to Ella the position of the left-hand side of the graph?

3-83   Generating Pythagorean Triples ★★ (A-APR.4)

A Pythagorean triple is a set of integers, a, b, and c, that could be sides of a right triangle if $a^2 + b^2 = c^2$. The steps below show how to generate Pythagorean triples:

1. Square an odd integer that is greater than 1.

2. Find two consecutive integers whose sum is equal to the square of the number in step 1.

The number you squared and the other two numbers are a Pythagorean triple.

Problem: Choose a number and generate a Pythagorean triple. Substitute it into the Pythagorean theorem to verify your results.

3-84   Pascal's Triangle and the Binomial Theorem ★★★ G (A-APR.5)

Pascal's triangle is a triangular array of numbers.

$$
\begin{array}{ccccccccc}
 & & & & 1 & & & & \\
 & & & 1 & & 1 & & & \\
 & & 1 & & 2 & & 1 & & \\
 & 1 & & 3 & & 3 & & 1 & \\
1 & & 4 & & 6 & & 4 & & 1
\end{array}
$$

Note that the first and last number in each row is 1. The other numbers are obtained by adding the two numbers to the upper right and left of the previous row.

Problem: How does each row of the triangle compare to the coefficients of the binomial $(x + y)^n$ where n is a positive integer? Write a general formula showing this relationship. Use this formula to find $(x + y)^8$.

Section 3: Algebra and Beyond

3-85   Rewriting Rational Expressions ★ (A-APR.6)

A rational expression is (or can be) written as the quotient of two polynomials.

Problem: Explain why rewriting a rational expression may also be called dividing polynomials. Explain the division algorithm.

3-86   Rewriting Rational Expressions ★★ (A-APR.6)

The procedure for rewriting a rational expression and checking the answer is the same as dividing whole numbers. For example, $\dfrac{21}{4} = 5\dfrac{1}{4}$.

You can check your work by multiplying the divisor by the quotient and adding any remainder. If you are correct, the result will equal the dividend. In the previous example, $4 \times 5 + 1 = 21$.

Problem: Rewrite the rational expressions. Check your answers.

(1) $\dfrac{x^2 + 3x - 5}{x + 4}$

(2) $\dfrac{x^2 + 5x - 12}{x + 3}$

(3) $\dfrac{2x^2 - 5x + 25}{x - 5}$

(4) $\dfrac{2x^2 + 3x - 10}{2x - 1}$

3-87   Rewriting Rational Expressions ★★★ (A-APR.6)

When rewriting rational expressions, the terms in the numerator must be written in descending order of the exponents of the variable. If a term is missing, insert the term with a zero coefficient.

Problem: Identify which rational expressions are written correctly. Correct those that are incorrect.

(1) $\dfrac{x^2 - 1}{x - 2} = x + 2 + \dfrac{3}{x - 2}$

(2) $\dfrac{x^2 - 14}{x + 7} = x + 7 + \dfrac{35}{x + 7}$

(3) $\dfrac{2x^3 + 1}{x + 1} = 2(x^2 - x + 1)$

(4) $\dfrac{3x^3 + 4x^2 + x - 5}{3x + 1} = (x)(x + 1) - \dfrac{5}{3x + 1}$

3-88 Simplifying Rational Expressions ★ (A-APR.6)

A rational expression is in simplest form if its numerator and denominator have no common polynomial factors.

To simplify a rational expression, factor the numerator and denominator. If the numerator and denominator have the same factors, the quotient is 1. The resulting rational expression is in simplest form. See the example that follows:

$$\frac{x^2 + 2x + 1}{x^2 + 3x + 2} = \frac{(x+1)(x+1)}{(x+1)(x+2)}$$

Because $\frac{x+1}{x+1} = 1$, $\frac{x+1}{x+2}$ is in simplest form.

Problem: Simplify the rational expressions.

(1) $\dfrac{x^2 + x - 2}{x^2 - 5x + 4}$

(2) $\dfrac{x^2 - 2x - 15}{x^2 - 9}$

(3) $\dfrac{2x^2 + 9x + 4}{x^2 + 6x + 8}$

(4) $\dfrac{x^2 + 6x - 16}{x^2 + 7x - 8}$

3-89 Multiplying and Dividing Rational Expressions ★★ (A-APR.7)

Multiplying and dividing rational expressions is easy if you know how to factor and multiply polynomials.

Problem: Two of the problems below have the same answer. Identify these two problems. Then find the answer to the other problem.

(1) $\dfrac{x^2 + 5x + 6}{x - 1} \cdot \dfrac{x - 1}{x + 3}$

(2) $\dfrac{x^2 - 4x + 3}{x + 1} \div \dfrac{x^2 - 9}{x + 1}$

(3) $\dfrac{x + 5}{x - 5} \div \dfrac{x + 5}{x^2 - 3x - 10}$

3-90   Multiplying and Dividing Rational Expressions ★★ (A-APR.7)

Noah is having trouble multiplying and dividing rational expressions because he refuses to factor first.

He was given this problem: $\dfrac{x^2 - 25}{x + 1} \div \dfrac{x + 5}{x - 1}$

He rewrote the problem correctly: $\dfrac{x^2 - 25}{x + 1} \cdot \dfrac{x - 1}{x + 5}$

He proceeded to multiply: $\dfrac{x^2 - 25}{x + 1} \cdot \dfrac{x - 1}{x + 5} = \dfrac{x^3 - 25x - x^2 + 25}{x^2 + 6x + 5}$

Even though he did not factor, he felt that this answer was in simplest form.

Problem: Explain how you would help Noah solve this problem.

3-91   Adding and Subtracting Rational Expressions with the Same Denominator ★★ (A-APR.7)

Follow the steps below to add rational expressions that have the same denominator:

1. Add the numerators.
2. Write this sum over the denominator because the sum of a rational expression is the sum of the numerators divided by the denominator.

Follow these steps to subtract rational expressions that have the same denominator:

1. Subtract the numerators.
2. Write the difference over the denominator because the difference of a rational expression is the difference of the numerators divided by the denominator.

Problem: The answers to some of the following problems are incorrect. Identify the errors and find the correct sums or differences.

(1) $\dfrac{x + 2}{x + 4} + \dfrac{x + 2}{x + 4} = \dfrac{x^2 + 4}{x + 4}$

(2) $\dfrac{x + 1}{x + 2} - \dfrac{x + 3}{x + 2} = \dfrac{4}{x + 2}$

(3) $\dfrac{x + 1}{x^2 - 1} + \dfrac{x + 2}{x^2 - 1} = \dfrac{2x + 3}{x^2 - 1}$

(4) $\dfrac{x + 2}{x - 5} - \dfrac{3x - 5}{x - 5} = \dfrac{-2x + 7}{x - 5}$

3-92   Finding the Least Common Denominator of Rational Expressions ★★ (A-APR.7)

To find the least common denominator (LCD) of rational expressions, follow these steps:

1. Find the least common multiple (LCM) of the denominators by factoring each denominator.

2. Multiply the greatest powers of the factors.

For example, the LCM of $(x^2 - 25)$ and $(x^2 - 10x + 25)$ is $(x - 5)^2(x + 5)$. Note that $(x^2 - 25)$ can be factored as $(x - 5)(x + 5)$, and $(x^2 - 10x + 25)$ can be factored as $(x - 5)^2$.

Problem: Match the LCD with the rational expressions in the problems.

(1) $(x + 1)(x + 2)$ **(A)** $\dfrac{1}{x^2 - 1}, \dfrac{1}{x - 1}$

(2) $(x - 1)^2$ **(B)** $\dfrac{1}{x^2 - 2x + 1}, \dfrac{1}{x - 1}$

(3) $x^2 - 1$ **(C)** $\dfrac{1}{x - 1}, \dfrac{1}{x + 1}$

(D) $\dfrac{1}{x + 1}, \dfrac{1}{x + 2}$

3-93   Adding and Subtracting Rational Expressions with Different Denominators ★★★ (A-APR.7)

Logan thinks he knows the procedure for adding and subtracting rational expressions. But he often rushes with his work and makes careless mistakes.

Problem: Find and correct the errors in Logan's homework.

(1) $\dfrac{x}{x + 5} - \dfrac{2}{x - 3} = \dfrac{x^2 - 5x - 10}{(x + 5)(x - 3)}$

(2) $\dfrac{x + 3}{x^2 - 4} + \dfrac{x}{x^2 + 3x + 2} = \dfrac{2x + 3}{(x^2 - 4)(x^2 + 3x + 2)}$

(3) $\dfrac{1}{x + 2} - \dfrac{4x + 2}{(x + 2)(x + 3)(x + 4)} = \dfrac{x^2 - 3x + 10}{(x + 2)(x + 3)(x + 4)}$

3-94 **Adding, Subtracting, Multiplying, and Dividing Rational Expressions ★★★ G (A-APR.7)**

Audrey heard her teacher say that rational expressions are closed under addition, subtraction, multiplication, and division. Her teacher said that closure means that when you add two rational expressions, the sum is a rational expression. This is also true for subtraction, multiplication, and division. But Audrey was confused because $\frac{x+1}{2x+3} + \frac{x+2}{2x+3} = \frac{2x+3}{2x+3} = 1$, which is not a rational expression.

Problem: What is the error in Audrey's reasoning? Create a subtraction, multiplication, and division problem involving rational expressions for which the answers are not rational expressions but can be expressed as rational expressions.

3-95 **Explaining the Steps in Solving an Equation ★ (A-REI.1)**

Sometimes providing a reason for each step in solving an equation is more difficult than actually solving an equation.

Problem: The steps for solving the equation $3(x-2) = 21$ are shown below. State the reason for each step.

  (1) $3x - 6 = 21$
  (2) $3x = 27$
  (3) $x = 9$

3-96   **Explaining the Steps in Solving an Equation ★★ (A-REI.1)**

Anthony sometimes uses a few more steps than necessary to solve an equation. For example, this is how he solved the following equation:

$$\frac{1}{2}x + x - 3 = 4x + 8 - 1$$

$$x - 3 = 3.5x + 8 - 1$$

$$-2.5x - 3 = 8 - 1$$

$$-2.5x = 8 - 1 + 3$$

$$-2.5x = 10$$

$$x = -4$$

Problem: Is Anthony correct? Explain your reasoning. Is there a more efficient way to solve the problem? If there is, solve it more efficiently.

3-97   **Solving Rational Equations ★★ (A-REI.2)**

A rational equation is an equation that contains rational expressions. (A rational expression is an expression that can be expressed as the quotient of two polynomials.) The best way to solve a rational equation is to eliminate all the denominators except denominators of 1. Follow these steps:

1. Find the least common denominator.

2. Multiply every term of the equation by the least common denominator.

3. Solve the equation that results.

4. Check your answers by substituting the value for each variable into the original equation.

Problem: Jodi used the following steps to solve $\frac{1}{5} + \frac{3}{x+4} = 1$: She found the least common multiple of 5 and $x + 4$, which is $5(x + 4)$. Then she multiplied $5(x + 4)\left(\frac{1}{5} + \frac{3}{x+4} = 1\right)$. Using the distributive property, she found $x + 4 + 15 = 1$. She solved the equation and said that $x = -18$, which did not check. Find and correct Jodi's error.

3-98   Solving Rational Equations — Extraneous Solutions
★★★ (A-REI.2)

An extraneous solution to a rational equation is a value that will make the denominator of the original equation equal zero. Because division by 0 is undefined, these values are not a solution to the original equation.

Whenever you solve a rational equation, check that your answer will not make the denominator equal to zero. If the denominator is equal to zero, the solution is not a solution to the equation.

Problem: Solve each equation if possible.

(1) $\dfrac{x}{x+2} = 4 - \dfrac{5}{x+2}$

(2) $\dfrac{2x}{x+1} = 3 - \dfrac{2}{x+1}$

(3) $\dfrac{x}{x-3} = \dfrac{3}{x-3} - 1$

3-99   Expressing Square Roots in Radical Form ★★ (A-REI.2)

Expressions such as $\sqrt{49}$ and $\sqrt{25}$ are called radicals or square roots. The symbol $\sqrt{}$ is the radical sign.

The word *radical* is taken from the Arabic word *jidr*, which means "plant root," because the Arab texts explained that square numbers grow out of root numbers. For example, 49 grows out of 7, and 25 grows out of 5.

The product and quotient property for square roots states that $\sqrt{ab} = \sqrt{a} \cdot \sqrt{b}$ if a and b are positive numbers, and $\sqrt{\dfrac{a}{b}} = \dfrac{\sqrt{a}}{\sqrt{b}}$ if a and b are positive.

Problem: Find and correct the problems that are simplified incorrectly.

(1) $\sqrt{36} = 6$

(2) $\sqrt{98} = 7\sqrt{2}$

(3) $\sqrt{.01} = \dfrac{1}{10}$

(4) $\sqrt{54} = 9\sqrt{6}$

3-100   **Finding Square Roots ★**

Finding a square root is the inverse of squaring a number. Since $4 \times 4 = 16$, $\sqrt{16} = 4$. $\sqrt{16}$ is read, "the square root of 16."

Problem: Explain why $\sqrt{-25}$ results in an error message on your calculator. List some other square roots that result in error messages.

3-101   **Expressing Radical Expressions in Simplest Form ★★ (A-REI.2)**

A radical is in simplest form when the following conditions are met:

- No radicand has a square root factor other than 1. (The radicand is the number beneath the radical sign.)
- The radicand is not a fraction.
- No radicals are in the denominator.

Problem: Mike received a grade of 60% on his quiz on simplifying radicals. The problems and his answers are shown below. Do you agree or disagree with his score? Explain your answer.

(1) $\dfrac{3}{\sqrt{7}} = \dfrac{3\sqrt{7}}{7}$ (2) $\dfrac{5\sqrt{3}}{4\sqrt{5}} = \dfrac{25\sqrt{15}}{4}$ (3) $\dfrac{9\sqrt{3}}{\sqrt{24}} = \dfrac{9}{\sqrt{8}}$

(4) $3\sqrt{\dfrac{48}{9}} = \sqrt{48}$ (5) $\sqrt{\dfrac{10}{36}} = \dfrac{\sqrt{10}}{6}$

3-102   Adding and Subtracting Radicals ★★ (A-REI.2)

To simplify sums and differences of radicals, follow two steps:

1. Express each radical in simplest form.

2. Add or subtract radicals with like radicands.

Problem: One expression is omitted from each problem below. Fill in the blanks with the correct expression.

(1) $6\sqrt{17} - \underline{\qquad} + 3\sqrt{17} = 7\sqrt{17}$

(2) $\sqrt{12} + \sqrt{3} = \underline{\qquad}$

(3) $\sqrt{18} + \underline{\qquad} = 4\sqrt{2}$

(4) $-11\sqrt{27} - 7\sqrt{12} = \underline{\qquad}$

3-103   Multiplying Binomials Containing Radicals ★★★ (A-REI.2)

If a and b are positive integers, then $\left(a + \sqrt{b}\right)$ and $\left(a - \sqrt{b}\right)$ are called conjugates.

Conjugates differ by the sign of one term. The product $\left(a + \sqrt{b}\right)\left(a - \sqrt{b}\right)$ is an integer.

Problem: Alberto says that the product of conjugates is like multiplying binomials of the form $(a - b)$ and $(a + b)$. Explain the similarities of these two products. Use examples to support your ideas.

3-104   Rationalizing the Denominator That Contains Radicals ★★★ (A-REI.2)

Rationalizing the denominator is the process of rewriting a fraction with an irrational denominator as a fraction with a rational denominator. Conjugates are used to rationalize binomial denominators that contain radicals.

Problem: Match each fraction with its simplest form.

(1) $\dfrac{2}{\sqrt{5}-2}$ (A) $2\sqrt{5}+4$

(2) $\dfrac{8}{3\sqrt{5}+4}$ (B) $-1-\sqrt{5}$

(3) $\dfrac{\sqrt{5}-4}{\sqrt{5}+2}$ (C) $\dfrac{24\sqrt{5}-32}{29}$

(4) $\dfrac{4}{1-\sqrt{5}}$ (D) $13-6\sqrt{5}$

3-105   Solving Radical Equations ★★ (A-REI.2)

A radical equation is an equation that has a variable in the radicand.

To solve a radical equation, isolate the radical and then simplify, if necessary, and square both sides. Since squaring both sides of an equation does not always result in an equation that is equivalent to the original equation, be sure to check every solution by substituting it in the original equation.

Problem: Solve for x.

(1) $\sqrt{2x+3}=9$ (2) $\sqrt{x^2+1}=1-x$ (3) $4\sqrt{x}=28$

3-106   Solving Simple Radical Equations — Extraneous Solutions ★★ (A-REI.2)

An extraneous solution is a solution that does not satisfy the original equation, although it was found by using appropriate problem-solving strategies.

Problem: Jayden looked at the equation $8 + \sqrt{3x} = 5$ and noticed that there is no real solution. Explain how he might have reached this conclusion just by looking at the equation.

3-107   Transforming Equations ★★ G (A-CED.4)

Equations are transformed by expressing them in terms of another variable.

Problem: Identify each formula below. Then solve for the variable after the semicolon.

(1) $C = 2\pi r$; r

(2) $V = \dfrac{Bh}{3}$; h

(3) $C = \dfrac{5}{9}(F - 32)$; F

(4) $P = 2(l + w)$; l

3-108   Solving Linear Equations in One Variable — Coefficients Are Letters ★★ (A-REI.3)

Liam's little brother Mason often plays tricks on him. One day, Mason decided to change some of the problems on Liam's math homework. Mason secretly changed some coefficients of x to capital letters.

When Liam started his homework, he noticed that in the following problems, he was supposed to solve for x. Liam was able to solve for x, but the solutions contained capital letters rather than just numbers.

Problem: Knowing this, solve each equation for x in terms of the capital letter.

(1) $Ax - 12 = 15$

(2) $Bx - 2 = 18$

(3) $5 - Cx(2 + 5) = 10$

(4) $15(3x) = Dx - 2$

3-109   Solving Two-Step Inequalities ★★ (A-REI.3)

When solving inequalities, the following list of transformations produces an equivalent inequality:

1. Add the same number to or subtract the same number from each side of the inequality.
2. Multiply or divide each side of the inequality by the same positive number.
3. Multiply or divide each side of the inequality by the same negative number and reverse the direction of the inequality.

Problem: Supply the missing inequality symbol in each inequality.

(1) $3(x+5) > -18$

$3x + 15\_\_\_\_ - 18$

$3x\_\_\_\_ - 33$

$x\_\_\_\_ - 11$

(2) $3x - 4x + 4 < 8$

$-x + 4\_\_\_\_8$

$-x\_\_\_\_4$

$x\_\_\_\_ - 4$

(3) $-3(-x + 8) - 14x \geq -2$

$3x - 24 - 14x\_\_\_\_ - 2$

$-11x\_\_\_\_22$

$x\_\_\_\_ - 2$

3-110   Using Squares of Binomials and Perfect Squares ★★ (A-REI.4)

Perfect squares are the result of squaring a number, such as $7^2 = 49$ or $(-3)^2 = 9$.

Squaring a binomial results in a trinomial such as $(x - 4)^2 = x^2 - 8x + 16$. The first and last terms are perfect squares.

Problem: In each example below, the square of half the coefficient of x and the perfect square are related. Write an explanation of this relationship.

(1) $(x + 6)^2 = x^2 + 12x + 36$

The square of half the coefficient of $x = \left(\frac{12}{2}\right)^2$.   Perfect square $= 36$.

(2) $(x - 1)^2 = x^2 - 2x + 1$

The square of half the coefficient of $x = \left(-\frac{2}{2}\right)^2$.   Perfect square $= 1$.

(3) $(x + a)^2 = x^2 + 2ax + a^2$

The square of half the coefficient of $x = \left(\frac{2a}{2}\right)^2$.   Perfect square $= a^2$.

3-111   Using the ± Symbol ★★

William Oughtred (1574–1660), an Englishman, first used the symbol ± in his work *Clavis Mathematicae*, which was published in 1631. The symbol is a short way of combining two mathematical sentences. For example, 7 ± 3 can be written as $7 + 3 = 10$ and $7 - 3 = 4$.

Problem: What two numbers are represented by each of the following? Express your answers in simplest form.

(1) 3 ± 15

(2) $7 \pm \sqrt{25}$

(3) $3 \pm \sqrt{50}$

(4) $\dfrac{8 \pm \sqrt{16}}{4}$

(5) $8 \pm \sqrt{9}$

(6) $4 \pm \sqrt{98}$

3-112   Solving Quadratic Equations by Completing the Square ★★★ (A-REI.4)

If an equation is not in the form $ax^2 = c$, $a \neq 0$, it may be possible to transform the equation so that it is in that form. This method, called completing the square, is described by the following steps:

1. Transform the equation so that the quadratic term plus the linear term equals a constant.

2. Divide each term by the coefficient of the quadratic term if the coefficient does not equal 1.

3. Complete the square:

   - Multiply the coefficient of x by $\dfrac{1}{2}$.
   - Square the value.
   - Add the result to both sides of the equation.
   - Express one side of the equation as the square of a binomial and the other as a constant.

4. Solve the equation.

Problem: Column A contains three equations. Column B contains a number that is added to each member of the equation. Column C contains solutions to the equations. Column B and column C are mixed up. Arrange the numbers and expressions so that they correspond to the equations in column A.

	A	B	C
(1)	$x^2 - 2x = 20$	4	$-3 + 3\sqrt{2}, -3 - 3\sqrt{2}$
(2)	$x^2 - 4x = 3$	9	$1 + \sqrt{21}, 1 - \sqrt{21}$
(3)	$x^2 + 6x - 9 = 0$	1	$2 + \sqrt{7}, 2 - \sqrt{7}$

3-113   Deriving the Quadratic Formula ★★★ (A-REI.4)

Given the equation $ax^2 + bx + c = 0$, Olivia knows that she can derive the quadratic formula: $x = \dfrac{-b \pm \sqrt{b^2 - 4ac}}{2a}$. In fact, she wrote the steps on index cards, but the cards got out of sequence.

Problem: Place each step in sequence so that Olivia's cards show the correct steps for deriving the quadratic formula.

- **(A)** Take the square root of each side of the equation.
- **(B)** Divide each term by a.
- **(C)** Solve for x, and simplify your answer.
- **(D)** Write the left side as a perfect square and the right side as a fraction.
- **(E)** Write the equation $ax^2 + bx + c = 0$.
- **(F)** Subtract c from both sides.
- **(G)** Complete the square and add $\dfrac{b^2}{4a^2}$ to both sides.

3-114   Transforming Equations into the Form $ax^2 + bx + c = 0$, $a \neq 0$ ★★ (A-CED.4)

All quadratic equations may be expressed in the form $ax^2 + bx + c = 0$, $a \neq 0$. This transformation is necessary so that the quadratic formula may be used.

Problem: Four quadratic equations are listed below. In which equations are a, b, and c correctly identified? Correct the values that are incorrect.

(1)	$x^2 + 3x = 4$	$a = 1$	$b = 3$	$c = 4$
(2)	$5x^2 - 6x = -10$	$a = 5$	$b = -6$	$c = 10$
(3)	$3x^2 + 4 = 7x$	$a = 3$	$b = 4$	$c = -7$
(4)	$4x^2 = 10x - 5$	$a = 4$	$b = -10$	$c = 5$

3-115   **Solving Quadratic Equations Using the Quadratic Formula If $b^2 - 4ac \geq 0$ ★★ (A-REI.4)**

The quadratic formula states: If $ax^2 + bx + c = 0$, $a \neq 0$, then $x = \dfrac{-b \pm \sqrt{b^2 - 4ac}}{2a}$.

Problem: Match each equation in the first column with its correct solution in the second.

(1) $x^2 + 3x + 1 = 0$ (A) $-1, -\dfrac{1}{4}$

(2) $x^2 + 4x = 6$ (B) $\dfrac{-3 + \sqrt{5}}{2}, \dfrac{-3 - \sqrt{5}}{2}$

(3) $4x^2 + 5x + 1 = 0$ (C) $\dfrac{4}{3}, 1$

(4) $3x^2 + 4 = 7x$ (D) $-2 + \sqrt{10}, -2 - \sqrt{10}$

3-116   **Using the Zero-Product Property ★ (A-REI.4)**

The zero-product property states that if the product of two or more factors is 0, at least one of the factors is 0, and if at least one of the factors is 0, the product is 0.

Problem: Write an explanation of why this property is true. Include examples to support your explanation.

3-117   Solving Quadratic Equations by Factoring ★★ (A-REI.4)

Many polynomial equations can be solved by factoring and applying the zero-product property. Follow these two steps:

1. If the polynomial is factored, solve it by using the zero-product property.

2. If the equation is not in standard form, transform it into standard form, factor it, and use the zero-product property. In the standard form of a polynomial equation, one side equals zero, and the other side is a simplified polynomial arranged in descending powers of the variable. Remember, not all polynomial equations can be factored.

Problem: Two of the problems below are correct, and two are partially correct. Identify and correct the problems that are partially correct.

(1) $(n + 17)(n + 7) = 0$

$n = -17$

$n = -7$

(2) $x^2 - 13x + 36 = 0$

$(x - 9)(x - 4) = 0$

$x = -9$

$x = -4$

(3) $y^2 - y = 6$

$y^2 - y - 6 = 0$

$(y - 3)(y + 2) = 0$

$y = 3$

$y = -2$

(4) $m^3 - 4m = 0$

$m(m^2 - 4) = 0$

$m = 0$

$m = 4$

3-118 Solving Quadratic Equations of the Form $ax^2 = c, a \neq 0$ ★★ (A-REI.4)

To solve equations of the form $ax^2 = c$ when $a \neq 0$, isolate the squared term and find the square root of $\frac{c}{a}$. If $\frac{c}{a} \geq 0$, there are two square roots that are real numbers. If $\frac{c}{a} < 0$, there are no real roots.

Problem: At least one problem below has no real roots. Find the real roots of the other problems.

(1) $x^2 = 49$ (2) $x^2 - 7 = 0$ (3) $3x^2 + 75 = 0$ (4) $2x^2 = 50$

3-119 Sums and Products of Roots ★★ (A-REI.4)

The sums and the products of the roots of quadratic equations in the form $ax^2 + bx + c = 0$, $a \neq 0$, where a, b, and c are real numbers, are each related to a ratio of a, $-b$, or c.

Problem: Look at the sum of the roots of each quadratic equation. Find the relationship, and express it as a ratio involving a, $-b$, or c. Then do the same for the product of the roots.

Equation	Roots
$x^2 + 5x + 6 = 0$	$-3, -2$
$x^2 - 9x + 18 = 0$	$3, 6$
$3x^2 - 3x - 1 = 0$	$\dfrac{3 + \sqrt{21}}{6}, \dfrac{3 - \sqrt{21}}{6}$
$4x^2 - 12x + 9 = 0$	$\dfrac{3}{2}, \dfrac{3}{2}$
$3x^2 - 8x + 4 = 0$	$\dfrac{2}{3}, 2$

3-120   Using the Discriminate ★★★ G (A-REI.4)

A quadratic equation of the form $ax^2 + bx + c = 0$, where a, b, and c are real numbers and $a \neq 0$, has a discriminate equal to $b^2 - 4ac$ which determines the number and kinds of solutions to the equation.

Study the chart.

If $b^2 - 4ac$ is:	then the equation will have:
negative	two (conjugate) imaginary roots
zero	one real root, called a double real root
positive	two different real roots

Problem: Write three quadratic equations according to the descriptions:

    1. One has two imaginary roots.

    2. One has one real root.

    3. One has two real roots.

Then solve each equation.

3-121   Producing Systems of Equations with the Same Solution ★ (A-REI.5)

Ava was given a system of equations, $y = 3x + 5$ and $2y = x$. She wanted to solve for y by multiplying the second equation by -3 and then adding this equation to the first equation.

Problem: Using Ava's method, find the solution to the new system of equations. How do you know it is a solution to the original system?

3-122 Solving a System Consisting of a Linear Equation and a Quadratic Equation ★★★ (A-REI.7)

The point, or points, of intersection of the graphs of two equations is the solution, or solutions, to both equations. If the point of intersection is not an integer, you should estimate the solution. But if you solve the system algebraically, you will find a precise answer.

Problem: Solve each system of equations.

(1) $y = x^2 + 4$
$\quad y = x + 4$

(2) $y = x^2$
$\quad y = x + 4$

3-123 Representing a System of Linear Equations as a Matrix Equation ★ (A-REI.8)

A system of linear equations can easily be represented as a matrix equation, provided the equations in the system are written in the standard form, $Ax + By = C$, where A, B, and C are integers and A and B are not both equal to zero. For example:

$\begin{matrix} x + 3y = 16 \\ 2x - 3y = -13 \end{matrix}$ can be written as $\begin{bmatrix} 1 & 3 \\ 2 & -3 \end{bmatrix} \begin{bmatrix} x \\ y \end{bmatrix} = \begin{bmatrix} 16 \\ -13 \end{bmatrix}$

Problem: Write each system of equations as a matrix equation.

(1) $3x - 2y = -9$
$\quad 2x + y = 8$

(2) $x + y = 3$
$\quad 2x - 5y = -22$

(3) $x = y + 4$
$\quad 2x - y = 12$

3-124   Using the Inverse of a Matrix to Solve a Matrix Equation ★★ (A-REI.9)

To solve a linear equation for x, such as $3x = 12$, you can divide each side by 3 or multiply each side by $\frac{1}{3}$, the multiplicative inverse of 3.

The system of linear equations, $5x - 4y = 23$ and $x + 3y = -3$, can be represented by the following matrix equation:

$$\begin{array}{ccc} A & X & B \end{array}$$
$$\begin{bmatrix} 5 & -4 \\ 1 & 3 \end{bmatrix}\begin{bmatrix} x \\ y \end{bmatrix} = \begin{bmatrix} 23 \\ -3 \end{bmatrix}$$

To solve the matrix equation for the matrix X, multiply both sides by the inverse of A.

Problem: Find the inverse of matrix A above. Then use the inverse to solve the matrix equation.

3-125   Using the Inverse of a 3 × 3 Matrix to Solve a Matrix Equation ★★ (A-REI.9)

Luis likes to talk in riddles. He said he could solve the following system of linear equations 1, 2, 3.

$$-8x + 2y + 11z = 29$$

$$-3x + y + 4z = 11$$

$$6x - y - 8z = -20$$

Problem: Let $A = \begin{bmatrix} -8 & 2 & 11 \\ -3 & 1 & 4 \\ 6 & -1 & -8 \end{bmatrix}$. Use a graphing calculator to find A^{-1} and use A^{-1} to solve for x, y, and z. Explain what Luis may have meant by 1, 2, 3.

3-126   Graphs and Solutions of Equations ★ (A-REI.10)

Mia is a visual learner. She finds a diagram, chart, or graph helpful when learning about solutions to an equation.

Problem: Matt showed Mia a graph he sketched of $y = x^3$. He said that every solution to this equation is on the graph. Mia said that $(-2, -6)$ is a solution to the equation, but that it is not on the graph. Explain how this might have happened.

3-127   Finding the Point Where Two Graphs Intersect ★★ (A-REI.11) 💻

Go to www.shodor.org/interactive/activities/Graphit.

Here is what to do:

1. Select a display by clicking on "Function," "Data," and "Light Grid Lines."
2. Under "Plot Type" click on "Connected." (Some items may already be selected.)

Problem: Find the point of intersection of the graphs of any two of the following four sets of equations. In the box to the right of $y(x) =$, enter the expression on the right side of the equation. After you enter the first pair of equations, click on "Plot/Update." The two equations will be graphed. You can click on "Show Tabular Data" to show the point of intersection. Repeat this procedure and graph another pair of equations.

(1) $y = x + 8$
     $y = |x|$ which is entered as $y = abs(x)$

(2) $y = (x - 1)/(x + 1)$
     $y = (x + 1)/(x - 1)$

(3) $y = e^x$ which is entered as $y = exp(x)$
     $y = x^2 + 1$ which is entered as $y = x \wedge 2 + 1$

(4) $y = \cos(x)$
     $y = x + 1$

3-128   **Graphing Solutions to a System of Linear Inequalities**
★★★ **(A-REI.12)** 🖥

Go to http://www.ronblond.com/M11/LinProg/index.html. You will see a coordinate plane, two inequalities, and their graphs.

Here is what to do:

1. Study the inequalities and their graphs that are displayed.

2. Move your cursor over points on the graph. As you move your cursor, the coordinates of the points will be displayed. It will be noted next to the inequality if the inequality is true or false.

3. Change the inequality symbols and the inequalities and note how these changes affect the graphs.

Problem: Write two inequalities so that $(3, 6)$ is a solution to both of them, $(0, 11)$ is a solution to one inequality, $(1, 4)$ is a solution to the other, and $(-1, 0)$ is a solution to neither.

3-129   **Writing and Solving Equations and Inequalities**
★★ **(A-CED.1)**

Equations and inequalities can be used to model real-world situations. Accurate modeling and algebraic reasoning will result in accurate solutions.

Problem: Write and solve an equation or inequality to model each situation.

(1) Manny wants to frame a 9-inch-square picture so that the total area of the picture and frame is less than 100 square inches. What is the maximum width of the frame?

(2) Chloe deposited a check for $376 in her savings account. Her new balance is $1,534. What was her previous balance?

(3) Jake deposited $500 in an investment account that has a guaranteed interest rate of 4%, compounded annually. How much money will be in the account after 10 years?

(4) Grace has taken three math tests and has an 86 test average. She feels that she can study hard and get scores of 100 on the rest of the tests to pull her test average up to 93. How many tests will she need to take to reach the 93 average (assuming she gets a score of 100 on each test)?

3-130   Creating and Graphing Equations ★★ G (A-CED.2)

Solutions to equations that have one variable are numbers. However, the solutions to equations that have two variables are pairs of numbers. This pair is called an ordered pair. The first number is a value of the term that is first alphabetically, and the second number is a value of the term that is second alphabetically.

Problem: Use two variables to write three equations of which $(3, -4)$ is a solution. Select one equation, and graph it in the coordinate plane.

3-131   Interpreting Solutions as Viable Options ★★ (A-CED.3)

A box has two square sides and four sides that are congruent rectangles. The measurement of each side of the square is x, and the measurements of the sides of the rectangle are 8 by x. The surface area is 72 square inches.

Problem: Sam said that the surface area of the box can be modeled by the equation $2x^2 + 32x = 72$. He solved the equation and said that $x = -18$ and $x = 2$. Is he correct? If he is incorrect, find his error.

3-132   A Quotation about Algebra ★★

Jean Le Rond d'Alembert (1717–1783) was a French mathematician and scientist. A specialty of his was differential equations. His later work dealt with the mathematics of music.

Problem: Write an explanation of this quote of Jean Le Rond d'Alembert: "Algebra is very generous; she often gives more than is asked of her."

Section 4

Functions

4-1   Domain and Range ★ (8.F.1)

A function consists of a domain (the input), a range (the output), and a rule. The rule assigns to each member of the domain exactly one member of the range.

Problem: Explain the term "exactly one," and create a table of input and output values to support your explanation.

4-2   Describing Graphs of Linear Functions ★★ (8.F.1)

Many plumbers are paid by the hour, plus a service charge.

Problem: EZ Plumbing charges a $90 service fee and a rate of $65 per hour. Quality Plumbing charges a $90 service fee and a rate of $70 per hour. These costs are represented by the functions below:

> EZ Plumbing: $f(x) = \$65x + \$90$
> Quality Plumbing: $g(x) = \$70x + \$90$

x represents the number of hours worked.

Sketch a graph of each function in the same coordinate plane. Then write an explanation of the similarities and differences between the graphs.

4-3   Finding and Comparing Rates of Change ★★ (8.F.2)

Functions can be represented in various ways: algebraically (by an equation), a graph in the coordinate plane, a table, or verbally.

Problem: Four different functions are represented below, each in a different way. Find the rate of change of each. Then arrange the rates of change in order from least to greatest.

(1) $y = x + 3$

(2)

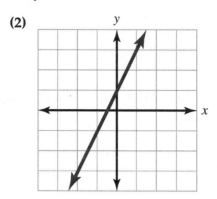

(3)

x	y
−1	2
2	−1
5	−4

(4) Mike gets paid time and a half for each hour he works on Sunday.

4-4   Identifying Linear Functions ★ (8.F.3)

All linear equations define linear functions whose graphs are lines.

Problem: Which of the functions below are linear functions? Explain how you know.

(1) The tip is equal to the cost of a meal multiplied by the tip rate.

(2)

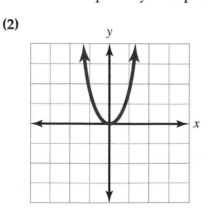

(3) $C = \pi d$

(4)

x	y
−2	−8
−1	−1
0	0
1	1
2	8

4-5   Identifying Linear Functions ★★ (8.F.3)

One way to represent a linear function is by the equation $y = mx + b$. Functions that are not linear cannot be represented by this equation.

Problem: Which of the following are linear functions? If the function is linear, write the equation.

(1) The cost of an item is reduced by 25%.

(2) The volume of a cube is the length of a side cubed.

(3) According to a catalogue, the cost of mailing a package is $8.99 if the order is less than $50 and $12.99 if the order is $50 to $99.99.

(4) Movie tickets for a child cost $7 on Saturday afternoon.

4-6   Interpreting the Initial Value of a Function ★ (8.F.4)

The initial value of a function is the value of the function when $x = 0$. For example, if $f(x) = 3x + 5$, then $f(0) = 3 \cdot 0 + 5 = 5$. The initial value of $f(x) = 5$.

Problem: The formula for finding the perimeter of a square is $P = 4s$ and can be represented by $f(x) = 4s$ and $f(0) = 0$. Courtney said that this function has no initial value because the length of a side of a square must be greater than 0. Do you agree with her? Explain your reasoning.

4-7   Functions and Graphs ★★ (8.F.5)

Graphs provide a visual representation of functions. By analyzing a graph, you can determine if a function is linear, nonlinear, increasing, or decreasing.

Problem: Which of the following graphs meet the criteria below? (Hint: Some meet more than one criterion. Some do not meet any.)

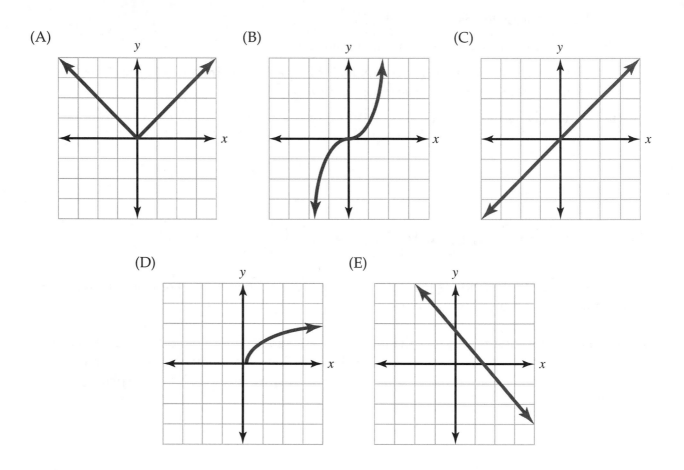

(1) The function is linear.

(2) The function is decreasing.

(3) The function is increasing.

(4) The function is increasing in quadrant I and decreasing in quadrant II.

4-8   **Increasing and Decreasing Functions ★★ G (8.F.5)**

Although every function assigns to each input exactly one output, graphs of functions vary.

The graph of a linear function, $f(x) = mx + b$, is a line with slope m and a y-intercept that is equal to b.

- If $m = 0$, the graph of a function is a horizontal line.
- If $m < 0$, the function is decreasing. As the values of x increase, the corresponding values of y decrease.
- If $m > 0$, the function is increasing. As the values of x increase, the corresponding values of y increase.

The graph of a nonlinear function is not a line. The shape of the graphs differ, depending on the particular function.

Problem: Sketch and graph each function.

(1) The function is increasing and linear. The graph is in quadrants I, II, and III.

(2) The function is nonlinear and is decreasing in quadrants I and II.

(3) The function is constant. The graph is in quadrants III and IV.

(4) The function is nonlinear and is increasing in quadrants I and IV.

4-9   **Understanding the Concept of a Function ★★ (F-IF.1)**

Andrew says that a function assigns to each element of the domain exactly one element of the range. He says that $(0, 0), (1, 2),$ and $(3, 2)$ are not on the graph of a function because 2 is paired with 1 and 3.

Problem: Does Andrew understand the concept of a function? Explain your answer.

4-10   Evaluating Functions ★ (F-IF.2)

The squaring function $f(x) = x^2$ can be represented by the equation $y = x^2$. It can be used to find the square of any number or the area of a square given the length of a side.

Problem: If $f(x) = x^2$, find the following.

    (1) $f(3)$ **(2)** $f(0.5)$ **(3)** $f(6)$ **(4)** $f(0.1)$

4-11   Using Sequences Defined Recursively ★★ (F-IF.3)

Leonardo of Pisa (1170–1250), known as Fibonacci, was an Italian mathematician best known for the sequence $\{1, 1, 2, 3, 5, 8, \ldots\}$, which is called the Fibonacci sequence. The sequence is defined recursively (the rule to find a term in the sequence uses previous terms): $f(0) = f(1) = 1$, $f(n) = f(n-1) + f(n-2)$, where n is an integer greater than 1.

Edward Lucas (1842–1891) is known for the Lucas sequence, $\{2, 1, 3, 4, 7, 11, \ldots\}$. This sequence is also defined recursively: $L(0) = 2, L(1) = 1, L(n) = L(n-1) + L(n-2)$, where n is an integer greater than 1.

Problem: Find the next four terms in each sequence above. What are the similarities of the sequences? What are the differences?

4-12   Identifying Key Features of a Graph ★★ (F-IF.4)

The perimeter of a rectangle is 20 feet. The area can be modeled by $A(x) = -x^2 + 10x$, where x is the length of a side. An adjacent side of the rectangle is $10 - x$.

Problem: Sketch the graph of the function above. Identify the vertex, symmetry, axis of symmetry, and where the graph is increasing and/or decreasing. Then restrict the domain so that it is applicable to finding the area of the rectangle.

4-13   Relating the Domain to the Relationships It Describes ★★ (F-IF.5)

The domain of a function may need to be restricted, depending on the situation the function models.

Problem: Find the domain of each function described below.

(1) The charge, c, for an SAT prep class is \$125 per person. This can be modeled by $c = f(p) = \$125p$. (The class is limited to 10 people.)

(2) Compiling a list of the cube roots of numbers can be modeled by $N = f(a) = \sqrt[3]{a}$.

(3) The area of an equilateral triangle can be modeled by $A = f(s) = \dfrac{s^2\sqrt{3}}{4}$.

(4) The sum of a number and its double can be modeled by $S = f(n) = 3n$.

4-14   Finding the Average Rate of Change ★★ (F-IF.6) 🖥

Many real-life problems can be solved using functions.

Go to www.gasbuddy.com.

Here is what to do:

1. Scroll down to Statistics and click on "Price Charts." The "Historical Price Charts" has tabs that will show the graphs of the average prices of gasoline (in cost per gallon) for the previous month, previous three months, previous six months, and so on.

2. Click on "1 Year." Let the first day correspond to 0 on the x-axis, and let the last day correspond to 1. This will represent one year. Calculate the rate of change of the average cost of 1 gallon of regular gasoline.

3. Click on "8 Years." Let the first day correspond to 0 on the x-axis, and let the last day correspond to 8. This will represent eight years. Calculate the average rate of change of the average cost of a gallon of regular gasoline per year.

Problem: How does the rate of change of the average cost of 1 gallon of regular gasoline for the year compare to the average rate of change of the average cost of a gallon of regular gasoline per year for the eight-year period?

4-15   Graphs of Functions ★★ (F-IF.7)

Graphs of functions can reveal the x- and y-intercepts, if they exist.

Problem: Graph the functions below. Identify which statements apply to the graphs. (Hint: Some statements may apply to more than one graph; others may not apply to any graph.)

Functions

(1) $f(x) = 2x^2 + 1$ **(2)** $h(x) = x^2 - 1$ **(3)** $k(x) = x - 1$

Statements

(A) The y-intercept is $(0, 1)$.   (B) The y-intercept is $(0, -1)$.

(C) There is no x-intercept.   (D) The x-intercept is $(1, 0)$.

(E) The x-intercept is $(-1, 0)$.   (F) The minimum is $(0, 1)$.

(G) The minimum is $(0, -1)$.   (H) There is no y-intercept.

4-16   Step Graphs ★★ G (F-IF.7)

A step graph looks like a series of steps rather than a curve or straight line. Step graphs have many uses.

For example, a mail order catalogue bases the shipping cost on the amount of the order. A step graph showing the amount of an order and the shipping cost is shown below.

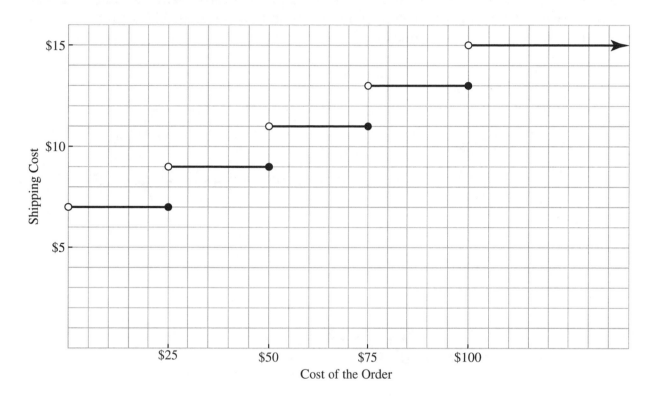

Problem: Using the step graph above, create a table showing the amount of the order and the shipping cost.

4-17   Using Factoring and Completing the Square in Quadratic Functions ★★ (F-IF.8)

Factoring and completing the square allows you to find three important features of a function: the zeros, extreme values, and symmetry of a graph.

Problem: Use factoring or completing the square to find the zeros, extreme values, and axis of symmetry of the functions. Some important points and lines are listed beneath the functions. Select those that pertain to each function.

Functions

(1) $f(x) = x^2 + 2x - 3$ **(2)** $y = x^2 - 16x - 17$ **(3)** $y = -x^2 + 7x - 12$

Points and Lines

$(-1, 0)$, $(1, 0)$, $(17, 0)$, $(4, 0)$, $(-3, 0)$, $(3, 0)$, $(8, -81)$, $(-1, -4)$, $(3.5, 0.25)$

$x = -1$, $x = 8$, $x = 3.5$

4-18   Classifying Functions as Exponential Growth or Exponential Decay ★★★ (F-IF.8)

Mason knows that $f(t) = ab^t$, where $b > 1$ and $a > 0$, represents exponential growth, and that $f(t) = ab^{-t}$, where $b > 1$ and $a > 0$, represents exponential decay.

Problem: Mason was asked to classify $f(t) = \left(\frac{1}{2}\right)^t$ as representing exponential growth or exponential decay. He was unable to classify this function because $b = \frac{1}{2}$, which is less than 1. His teacher suggested that he use the properties of exponents to rewrite the problem and then decide how to classify the function. How could Mason rewrite the problem? Does the function represent exponential growth or exponential decay?

4-19   Comparing Properties of Functions ★★ (F-IF.9)

Functions can be represented in a variety of ways: an equation, a table of values, a graph, or verbally. Because each representation has advantages and disadvantages, it is important to be able to use each representation to analyze functions.

Problem: Four different quadratic functions are represented below. Which function has the largest minimum? Which function has the smallest minimum?

(1) The square of a number is the product of the number and itself.

(2) $y = 2x^2 - 3$

(3)

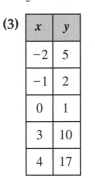

x	y
−2	5
−1	2
0	1
3	10
4	17

(4)

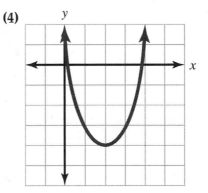

4-20   Writing Functions ★ (F-BF.1)

Functions can be used to represent the relationship between two quantities. For example, the candy in a one-pound bag that costs $2.49 can be melted and will make 50 pieces of candy starfish. A function $T(x)$ can be written to relate the cost of the candy to the number of bags, and another function $P(x)$ can be written to relate the number of pieces to the number of bags.

Problem: Write $T(x)$ and $P(x)$. Find $\left(\dfrac{T}{P}\right)(x)$. What does this represent?

4-21   Writing Sequences ★★★ (F-BF.2)

Figurate numbers are numbers associated with geometric figures. The ancient Greeks found figurate numbers unusual and interesting.

Triangular numbers are an example of figurate numbers that can form an arrangement that has three sides and three angles. The first three triangular numbers are shown below:

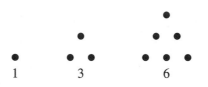

Note that the second triangular number is two more than the first, and the third triangular number is three more than the second.

Problem: List the first ten triangular numbers. Then write the sequence in two ways: recursively (in terms of preceding terms) and with an explicit formula. Find the 100th term in the sequence.

4-22   Translations and Dilations of Graphs ★★ (F-BF.3)

The size and shape of a graph of a function do not change, even though the graph may be moved up, down, to the right, or to the left. But if the function is multiplied by a nonzero number other than 1, the size of the graph will change.

Problem: Consider the graph of $f(x) = x^2$. Describe the graph of each function.

(1) $f(x) = x^2 + 3$ **(2)** $f(x) = x^2 - 3$ **(3)** $f(x) = (x - 3)^2$ **(4)** $f(x) = (x + 3)^2$

(5) $f(x) = 3x^2$ **(6)** $f(x) = -3x^2$ **(7)** $f(x) = \dfrac{1}{3}x^2$

4-23   Odd and Even Functions ★★ (F-BF.3)

Ella is learning to use the graphing calculator. She graphed $f(x) = (2x)^2$ and $f(x) = (-2x)^2$ and found that the graphs coincide. When she graphed $f(x) = (2x)^3$ and $f(x) = (-2x)^3$, she found two different graphs.

Problem: Explain why this happened.

4-24   Finding the Inverse of a Function ★★ (F-BF.4)

Mrs. Posik is replacing 7 posts and railings on her deck. The cost is $767, which includes all permits and taxes. The installer is offering her the option of placing a solar light on as many posts as she wishes at the cost of $87 per light. Her daughter wrote a function, $f(x) = \$767 + \$87x$, to find the total cost, where x is equal to the number of solar lights. She constructed this table of values:

x	0	1	2	3	4	5	6	7
$f(x)$	$767	$854	$941	$1,028	$1,115	$1,202	$1,289	$1,376

Problem: Find the inverse of $f(x)$. Interchange the values in the table above to find the domain and range of $f^{-1}(x)$. What does $f^{-1}(x)$ represent?

4-25   Determining If Two Functions Are Inverses ★★ (F-BF.4)

Two functions are inverses of each other if and only if $f(g(x)) = x$ for all x in the domain of g and $g(f(x)) = x$ for all x in the domain of f.

Problem: Match each function in the column on the left with its inverse in the column on the right. Verify that the functions are inverses. Assume that the domain is all real numbers unless the domain is specified.

Functions	Inverses
(1) $f(x) = x^3 - 1$	(A) $g(x) = \sqrt[3]{x - 3}$
(2) $f(x) = \dfrac{1}{2x}; x \neq 0$	(B) $g(x) = \dfrac{1}{2x}; x \neq 0$
(3) $f(x) = x^2; x \geq 0$	(C) $g(x) = \sqrt[3]{x + 1}$
(4) $f(x) = \dfrac{x - 4}{2}$	(D) $g(x) = \sqrt{x}; x \geq 0$
(5) $f(x) = x^3 + 3$	(E) $g(x) = 2x + 4$

4-26   Using Exponential and Logarithmic Functions ★★ (F-BF.5)

The exponential function is of the form $f(x) = b^x$, where $b > 0$ and $b \neq 1$.

The logarithmic function is the inverse of the exponential function. $y = \log_b x$ if and only if $x = b^y$, where x and b are positive real numbers and $b \neq 1$.

Problem: Six logarithmic functions are listed below. Match each with its inverse and then solve for the variable.

(1) $\log_2 x = 3$	(A) $x = 3^2$
(2) $\log_b 81 = 4$	(B) $b^2 = 81$
(3) $\log_2 \dfrac{1}{64} = y$	(C) $4^y = \dfrac{1}{64}$
(4) $\log_3 x = 2$	(D) $x = 2^3$
(5) $\log_b 81 = 2$	(E) $2^y = \dfrac{1}{64}$
(6) $\log_4 \dfrac{1}{64} = y$	(F) $b^4 = 81$

4-27 Linear and Exponential Models ★ (F-LE.1)

A linear function can be described by a linear equation, $y = mx + b$, where $m \neq 0$.

An exponential function can be described by an exponential equation, $y = ab^x$, where x is a real number and $b > 0$.

Problem: Jamie claims that $f(x) = 2x$ and $g(x) = 2^x$ are the same functions. She created the following table of values for each function to support her claim. Do you agree with her? Explain your reasoning.

x	1	2
$f(x)$	2	4
$g(x)$	2	4

4-28 Constructing Linear and Exponential Functions ★★★ (F-LE.2)

All functions can be described verbally, by values in a table, and by a graph.

Problem: Construct a linear or exponential function from the representations below.

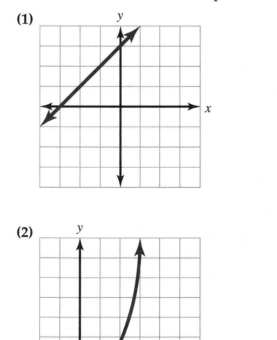

(1)

(2)

(3)

x	−1	0	2	3
$f(x)$	2.5	5	20	40

(4) 1 is the first term of the sequence. Each consecutive term is 5 times the preceding term.

(5) 0 is the first term of the sequence. Each consecutive term is 5 more than the preceding term.

4-29   Comparing Exponential, Linear, and Polynomial Functions ★★★ (F-LE.3) 🖳

Go to www.shodor.org/interactivate/activities/Graphit.

Here is what to do:

1. Select a display by clicking on "Function," "Data," and "Light Grid Lines."
2. Under "Plot Type" click on "Connected." (Some items may already be selected.)

Problem: Determine which quantity (those growing exponentially, those increasing linearly, or those defined by a polynomial function) exceeds the other two. Enter an exponential function such as $y(x) = 2\hat{\ }x$, a linear function such as $y(x) = x$, and a polynomial function such as $y(x) = x\hat{\ }3$ in the box $y(x) =$. After you enter the equations, click on "Plot/Update." The three equations will be graphed. You can click on "Show Tabular Data" to show the values of x and the values of the functions. Depending on the functions you have written, you may wish to change the maximum value to 100 and click on "Set." Write an explanation of which quantity is increasing fastest. Use data from the graph and table to support your reasoning.

4-30   Solving Exponential Equations ★ (F-LE.4)

Exponential equations can be solved by following these steps:

1. Isolate the exponential expression on one side of the equation.
2. Take the logarithm of each side.
3. Use the laws of logarithms.
4. Solve for x.

Problem: Write the missing expressions as you solve for x in the equation: $9e^{2x} = 45$

(1) $e^{2x} =$ _____

(2) $\ln e^{2x} =$ _____

(3) $2x =$ _____

(4) $x =$ _____

(5) $x \approx$ _____

4-31   Interpreting Parameters in the Compound Interest Formula ★★ (F-LE.5)

If you invest money in an account in a bank, interest may be compounded in a variety of ways. For example, interest may be compounded annually, semiannually, quarterly, or monthly.

The amount of money in the account can be found by using the compound interest formula: $A = P\left(1 + \frac{r}{n}\right)^{nt}$ where:

A = the amount of money in the account

P = the principal, which is the amount of money invested

r = the interest rate, expressed as a decimal

n = the number of times interest is compounded per year

t = the number of years for which the money is invested

Problem: Connor wrote the following formula for finding compound interest: $A = 10,000\left(1 + \frac{0.05}{4}\right)^{40}$. Find P, r, n, and t. Then explain the meaning of each variable.

4-32   Understanding Radian Measures ★ (F-TF.1)

The central angle of a circle is an angle whose vertex is at the center of the circle. When the arc that a central angle intercepts is the same length as the radius of the circle, the measure of the central angle is 1 radian.

Problem: Explain why the size of a circle does not affect the measure of a radian.

**4-33   Extending Trigonometric Functions to All Real Numbers
★★ (F-TF.2)**

An angle may be formed by rotating a ray about its end point. Imagine an angle whose vertex is at the origin of the coordinate plane. One of the sides of the angle is on the *x*-axis. This is called the initial side of the angle. This side is rotated counterclockwise around the origin. The ending position of the side is called the terminal side of the angle.

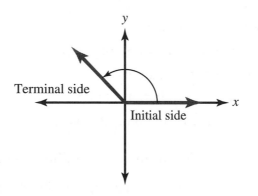

Problem: Sharon understands how to use the method of rotating a ray around the origin to find the values of the trigonometric functions where the measure of the central angle ranges from 0 to 360°. Explain how trigonometric functions can be defined if the central angle is larger than 360°.

4-34   Using Special Right Triangles ★ (F-TF.3)

The 30°-60°-90° triangle and the 45°-45°-90° triangle are known as special right triangles. If the vertices of the acute angles of the triangles are placed in the coordinate plane as shown below, it is easy to find the sine, cosine, and tangent of the angle. Remember: $\sin\theta = \dfrac{y}{r}$, $\cos\theta = \dfrac{x}{r}$, and $\tan\theta = \dfrac{y}{x}$.

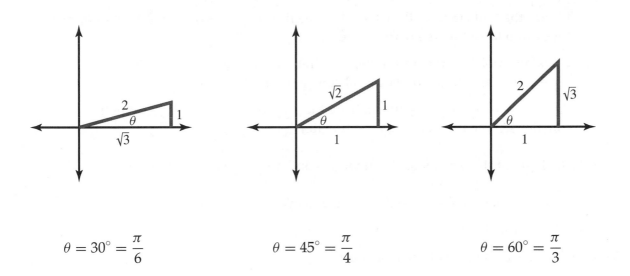

$$\theta = 30° = \frac{\pi}{6} \qquad\qquad \theta = 45° = \frac{\pi}{4} \qquad\qquad \theta = 60° = \frac{\pi}{3}$$

Problem: Find the $\sin\theta$, $\cos\theta$, and $\tan\theta$ in each triangle above.

4-35   **Using the Unit Circle to Explain the Symmetry and Periodicity of the Trigonometric Functions ★★★ (F-TF.4)** 🖥

Go to http://www.mathsisfun.com/algebra/trig-interactive-unit-circle.html.

Here is what to do:

1. Notice the unit circle on the left of the screen. The graphs of $\sin\theta$ (in red), $\cos\theta$ (in blue), and $\tan\theta$ (in green) are on the right of the screen.

2. Click on a point on the unit circle, and drag the point along the circle. This represents the rotation of the initial side of the angle.

3. As you rotate the point, you will trace the graphs of the three trigonometric functions. Note the values of each function.

Problem: Look at the graphs of the functions and answer the questions below.

(1) Which function is even, and how do you know?

(2) Which functions are odd, and how do you know?

(3) What is the period of each function?

4-36   **Choosing Trigonometric Functions to Model Periodic Phenomena ★★★ (F-TF.5)**

The distance from the seat of a Ferris wheel to the ground depends on the radius of the Ferris wheel, the boarding height (the distance from the seat to the ground when a person is boarding), and the number of degrees the Ferris wheel has rotated.

Based on the information above, Michael tried to model the movement of a Ferris wheel, using distances measured in meters. He set the viewing rectangle on his graphing calculator to $X\min = \dfrac{-\pi}{2}$, $X\max = \dfrac{3\pi}{2}$, $Y\min = 2$, and $Y\max = 20$, and graphed $y = 9\sin(x) + 11$.

Problem: Answer the following questions.

(1) What does Michael's graph represent?

(2) What is the radius of the Ferris wheel?

(3) How far is the wheel from the ground when a rider boards?

4-37   **Restricting the Domain of a Trigonometric Function to Find Its Inverse ★★★ G (F-TF.6)**

Tamara knows that all one-to-one functions have an inverse, which can be found by inter-changing the domain and range. She also knows how to apply the vertical line test, which states that a function is one-to-one if no vertical line intersects the function more than once.

For example, $f(x) = x^2$ is not a one-to-one function. It does not have an inverse because when the range and domain are switched, 4 is paired with 2 and -2. But if she looks at only the part of the graph of $f(x)$ where $x \geq 0$ or $x \leq 0$, $f(x) = x^2$ is one-to-one and has an inverse on these intervals.

Problem: How does this line of reasoning apply to finding the inverse of the sine, cosine, and tangent functions?

4-38   **Using Inverse Trigonometric Functions ★★ (F-TF.7)**

Inverse trigonometric functions can be used to find the measure of an angle, given two sides of a right triangle.

Problem: A motion detector is mounted on a home 10 feet from the ground and detects movements that are up to 30 feet away from the house. Determine the angle of depression from the motion detector to the ground. Round your answer to the nearest tenth.

4-39   **Proving a Pythagorean Identity ★★ (F-TF.8)**

The Pythagorean identity, $\sin^2 \theta + \cos^2 \theta = 1$, can be proved in a variety of ways.

Problem: Make Pythagoras proud by proving that $\sin^2 \theta + \cos^2 \theta = 1$ by using the following information.

The equation of a circle with center (h, k) and radius r is $(x - h)^2 + (y - k)^2 = r^2$. The unit circle is centered at the origin and has a one-unit radius. The terminal side of an angle θ in standard position intersects the unit circle at (x, y). The y-value of this point is $\sin \theta$. The x-value of this point is $\cos \theta$.

4-40   Proving the Addition Formula for the Sine Function
★★★ (F-TF.9)

Sometimes formulas may be used to prove other formulas. For example, the difference formula for the cosine function, $\cos(\alpha - \beta) = \cos\alpha\cos\beta + \sin\alpha\sin\beta$, and the cofunction formulas, $\sin x = \cos\left(\dfrac{\pi}{2} - x\right)$ and $\cos x = \sin\left(\dfrac{\pi}{2} - x\right)$, can be used to prove the addition formula for the sine function, $\sin(\alpha + \beta) = \sin\alpha\cos\beta + \cos\alpha\sin\beta$.

Problem: Starting with $\sin x = \cos\left(\dfrac{\pi}{2} - x\right)$, let $x = \alpha + \beta$. Place the next four expressions in order to prove $\sin(\alpha + \beta) = \sin\alpha\cos\beta + \cos\alpha\sin\beta$.

Step 1: $\sin(\alpha + \beta) =$ (A) $\sin\alpha\cos\beta + \cos\alpha\sin\beta$

Step 2: $\sin(\alpha + \beta) =$ (B) $\cos\left(\dfrac{\pi}{2} - \alpha\right)\cos\beta + \sin\left(\dfrac{\pi}{2} - \alpha\right)\sin\beta$

Step 3: $\sin(\alpha + \beta) =$ (C) $\cos\left[\left(\dfrac{\pi}{2} - \alpha\right) - \beta\right]$

Step 4: $\sin(\alpha + \beta) =$ (D) $\cos\left[\dfrac{\pi}{2} - (\alpha + \beta)\right]$

4-41   A Quotation Applicable to Functions ★

Nicolai Lobachevsky (1792–1856) was a Russian mathematician. He said: "There is no branch of mathematics which may not be applied to the real world."

Problem: Explain how Lobachevsky's words may be applied to functions.

Geometry

5-1 Naming Lines, Rays, and Segments ★

Lines, rays, and segments are named by points.

A line has no end points. It continues in both directions.

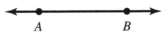

A ray has one end point and continues forever. A good example of a ray is a beam of light.

A segment (or line segment) has two end points.

Problem: Write the name, symbol, and number of end points for each figure.

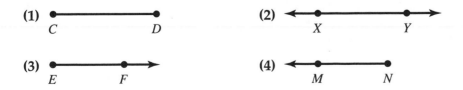

5-2   Intersection of Lines, Segments, and Rays ★

The intersection of two figures, designated by the symbol ∩, is the set of points that lie in both figures. Lines, segments, and rays intersect to form geometric figures.

For example, in the figure below, $\overrightarrow{XY}$ intersects $\overline{AB}$ at point Z.

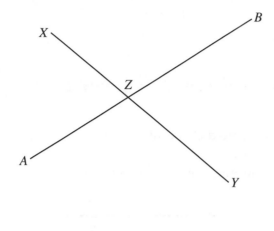

$$\overrightarrow{XY} \cap \overline{AB} = Z$$

Problem: Use the number line to describe each geometric figure below.

←———•———•———•———•———→
     A   C   B   D

(1) $\overline{AB} \cap \overline{CD}$ **(2)** $\overline{AC} \cap \overline{CB}$ **(3)** $\overline{AC} \cap \overline{BD}$

(4) $\overleftrightarrow{AB} \cap \overleftrightarrow{BD}$ **(5)** $\overrightarrow{AC} \cap \overrightarrow{BD}$ **(6)** $\overrightarrow{AC} \cap \overrightarrow{DB}$

5-3   Unions of Lines, Segments, and Rays ★★

The union of two geometric figures is the set of points that are in at least one of the figures. The union is designated by the symbol ∪.

For example, in the figure below, $\overline{AB} \cup \overrightarrow{CD} = \overrightarrow{AD}$.

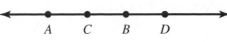

Problem: Use the figure below to name the geometric figures.

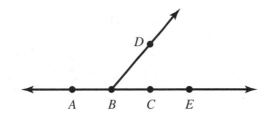

(1) $\overrightarrow{BD} \cup \overrightarrow{BC}$ (2) $\overline{AC} \cup \overline{CE}$ (3) $\overline{AC} \cup \overrightarrow{BE}$

(4) $\overline{AC} \cup \overline{BE}$ (5) $\overrightarrow{BD} \cup \overrightarrow{BA}$ (6) $\overrightarrow{CE} \cup \overrightarrow{CA}$

5-4   Naming Angles ★

An angle is formed by two rays with a common end point. The vertex is another name for the end point. The rays are the sides of the angle.

There are several ways to name an angle. Angles may be named by using a point on one side, the vertex, and a point on the other side. They may also be named by a number or letter inside the angle, or by the letter that identifies the vertex.

Problem: Match each angle below with its name. Some of the names may be used more than once, and some may not be used at all.

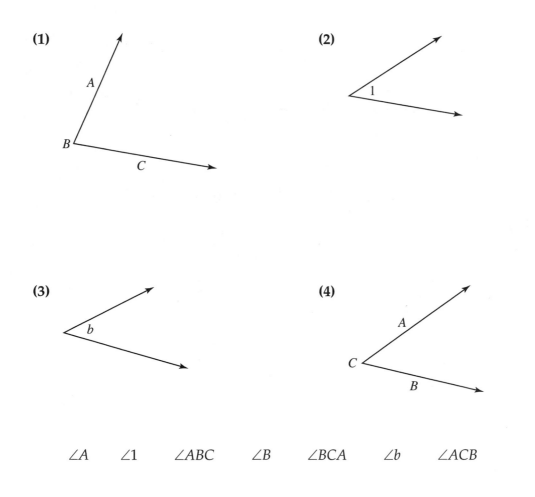

(1)

(2)

(3)

(4)

∠A   ∠1   ∠ABC   ∠B   ∠BCA   ∠b   ∠ACB

5-5   **Types of Angles** ★

Angles are grouped according to their degrees.

- An acute angle is an angle whose measure is greater than 0° and less than 90°.
- A right angle is an angle whose measure is 90°.
- An obtuse angle is an angle whose measure is greater than 90° and less than 180°.
- A straight angle is an angle whose measure is 180°.

Problem: Give the name, or names, of the angles.

(1) A 30° angle   **(2)** The sum of two acute angles

(3)   **(4)** The sum of two right angles

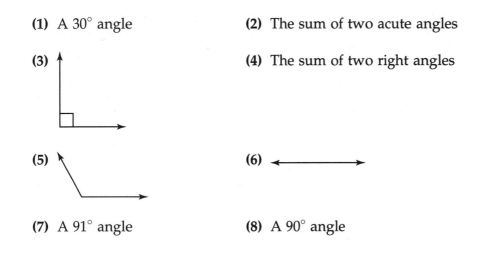

(5)   **(6)**

(7) A 91° angle   **(8)** A 90° angle

5-6   Complementary and Supplementary Angles ★

Complementary angles are two angles whose sum equals 90°. One angle is the complement of the other.

Supplementary angles are two angles whose sum equals 180°. One angle is the supplement of the other.

Problem: Each row below contains five angles. Two are complementary, two are supplementary, and one is neither. Identify the complementary angles and supplementary angles in each row.

(1)   15°   115°   125°   65°   75°

(2)   40°   50°   60°   150°   120°

(3)   90°   70°   100°   80°   20°

(4)   1°   90°   90°   89°   178°

5-7   Pairs of Angles — Adjacent, Vertical, Complementary, and Supplementary Angles ★

Special pairs of angles have their own names and distinguishing features.

- Adjacent angles are two angles that have a common vertex, a common side, and no common interior points.
- Vertical angles are two nonadjacent angles formed by two intersecting lines. Vertical angles always have the same measure.
- Complementary angles are two angles whose sum is 90°.
- Supplementary angles are two angles whose sum is 180°.

Problem: Consider the angles below. Identify the angles as being adjacent, vertical, complementary, and/or supplementary.

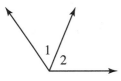   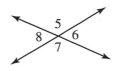

    (1) ∠1 and ∠2   **(2)** ∠3 and ∠4   **(3)** ∠5 and ∠6

    (4) ∠5 and ∠8   **(5)** ∠6 and ∠7   **(6)** ∠6 and ∠8

5-8   Angles Formed by a Transversal ★★

A transversal is a line that intersects two or more lines in the same plane at different points. As it does, it forms several special types of angles.

- Interior angles are angles inside the region bounded by the two lines.
- Exterior angles are angles outside the region bounded by the two lines.
- Same-side interior angles are two nonadjacent interior angles that are on the same side of the transversal.
- Alternate interior angles are two nonadjacent interior angles that are on opposite sides of the transversal.
- Alternate exterior angles are two nonadjacent exterior angles that are on opposite sides of the transversal.
- Corresponding angles are two nonadjacent angles (one is an interior angle and the other is an exterior angle) on the same side of the transversal.

Problem: Label the eight angles on the figure below with a number from 1 to 8 using the clues below. The odd-numbered angles are exterior angles.

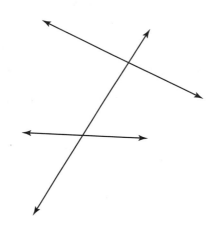

∠5 and ∠4 are vertical angles.

∠2 and ∠4 are same-side interior angles.

∠7 and ∠2 are corresponding angles.

∠4 and ∠6 are alternate interior angles.

∠8 and ∠7 are vertical angles.

∠2 and ∠3 are vertical angles.

∠1 and ∠5 are alternate exterior angles.

5-9   **Parallel Lines and Transversals ★★★ (8.G.5)**

Parallel lines are lines that never intersect. The word *parallel* is taken from the Greek word *parallelos*, which means "beside one another." The symbol for parallel lines is ||.

When two parallel lines are cut by a transversal, special pairs of angles are formed:

- Corresponding angles
- Alternate interior angles
- Alternate exterior angles
- Vertical angles
- Supplementary angles
- Same-side interior angles
- Linear pairs

Problem: In the figure below, $l_1 \| l_2$. Angles are numbered by their vertices. Find the measures of all the angles if the measure of $\angle 5 = 95°$. Then find the measure of all the angles if the measure of $\angle 2 = x°$.

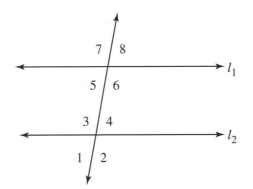

**5-10   Perpendicular Lines and Unknown Angle
Measurements ★★ (7.G.5)**

The word *perpendicular* is taken from two Latin words: *per*, which means "thoroughly," and
pendre, which means "to hang." A weight hanging from a horizontal bar attached to a base
would be perpendicular to the base. The symbol for perpendicular is ⊥.

Two perpendicular lines form four right angles. A right angle is an angle with a measure
of 90°.

Problem: In the figure below, $l_1 \perp l_2$. The $m \angle 1 = 30°$.

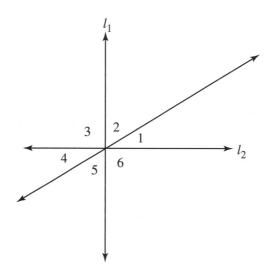

(1) Identify four right angles.

(2) Write an equation to express the sum of the measures of $\angle 1$ and $\angle 2$.

(3) Write an equation to express the sum of the measures of $\angle 1$, $\angle 2$, and $\angle 6$.

(4) Find the measures of $\angle 2$ and $\angle 4$.

5-11   Identifying and Sketching Common Polygons ★

A polygon is a figure made up of line segments that form the sides of the polygon. Polygons can have any number of sides, but they must have at least three. Following are some common polygons and the number of their sides:

- Triangle: 3
- Quadrilateral: 4
- Pentagon: 5
- Hexagon: 6
- Heptagon: 7
- Octagon: 8
- Nonagon: 9
- Decagon: 10

Problem: Sketch (neatly) and label each of the polygons above. Compare your sketches to those of a classmate. Are your sketches of the different polygons identical? Explain your answer.

5-12   Drawing Polygons in the Coordinate Plane ★★ (6.G.3)

A polygon is a closed plane figure whose sides are line segments. For example, a polygon that has four sides is a quadrilateral.

Quadrilaterals can be classified by the lengths of their sides and the number of parallel sides.

Problem: The vertices of a polygon are $A(2, -3), B(2, 5), C(-1, 1),$ and $D(-1, -3)$. Graph the points in the coordinate plane. Join A to B, B to C, C to D, and D to A with segments. What type of polygon is formed? Find the length of the longest side.

5-13   **Diagonals of Polygons ★**

A diagonal is a line segment drawn from one vertex to another nonadjacent vertex. The word *diagonal* comes from two Greek terms: *dia*, which means "across," and *gonia*, which means "angle."

Problem: Draw the diagonals in each figure. Then complete the table.

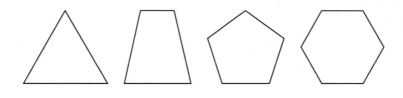

Number of Sides	Number of Diagonals
3	
4	
5	
6	
n	

5-14   **Sum of the Angles of a Polygon** ★

The sum of the measures of the angles of a polygon can be found if the number of sides is known.

Use the formula $S = (n - 2)(180°)$ where S represents the sum of the measures of the angles and n stands for the number of sides.

Problem: Complete the chart.

Type of Polygon	Number of Sides	Sum of the Measures of the Angles
Triangle		
	4	
Pentagon		
	6	
	7	
Octagon		

5-15   **The Measure of Each Interior Angle of a Regular Polygon** ★★

A regular polygon has congruent sides and congruent angles.

An interior angle of a regular polygon is an angle formed by two adjacent sides. The measure of each interior angle is $\frac{(n - 2)(180°)}{n}$, where n is the number of sides.

Problem: The measure of each interior angle of a regular polygon is shown below. Find the number of sides.

(1) 60°   **(2)** 120°   **(3)** 90°   **(4)** $128\frac{4}{7}°$ **(5)** 135°   **(6)** 108°

5-16   The Measure of Each Exterior Angle of a Regular Polygon ★★

An exterior angle of a polygon is formed by using an auxiliary ray.

In the figure below, an auxiliary ray $\overrightarrow{DF}$ is used to form $\angle EDF$. $\angle EDF$ is an exterior angle of the pentagon.

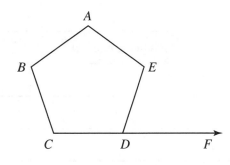

The measure of each exterior angle of a regular polygon is $\dfrac{360°}{n}$. n represents the number of sides. In the figure above, the $m\angle EDF = \dfrac{360°}{5} = 72°$.

Problem: Consider the following regular polygons: a triangle, quadrilateral, hexagon, heptagon, octagon, nonagon, and decagon. Which one of these polygons has exterior angles whose measures are mixed numbers? Find the measures of the exterior angles of this polygon.

5-17   **The Sum of the Measures of Each Exterior Angle of a Polygon ★★**

In the figure below, $\angle BCD$ is an exterior angle of $\triangle ABC$. To find the measure of $\angle BCD$, use the formula $\dfrac{360°}{n}$, where n is the number of sides of a regular polygon.

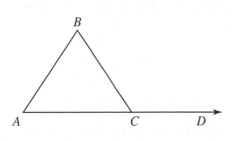

Problem: Complete the chart. What do you notice about the sum of the measures of the exterior angles?

Regular Polygon	Number of Sides	Measure of Each Exterior Angle	Sum of the Measures of the Exterior Angles
Triangle	3	120°	360°
Quadrilateral			
Pentagon			
Hexagon			
Octagon			
Decagon			
N-gon	n		

5-18   **Classifying Triangles by the Lengths of Their Sides** ★

Triangles come in various shapes and sizes. They may be classified according to the lengths of their sides.

To classify triangles by the lengths of their sides, use the following definitions:

Equilateral triangle: All three sides have the same length.

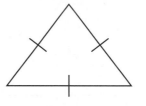

Isosceles triangle: At least two sides have the same length.

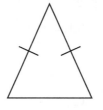

Scalene triangle: All three sides have different lengths.

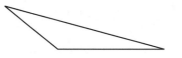

Problem: Given the sides, classify each triangle below as equilateral, isosceles, or scalene.

    (1) 3 feet, 3 feet, 1 yard

    (2) 1.5 feet, 1 foot, 12 inches

    (3) 30 centimeters, 30 centimeters, 30 millimeters

    (4) 1 yard, 4 feet, 5 feet

5-19   Classifying Triangles by the Measures of Their Angles ★

To classify triangles by the measures of their angles, it may be necessary to find the measure of each angle in the triangle. (Hint: The sum of the angles of any triangle equals 180°.)

To classify triangles according to the measures of their angles, use the following definitions:

Equiangular triangle: All angles are equal.

Acute triangle: All angles are acute (less than 90°).

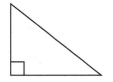

Right triangle: One angle measures 90°.

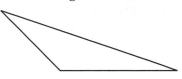

Obtuse triangle: One angle is obtuse (larger than 90°).

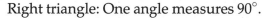

Problem: The measure of *at least one* angle of six triangles is listed below. Classify the triangles as equiangular, acute, right, or obtuse.

(1) 60, 20, 100	**(2)** 60, 60	**(3)** 90, 30, 60
(4) 120	**(5)** 45, 90	**(6)** 80, 80, 20

5-20   Included Sides and Angles of a Triangle ★★

A triangle has three sides and three angles.

An angle is included between two sides of a triangle if the end point of the two line segments is the vertex of the angle. In the triangle below, $\angle C$ is included between $\overline{BC}$ and $\overline{AC}$.

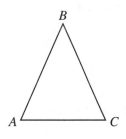

A side is included between two angles of a triangle if each end point of the side is a vertex of each angle. In the triangle above, $\overline{BC}$ is included between $\angle B$ and $\angle C$.

Problem: The triangles below are named by their vertices. Decide whether each statement is true or false. If it is false, explain why. (Hint: You may wish to sketch the triangle.)

(1) Consider $\triangle DEF$. $\angle D$ is included between $\overline{EF}$ and $\overline{ED}$.

(2) Consider $\triangle HIJ$. $\angle H$ is included between $\overline{HI}$ and $\overline{HJ}$.

(3) Consider $\triangle ACD$. $\overline{CD}$ is included between $\angle C$ and $\angle D$.

(4) Consider $\triangle ACH$. $\overline{AH}$ is included between $\angle A$ and $\angle C$.

5-21   Opposite Sides and Angles of a Triangle ★

In a triangle, the side opposite an angle does not have the vertex of the angle as an end point. The angle opposite a side of a triangle has a vertex that is not an end point of the segment. This is illustrated below:

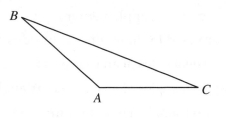

In $\triangle ABC$, $\overline{BC}$ is the side opposite $\angle A$. $\angle A$ is the angle opposite $\overline{BC}$.

In any triangle the longest side is opposite the largest angle, and the largest angle is opposite the longest side. Conversely, the shortest side is opposite the smallest angle, and the smallest angle is opposite the shortest side.

Problem: Consider the following triangles. Identify the longest and shortest sides of each. (Hint: The sum of the measures of the angles of any triangle equals 180°.)

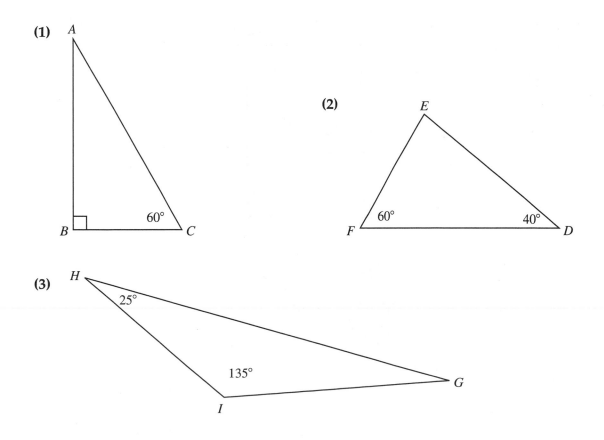

5-22   Finding the Measures of the Angles in a Triangle ★★ G

There are many true statements about triangles, including these:

- Vertical angles are congruent.
- Angles that form a linear pair are supplementary.
- Tick marks (or slashes) are used to show congruent sides and congruent angles.
- The angles opposite congruent sides of an isosceles triangle are congruent.
- The sides opposite congruent angles of an isosceles triangle are congruent.
- Each angle of an equilateral triangle has a measure of 60°.
- The sum of the measures of the angles in a triangle equals 180°.

Problem: Using the information listed above, find the measures of the numbered angles in the triangles below.

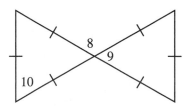

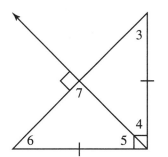

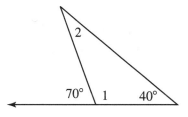

5-23   Using the Triangle Inequality Theorem ★★

The triangle inequality theorem states that the sum of the lengths of any two sides of a triangle is greater than the length of the third side. The examples below show why this is true.

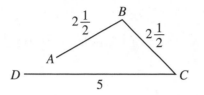

The three segments, $\overline{AB}$, $\overline{BC}$, and $\overline{CD}$, cannot be a triangle if $AB = BC = 2\frac{1}{2}$ inches and $CD = 5$ inches.

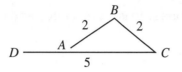

The three segments, $\overline{AB}$, $\overline{BC}$, and $\overline{CD}$, cannot be a triangle if $AB = BC = 2$ inches and $CD = 5$ inches.

Problem: The triangles below are not drawn to scale. Some cannot be triangles if the lengths of the sides are as they are labeled. Identify the triangles that could have sides of the indicated lengths. Correct the lengths of the longest sides of the other triangles.

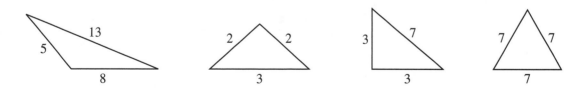

5-24   Drawing Triangles with Given Conditions ★★ G (7.G.2)

Knowing the lengths of the sides and/or the measures of the angles in a triangle may not be enough to sketch the triangle accurately. Depending on the information, it may be impossible to sketch the triangle at all, or it may be possible to sketch one triangle, or it may be possible to sketch several triangles.

Problem: Determine how many types of triangles may be drawn with the information provided.

    (1) Only two sides are 5 units long.

    (2) Two sides are 6 units long, and one angle measures 120°.

    (3) The sides are 2, 3, and 6 units long.

    (4) Two sides are 7 units long and only one angle measures 45°.

    (5) One side is 4 units long, one side is 6 units long, and one angle is 100°.

5-25   Using the Pythagorean Theorem to Find the Length of the Hypotenuse ★ (8.G.7)

Pythagoras (570–500 BC) was one of history's most interesting mathematicians. He believed that everything followed a strict pattern and "the essence of all things is numbers."

The Pythagorean theorem, which states $a^2 + b^2 = c^2$, where a and b are the lengths of the legs of a right triangle and c is the length of the hypotenuse, is credited to him.

Problem: The lengths of the legs of right triangles are listed or pictured below. Find the length of the hypotenuse of each triangle.

(1) 3, 4   **(2)** 9, 12   **(3)**   **(4)**

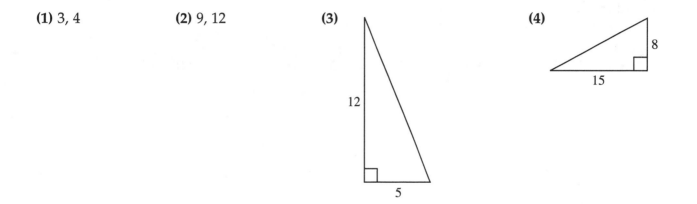

5-26   Explaining a Proof of the Pythagorean Theorem ★★ (8.G.6) 🖳

Go to http://www.math.hmc.edu/funfacts/ffiles/10007.2.shtml.

Here is what to do:

1. Read the proof carefully.

2. Make any notations and figures that you feel are helpful.

Problem: Write a brief explanation of the proof of the Pythagorean theorem in your own words.

5-27   Using the Pythagorean Theorem to Find the Length of a Leg ★★ (8.G.7)

$a^2 + b^2 = c^2$ is the Pythagorean theorem, named after the Greek mathematician Pythagoras who lived in the sixth century BC. The theorem applies to right triangles where a and b stand for the lengths of the legs, and c stands for the length of the hypotenuse.

To find the length of a missing leg, substitute the length of the leg you know for a or b (it does not matter which variable), substitute the length of the hypotenuse for c, square each number, and solve.

Problem: The length of one of the triangle's legs and the length of the hypotenuse (the longer segment) are shown for right triangles. Find the length of the other leg. Express your answers in radical form.

    (1) 6, 7   **(2)** 1, 5   **(3)** 5, 10   **(4)** $\sqrt{5}$, 7

5-28   **Applying the Pythagorean Theorem to Find the Distance between Two Points ★★ (8.G.8)**

The Pythagorean theorem can be used to find the distance between any two points in the coordinate plane, provided that the points do not lie on a horizontal or vertical line.

Using her knowledge of the Pythagorean theorem, Aubrey tried to find the distance between $(3, 1)$ and $(-2, -2)$. She drew a line containing these points and then drew a right triangle so that the line containing $(3, 1)$ and $(-2, -2)$ is the hypotenuse, as shown below. She said that $a = 3$ and $b = 5$. After applying the Pythagorean theorem, she found $c = \sqrt{34}$.

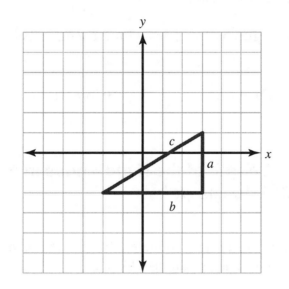

Problem: Is Aubrey correct? Is there another triangle she could have drawn? If there is, how would drawing this triangle affect the distance between the two points?

5-29   Testing for Acute and Obtuse Triangles ★★

The Pythagorean theorem states that $a^2 + b^2 = c^2$ for any right triangle if a and b stand for the lengths of the legs and c stands for the length of the hypotenuse.

It follows that if $c^2 \neq a^2 + b^2$ the triangle is not a right triangle.

If $c^2 < a^2 + b^2$, where c is the longest side, the triangle is acute. (Remember that an acute triangle has three acute angles.)

If $c^2 > a^2 + b^2$, where c is the longest side of a triangle, the triangle is obtuse. (Remember that an obtuse triangle has one obtuse angle.)

Problem: Which of the triangles having sides with the lengths below are acute? Which are obtuse?

    (1) 5, 5, 7   **(2)** 6, 8, 9   **(3)** 6, 8, 11   **(4)** 9, 12, 16

5-30   Finding the Length of the Hypotenuse in a 45°-45°-90° Triangle ★★

A 45°-45°-90° triangle is an isosceles right triangle. The legs of this triangle are congruent. The hypotenuse equals the length of a leg multiplied by $\sqrt{2}$.

In the figure below, $\overline{AB}$ is the hypotenuse, and $\overline{AC}$ and $\overline{BC}$ are legs. $AB = AC\sqrt{2}$ and $AB = CB\sqrt{2}$. If $AC = 7$, then $AB = 7\sqrt{2}$. Since $\overline{AC} \cong \overline{BC}$, $CB = 7\sqrt{2}$.

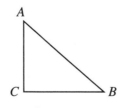

Problem: Find the length of the hypotenuse (in simplest form) if a leg of a 45°-45°-90° triangle has the following lengths.

    (1) 4   **(2)** $\sqrt{6}$ **(3)** $\sqrt{2}$ **(4)** $7\sqrt{2}$

5-31   Finding the Length of a Leg in a 45°-45°-90° Triangle ★★

The legs of a 45°-45°-90° triangle, as in any isosceles triangle, are congruent.

To find the length of a leg, divide the length of the hypotenuse by $\sqrt{2}$ and simplify, if possible.

Another way of stating this is to multiply $\frac{1}{2}$ the hypotenuse by $\sqrt{2}$ and simplify, if possible. For example, if the hypotenuse is $12\sqrt{2}$ centimeters, the leg equals $\frac{1}{2} \cdot 12\sqrt{2} \cdot \sqrt{2} = 12$.

Problem: The length of the hypotenuse of 45°-45°-90° triangles are listed in the first column. Match each with the length of its leg expressed in simplest form. Some "legs" will not be used.

Hypotenuses
(1) 8
(2) 4
(3) 38
(4) $6\sqrt{2}$

Legs
(A) $2\sqrt{2}$
(B) $4\sqrt{2}$
(C) 12
(D) $3\sqrt{4}$
(E) 6
(F) $19\sqrt{2}$

5-32   Finding the Length of the Hypotenuse in a 30°-60°-90° Triangle ★★

The length of the hypotenuse of a 30°-60°-90° triangle is related to its legs.

The hypotenuse is twice the length of the shorter leg. For example, if the shorter leg of a 30°-60°-90° triangle is 6, the length of the hypotenuse is 12.

The hypotenuse is $\frac{2}{3}$ of the length of the longer leg times $\sqrt{3}$. For example, if the longer leg of a 30°-60°-90° triangle is $6\sqrt{3}$, the length of the hypotenuse is $\frac{2}{3} \cdot 6\sqrt{3} \cdot \sqrt{3} = 12$.

Problem: Find the hypotenuse of a 30°-60°-90° triangle, given the length of a leg.

(1) The longer leg is $10\sqrt{3}$.
(2) The shorter leg is 7.
(3) The longer leg is $5\sqrt{3}$.
(4) The longer leg is $9\sqrt{3}$.
(5) The shorter leg is 8.
(6) The shorter leg is 10.

5-33   Finding the Lengths of the Legs in a 30°-60°-90° Triangle ★★

In a 30°-60°-90° triangle, the shorter leg is opposite the 30° angle. The longer leg is opposite the 60° angle. The relationship between the legs and the hypotenuse is stated below:

- The length of the shorter leg is $\frac{1}{2}$ of the hypotenuse.

- The length of the longer leg is $\frac{1}{2}$ of the hypotenuse times $\sqrt{3}$, or the length of the shorter leg times $\sqrt{3}$.

- The hypotenuse is the longest side of the triangle.

Problem: The length of the hypotenuse of 30°-60°-90° triangles are listed below. Find the lengths of the smaller and longer legs.

    (1) 15   **(2)** 10   **(3)** 6   **(4)** 20

5-34   **Finding the Missing Lengths of the Sides of a 45°-45°-90° and a 30°-60°-90° Triangle ★★★**

The triangles below will allow you to apply your understanding of the relationships between the legs and the hypotenuse of special right triangles.

Problem: Using the information given, find the missing lengths of the sides of the triangles.

$AB = 12\sqrt{2}$ $DE = 12\sqrt{3}$ $GI = 11\sqrt{3}$ $JL = 1$

$m\angle C = 45°$ $m\angle D = 60°$ $m\angle H = 60°$ $m\angle J = 90°$

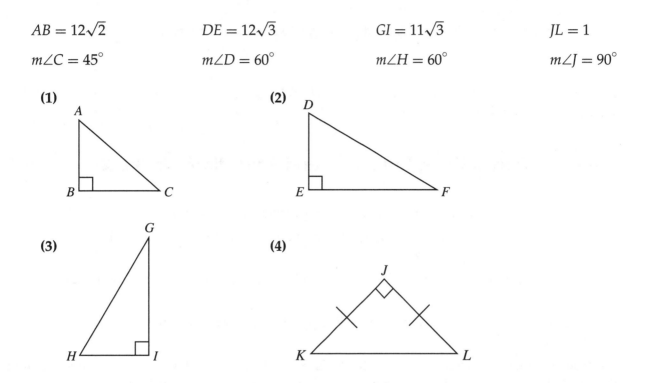

5-35   **Properties of Rotations, Reflections, and Translations ★ (8.G.1)**

Jamal was working on a report about rotations, reflections, and translations. To include figures in his report, he drew several figures on a sheet of paper and photocopied them. Then he cut them out. To show rotations, reflections, and translations, he turned, flipped, slid, and pasted the figures on a sheet of paper so that they were the same size as the original figures but in different positions.

Problem: Do you think this is a good strategy? Explain your answer.

5-36   **Translations, Rotations, and Reflections ★ (8.G.2)**

Three rigid forms of motion are translations, rotations, and reflections:

- A translation is made when a figure is moved along a line. Sometimes this motion is referred to as a "slide" or "glide."

- A rotation is made when a figure is moved around a point. This is also called a "turn."

- A reflection is made when a figure is flipped over a line. This motion is often called a "flip."

Problem: In the figure below, the letter M is printed in bold. It has been translated, rotated 90°, and reflected. Three lighter figures are the result of each and are labeled 1, 2, and 3. Identify which is the result of a translation, rotation, or reflection. More than one answer is possible.

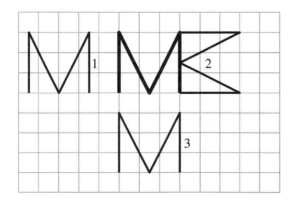

5-37   Identifying Congruent Triangles ★ (8.G.2)

Congruent triangles have the same shape and are the same size. They may be flipped or turned, but as long as the size and shape are the same, the triangles are congruent. The symbol for congruency is ≅.

Problem: Of the six triangles pictured below, some are congruent. Identify the congruent triangles.

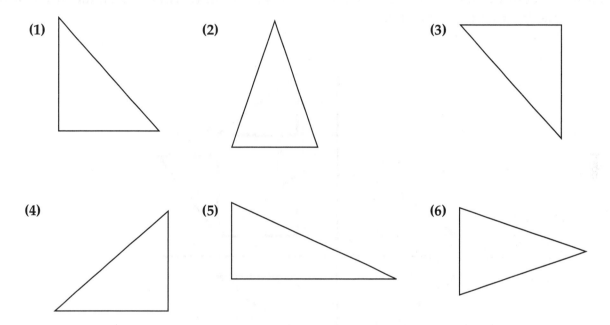

(1)   (2)   (3)

(4)   (5)   (6)

5-38   Translations, Rotations, and Reflections of a Right Triangle ★★ (8.G.2)

The three rigid forms of motion are translations (slides or glides), rotations (turns), and reflections (flips). When a figure is moved in any of these ways, its size and shape remain the same. Only its position changes.

Problem: Consider the right triangle whose vertices are $(2, 4), (2, 1),$ and $(6, 1)$. Identify which triangle results from the following.

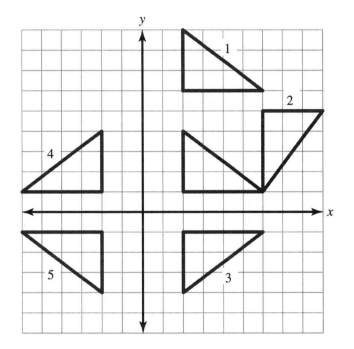

(1) A reflection over the y-axis

(2) A rotation around point $(6, 1), 90°$ clockwise

(3) A reflection over the x-axis

(4) A rotation of $180°$ around the origin

(5) A reflection over the y-axis and a reflection over the x-axis

(6) A translation 5 units up

5-39   Using Undefined Terms ★ (G-CO.1)

Geometry is based on three undefined terms: point, line, and plane. Although these terms do not have precise definitions, they can be described as follows:

- A point is represented by a dot. It has no length, width, or thickness.
- A line has only length and extends infinitely in two directions.
- A plane has length and width. It can be thought of as a wall (with no windows or other openings) that extends infinitely in two directions.

Using these three terms, all other terms in geometry can be defined.

Problem: The precise definitions of angle, circle, perpendicular lines, parallel lines, and line segments are listed below. Match each term with its definition.

(1) Two lines that form right angles

(2) A figure formed by two rays with a common end point

(3) Two points on the line and all the points between them

(4) The set of points in a plane that are a given distance from a given point in the plane

(5) Lines that do not intersect and are coplanar

5-40   Describing Transformations as Functions ★★ (G-CO.2)

Transformations can be described as functions that pair points in the coordinate plane with other points. For example, a translation of 4 units to the left pairs every ordered pair (x, y) with $(x - 4, y)$.

Problem: Consider $\triangle ABC$ with vertices $A(2, 5), B(2, -1),$ and $C(-3, 3)$. Find the vertices of each triangle described below. Then identify the transformation.

(1) (x, y) is paired with $(x, y + 2)$.

(2) (x, y) is paired with $(-y, x)$.

(3) (x, y) is paired with $(x, -y)$.

(4) (x, y) is paired with $(-x, -y)$.

5-41   Describing Dilations ★★ (G-CO.2)

Andrew is a good math student who knows that reflections, rotations, and translations produce congruent figures and that dilations produce similar figures. But sometimes he reaches incorrect conclusions.

Problem: Andrew made a generalization about the vertices of polygons. He said that when (x, y) is paired with (kx, y) where k is greater than 1, the polygons are larger than and similar to the original. If k is less than 1, the polygons are smaller than and similar to the original. Do you agree? Explain your reasoning.

5-42   Rotations and Reflections of Regular Polygons ★★ (G-CO.3)

A regular polygon is both equiangular and equilateral, meaning that all of its angles are congruent and all of its sides are congruent.

Problem: Taylor made the following generalization about a regular polygon that has n sides (an n-gon): it has n lines of symmetry. A reflection in any of the lines of symmetry will carry the n-gon onto itself. A rotation of $\dfrac{360°}{n}$ about the intersection of these lines of symmetry will also carry the n-gon onto itself. Do you agree? Explain your answer.

5-43   ## Defining Rotations, Reflections, and Translations in Terms of Line Segments ★★★ G (G-CO.4)

Geometric terms are often defined and clarified by using geometric figures. For example, a line segment can be defined as a part of a line between two points that are the end points of the segment. $\overline{AB}$ is shown below.

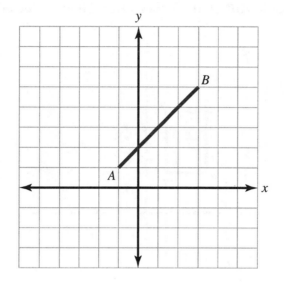

Problem: David missed several days of school because of the flu. He is now confused about rotations, reflections, and translations. Explain these terms to him in terms of $\overline{AB}$. Then demonstrate them by showing him how to rotate, reflect, and translate $\overline{AB}$. (Hint: You may find it helpful to include figures.)

5-44   **Specifying a Sequence of Transformations That Will Carry a Given Figure onto Another ★★ (G-CO.5)**

Rotations, reflections, and transformations will carry a figure onto another figure. This other figure depends on the original figure, the specific transformation, and the sequence of the transformations.

Problem: Consider rectangle *ABCD*. It has been translated, reflected, and rotated to carry it onto rectangle *A'B'C'D'*.

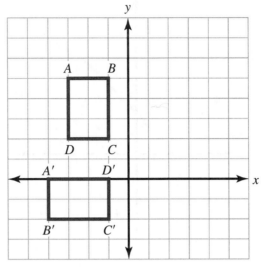

Arrange the transformations in order.

    (1) Rotated 90° clockwise about the origin

    (2) Translated 3 units down, 1 unit right

    (3) Reflected in the *y*-axis

5-45   **Predicting the Effects of Rigid Motions ★★ (G-CO.6)**

Molly knows that when a figure is rotated, reflected, or translated, the resulting figure is congruent to its preimage.

Problem: Molly sketched $\triangle ABC$ with vertices $A(1, 2), B(3, 4), C(1, 3)$ and translated it 2 units down and 1 unit to the left to find $A'(0, 0), B'(2, 1),$ and $C'(0, 1)$. $\triangle A'B'C'$ should be congruent to $\triangle ABC$, but it did not seem to be congruent based on the sketch. Was Molly, in fact, correct in thinking the triangles were congruent, despite her sketch? If she was wrong, what was her mistake?

5-46   Writing a Statement of Congruence and Identifying Corresponding Parts ★★ (G-CO.7)

When a triangle is rotated, reflected, or translated, the resulting triangle is congruent to the original because rotations, reflections, and translations are rigid motions.

Two triangles are congruent if and only if corresponding angles are congruent and corresponding sides are congruent. $\triangle UVW \cong \triangle XYZ$ is a congruence statement for the triangles below.

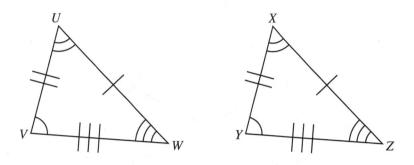

Problem: Consider the triangles that follow. Write a statement of congruence. List three congruent angles and three congruent sides.

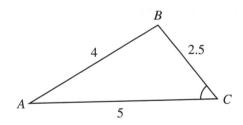

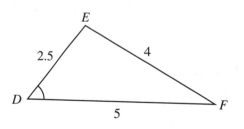

5-47   Identifying Corresponding Parts in Overlapping Triangles ★★

Sometimes a geometric figure is made up of several different figures. Four triangles are in the diagram below: $\triangle ABF, \triangle EDF, \triangle ACD,$ and $\triangle ECB$.

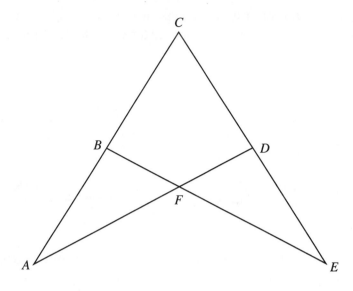

Problem: Consider the figure above. $\triangle ACD \cong \triangle ECB$. Fill in the blanks.

(1) $\overline{AB} \cong$ _____   **(2)** $\overline{BC} \cong$ _____

(3) $\angle A \cong$ _____   **(4)** $\angle CBF \cong$ _____

5-48   Using SSS, SAS, and ASA to Verify Congruent Triangles ★★

Three ways to prove that two triangles are congruent are listed below:

- SSS: If three sides of one triangle are congruent to corresponding sides of the other triangle, the two triangles are congruent.
- SAS: If two sides and the included angle of one triangle are congruent to the corresponding parts of the other triangle, the triangles are congruent.
- ASA: If two angles and the included side of one triangle are congruent to the corresponding parts of the other triangle, the two triangles are congruent.

Problem: Decide which triangles below are congruent, and write a congruence statement to verify your choices. Choose from SSS, SAS, or ASA.

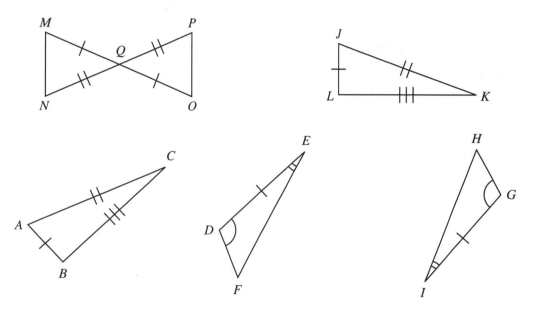

5-49   Explaining the Criteria for Triangle Congruence ★★ (G-CO.8)

Anna knows how to show the SSS, SAS, and ASA criteria for triangle congruence. For example, SSS can be shown by rotating, reflecting, or translating each side of a triangle, then translating each segment to form a triangle that is congruent to the original.

Problem: Suppose Anna rotated, reflected, or translated two sides of a triangle and the angle that is adjacent to only one of the sides. She then drew a segment that formed a triangle. Would this triangle be congruent to the original? Explain your answer.

5-50   **Proving Vertical Angles Are Congruent ★ (G-CO.9)**

Alec knows that vertical angles are congruent, but he is having trouble proving that they are.

Problem: Help Alec out. Consider the figure and complete the proof by writing the reason for each statement.

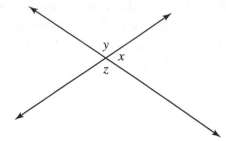

    (1) $\angle y$ and $\angle z$ are vertical angles.

    (2) $m\angle x + m\angle y = 180°$

    (3) $m\angle x + m\angle z = 180^o$

    (4) $m\angle x + m\angle y = m\angle x + m\angle z$

    (5) $m\angle y = m\angle z$

    (6) $\angle y \cong \angle z$

5-51   Proving the Isosceles Triangle Theorem ★★ (G-CO.10)

An isosceles triangle is a triangle that has at least two congruent sides. In the figure below, $\triangle ABC$ is isosceles because $\overline{AB} \cong \overline{CB}$.

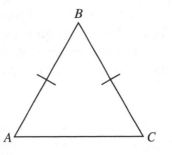

Problem: Vinnie was asked to prove the isosceles triangle theorem, which states that if two sides of a triangle are congruent, then the angles opposite those sides are congruent. He knows the proof involves drawing an angle bisector and then proving that two triangles are congruent. How would you help Vinnie complete the proof, using the figure above?

5-52   Proving the Diagonals of a Parallelogram Bisect Each Other ★★ (G-CO.11)

Sasha wants to prove that the diagonals of a parallelogram bisect each other. She drew the diagonals of parallelogram *ABCD* as shown on the figure below.

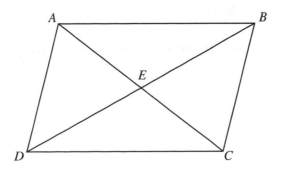

Problem: Explain what Sasha must prove. How can she prove it?

5-53   **Constructing the Perpendicular Bisector of a Segment**
★★ (G-CO.12)

A perpendicular bisector of a segment is a line, ray, or segment that is perpendicular to the segment at its midpoint. Although you can draw a perpendicular bisector using a ruler and protractor, constructing a perpendicular bisector requires a straightedge and a compass. (Hint: Remember that a construction of a figure is done only with a compass and straightedge, or ruler. A drawing may be done with the tools used for a construction and other tools, such as a protractor.)

Problem: Mason tried to construct the perpendicular bisector of $\overline{AB}$. He drew four arcs with the same radius (two from A and two from B). He was supposed to label one point of the intersection of the arcs C and the other point D, so that $\overleftrightarrow{CD}$ is the perpendicular bisector of $\overline{AB}$. But the arcs did not intersect. What did Mason do wrong?

5-54   **Constructing a Regular Hexagon Inscribed in a Circle**
★★ (G-CO.13) 🖥

Go to http://www.mathopenref.com/constinhexagon.html and view a virtual construction of a regular hexagon inscribed in a circle.

Do the following:

1. Click on "run" to view an animated construction.
2. Scroll down and click on "printable step-by-step instruction sheet" to read about how to inscribe a regular hexagon in a circle.

Problem: Follow the instructions and construct a regular hexagon in a circle on your paper.

5-55   Describing the Effects of Dilations, Translations, Rotations, and Reflections ★★ (8.G.3)

Translations, rotations, and reflections produce figures that are congruent to the preimage. Dilations produce figures that are similar to the preimage.

Problem: Consider the triangle with vertices $A(-1,-2), B(3,1)$, and $C(4,-3)$. Identify which transformation produces each of the triangles described below.

(1) $A'(1,2), B'(-3,-1)$, and $C'(-4,3)$

(2) $A'(-1,2), B'(3,-1)$, and $C'(4,3)$

(3) $A'(0,1), B'(4,4)$, and $C'(5,0)$

(4) $A'(-2,-4), B'(6,2)$, and $C'(8,-6)$

5-56 **Describing a Sequence That Exhibits Similarity between Two Figures** ★★★ (8.G.4)

If you are given a two-dimensional figure, a sequence of rotations, reflections, translations, and dilations will always produce a similar figure.

Problem: $\triangle ABC \sim \triangle DEF$ is shown below. Starting with $\triangle ABC$, identify which sequences will exhibit the similarity between the triangles.

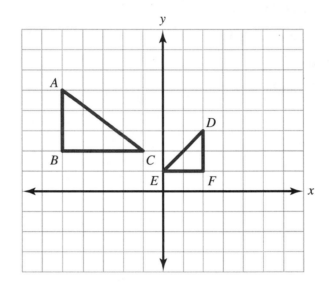

(1) Rotate 180° about the origin, reflect in the *x*-axis, translate 1 unit left, and dilate by a scale factor of $\frac{1}{2}$.

(2) Rotate 90° clockwise about the origin, reflect in the *x*-axis, translate 1 unit left, and dilate by a scale factor of $\frac{1}{2}$.

(3) Reflect in the *x*-axis, translate 1 unit left, and dilate by a scale factor of $\frac{1}{2}$.

(4) Reflect in the *y*-axis, translate 1 unit left, and dilate by a scale factor of $\frac{1}{2}$.

5-57   Verifying the Properties of Dilations ★★ (G-SRT.1)

Thomas tried to verify that the dilation of a line is longer or shorter by a given factor. He drew $\overline{AB}$ 4 units long with end points $(-3, 3)$ and $(1, 3)$. He dilated the segment by a scale factor of 3 and found $(-3, 3) \rightarrow (-9, 9)$ and $(1, 3) \rightarrow (3, 9)$. The length of $\overline{A'B'}$ was 12 units long, which is three times the length of $\overline{AB}$. He dilated $\overline{AB}$ by a scale factor of $\frac{1}{3}$ and found $(-3, 3) \rightarrow (-1, 1)$ and $(1, 3) \rightarrow \left(\frac{1}{3}, 1\right)$. The length of $\overline{A''B''}$ was $\frac{4}{3}$ units long, which was $\frac{1}{3}$ the length of $\overline{AB}$. He concluded that the dilation of a segment is longer than the segment if the scale factor is greater than 1 and smaller than the segment if the scale factor is less than 1.

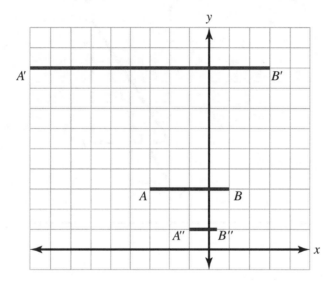

Problem: Dilate $\overline{CD}$ with $C(1, 3)$ and $D(6, -2)$ by -2. Compare the length of $\overline{CD}$ with the length of $\overline{C'D'}$. Does this support Thomas's conclusion about the lengths of segments and dilations? Explain your answer.

5-58   Using the Definition of Similarity to Decide If Two Figures Are Similar ★ (G-SRT.2)

Two polygons are similar if their corresponding angles are congruent and the lengths of their corresponding sides are in proportion. The symbol ~ means "is similar to." It was first used by Gottfried Wilhelm Leibniz in an article published in 1679.

Problem: Michelle said that she can tell by looking at the figure below that $\triangle ABC \sim \triangle DEF$, without using the definition of similar triangles. What might she be thinking?

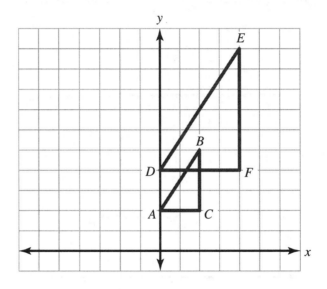

5-59   Establishing the AA Criterion for Similar Triangles ★★ (G-SRT.3)

$\triangle ABC$ is dilated by a scale factor of k with respect to the origin to form $\triangle A'B'C'$.

Problem: Marcus reasoned that $\angle A \cong \angle A'$ and $\angle B \cong \angle B'$. He therefore concluded that $\triangle ABC \sim \triangle A'B'C'$. Is he correct? Explain your reasoning.

5-60   Using AA, SSS, and SAS to Prove That Triangles Are Similar ★★

Similar triangles have the same shape, but they are not necessarily the same size. Each of the methods below can be used to show that two triangles are similar:

- AA: If two angles of one triangle are congruent to two angles of another triangle, the triangles are similar.
- SSS: If the corresponding sides of one triangle are in proportion to the corresponding sides of the other triangle, the triangles are similar.
- SAS: If a pair of corresponding angles is congruent and the sides that include these angles are in proportion, the triangles are similar.

Problem: Decide which of the pairs of triangles are similar. Verify your choices using AA, SSS, or SAS.

(1)

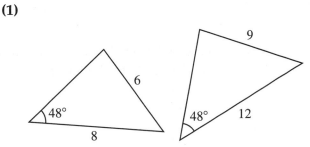

(2)

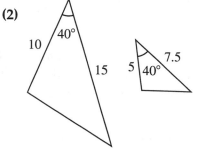

(3)

(4)

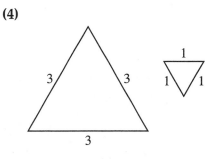

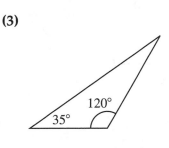

5-61   **Writing a Similarity Statement and Finding
the Scale Factor ★★**

Because similar triangles have the same shape but are not necessarily the same size, the pairs of corresponding sides are proportional.

A similarity statement is a correspondence between figures, and the vertices of the angles must be listed in corresponding order. In the figure below, $\triangle ABC \sim \triangle EDF$.

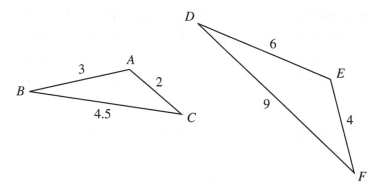

The scale factor is the ratio of the corresponding sides. In the figure above, the scale factor of $\triangle ABC$ to $\triangle EDF$ is 1:2.

Problem: Write a similarity statement for each pair of triangles below. Then find the scale factor. (Hint: Use the ratio of the length of the side of the first triangle to the length of the corresponding side of the second triangle.)

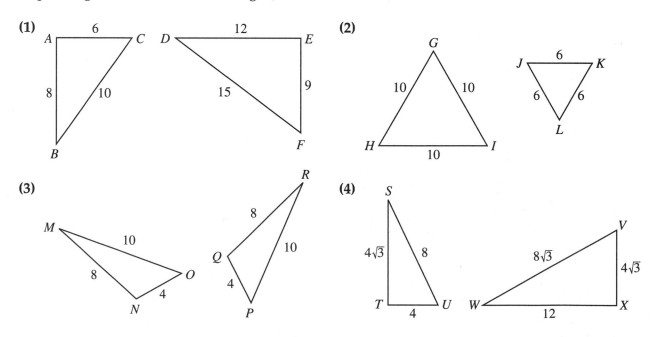

5-62   Proving the Triangle Proportionality Theorem
★★★ (G-SRT.4)

The triangle proportionality theorem states that if a line segment parallel to one side of a triangle intersects the other two sides, it divides those sides proportionally. The theorem can be proved using the properties of similar triangles and the properties of proportions.

Problem: Lee Ann tried to prove the triangle proportionality theorem. She drew a figure so that $AB \parallel DE$. She said that $\angle CAB \cong \angle CDE$ and $\angle C \cong \angle C$, therefore $\triangle ABC \sim \triangle DEC$. She concluded that $\dfrac{AC}{DC} = \dfrac{BC}{EC}$. Is she correct so far? If she is, complete the proof. If she is not, correct her work, then complete the proof.

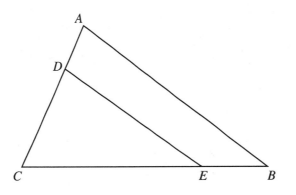

5-63 Finding the Lengths of the Sides of Similar Triangles ★★★ (G-SRT.5)

If two triangles are similar, their corresponding angles are congruent, and corresponding sides are in a constant ratio called the scale factor.

If the lengths of two corresponding sides of a triangle are given, you can find the scale factor. This is usually the ratio of the length of a side of the first triangle to the corresponding length of a side of the second triangle. You can then write a proportion and solve to find the length of the other side.

For example, in the figure below, $\triangle ABC \sim \triangle EFD$. $BC:FD = 2:1$. Likewise, $AC:ED = 2:1$ and $AB:EF = 2:1$.

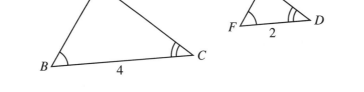

Problem: Each pair of triangles below is similar. Write a proportion and solve for x and y.

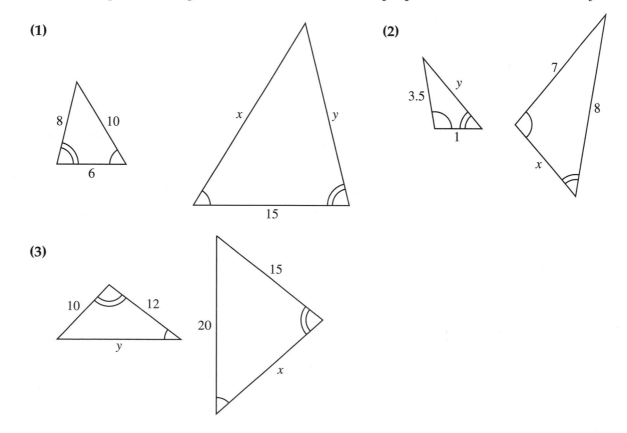

5-64   **Working with Scale Drawings of Geometric Figures**
             ★★ (7.G.1)

Scale is the ratio of the dimensions on a drawing to the dimensions of a real object.

Raul and his father want to plant a vegetable garden in their yard. Raul made a scale drawing of the rectangular garden shown below.

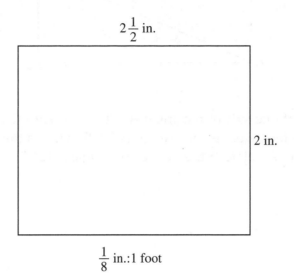

$2\frac{1}{2}$ in.

2 in.

$\frac{1}{8}$ in.:1 foot

Problem: Answer the questions.

   (1) What are the dimensions of the actual garden?

   (2) What is the area of the actual garden?

   (3) Using a ruler, reproduce Raul's scale drawing with a scale of $\frac{1}{4}$ inch:1 foot. Give the length and width of your scale drawing.

   (4) Using the scale of your drawing, find the dimensions of the actual garden.

   (5) How does the area of the actual garden of your scale drawing compare to the area of the actual garden in Raul's scale drawing?

5-65   **Finding the Area of a Triangle by Using a Rectangle ★ (6.G.1)**

The area of a rectangle is found by multiplying its length by its width, $A = l \times w$. A diagonal of a rectangle divides the rectangle into two congruent triangles, as shown below.

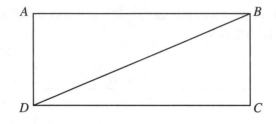

Problem: If the length of one side of rectangle *ABCD* is 10 centimeters and the length of an adjacent side is 6 centimeters, what is the area of △*ABD*? What is the area of △*DBC*? How do the areas of the two triangles relate to the area of rectangle *ABCD*?

5-66   Finding the Area of a Triangle ★

The formulas for finding the area of a triangle are $A = \frac{1}{2}bh$ or $\frac{bh}{2}$. In the formulas, A is the area, b equals the length of the base of the triangle, and h equals the height, which is also called the altitude. The height and the base form a right angle.

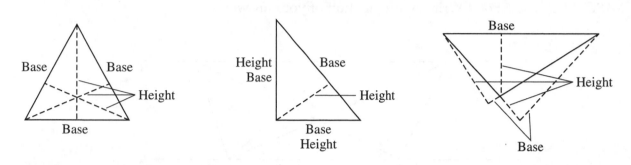

Each triangle in the figure above has three altitudes. Notice that each altitude of an acute triangle is inside the triangle. Each leg of a right triangle is an altitude, and the other altitude is inside the triangle. Two altitudes of an obtuse triangle are outside the triangle, and the other is inside the triangle.

When finding the area of any triangle, always be sure that the units of measurement are the same. Area is measured in square units.

Problem: Find the area of each triangle below.

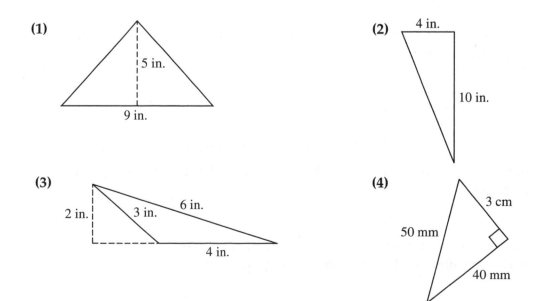

5-67   Finding the Area of a Triangle ★★★

Sometimes it is possible to compare areas without knowing any of the lengths. This requires careful analysis of what you already know.

Problem: In the figure below, $l_1 \parallel l_2$. Which of the following triangles has the largest area: $\triangle ABC$, $\triangle DBC$, or $\triangle EBC$? Write an explanation of your answer.

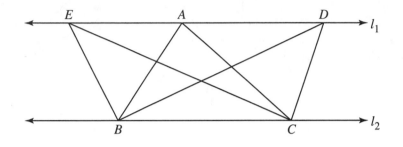

5-68   Definitions of Trigonometric Ratios for Acute Angles of a Right Triangle ★ (G-SRT.6)

Three trigonometric ratios are the sine, cosine, and tangent. Each is a ratio of a side of a right triangle to another side:

- The sine of an acute angle θ of a right triangle is the ratio of the leg opposite the angle to the hypotenuse.
- The cosine θ is the ratio of the leg adjacent to the angle to the hypotenuse.
- The tangent θ equals the ratio of the leg opposite the angle to the leg adjacent to the angle.

Problem: If θ is an acute angle in a right triangle, sin θ, cos θ, and tan θ are the same if the right triangles are similar. Do you agree? Explain your reasoning.

5-69   **Using the Sine and Cosine of Complementary Angles**
          ★ (G-SRT.7)

When working with all trigonometric functions and right angles, you must first select an acute angle and then write the ratio.

Problem: As part of her homework, Eva's teacher asked the class to write one trigonometric ratio using the figure below.

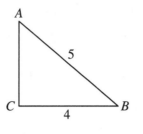

Eva said $\sin \theta = \dfrac{4}{5}$ but her friend Chelsea said that $\cos \theta = \dfrac{4}{5}$. Their teacher looked at their figures and said they were both correct. Explain how this could be.

5-70   **Using Trigonometric Ratios and the Pythagorean Theorem**
          to Solve Problems ★★★ G (G-SRT.8)

The Pythagorean theorem can be used to find the length of a side of a right triangle if the lengths of two sides are known.

However, if the length of a side of a right triangle and an angle are given, trigonometric ratios may be used to find the length of the other side. Whether you use the sine, cosine, or tangent ratio depends on what information is provided.

Problem: Solve each problem.

    (1) Find the height of a flagpole if its shadow is 65 feet long and the angle of elevation of the sun is 26°.

    (2) Danielle is making a triangular flower garden, whose sides will be set by plastic edging. One side is 15 feet long and the other side, which is perpendicular to the first side, is 10 feet long. How much edging will Danielle need to enclose the garden?

5-71   **Deriving the Formula $A = \frac{1}{2}ab \sin C$ to Find the Area of a Triangle ★★ (G-SRT.9)**

The area of a triangle can be found by using the formula $A = \frac{1}{2}bh$, where b is the base and h is the height. It can be used to find the area of a triangle when the length of the base and height are given.

You can use this formula to derive the formula $A = \frac{1}{2}ab \sin C$ for finding the area of a triangle, where the lengths of two sides of a triangle and the measure of the included angle are given.

Problem: Use the figure that follows to complete the steps to derive the formula $A = \frac{1}{2}ab \sin C$.

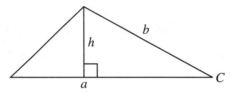

(1) Express the sine of $\angle C$ in terms of h and b.

(2) Use the equation in step 1 to solve for h.

(3) Use the formula $A = \frac{1}{2}ah$ to solve for h.

(4) Substitute the expressions for h in steps 2 and 3. Solve for A.

5-72   Proving the Law of Sines ★★ (G-SRT.10)

The law of sines states that the lengths of the sides of a triangle are proportional to the sines of the corresponding opposite angles. Stated algebraically, for any $\triangle ABC$, $\dfrac{\sin A}{a} = \dfrac{\sin B}{b} = \dfrac{\sin C}{c}$.

Natalie said that the formula for finding the area of a triangle can be used to prove the law of sines.

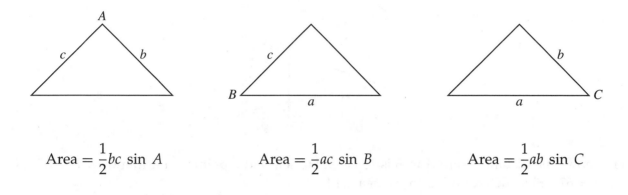

$$\text{Area} = \frac{1}{2}bc \ \sin \ A \qquad \text{Area} = \frac{1}{2}ac \ \sin \ B \qquad \text{Area} = \frac{1}{2}ab \ \sin \ C$$

She explained that the area of the three congruent triangles above can be written in three ways. Since the triangles are congruent, their areas are the same. Because of this, Natalie says that the law of sines is apparent. But her friend Emily said that it was not apparent. She said, correctly, that some steps of Natalie's reasoning are missing.

Problem: What are the missing steps?

5-73   Using the Law of Sines ★★ (G-SRT.11)

The law of sines, which applies to any $\triangle ABC$, states that $\dfrac{\sin A}{a} = \dfrac{\sin B}{b} = \dfrac{\sin C}{c}$. You can always find a missing side or missing angle of a triangle if you are given one side and two angles, or two sides and the angle opposite one of the sides.

Problem: A surveyor wants to determine the distance across a river from B to C as shown in the figure below.

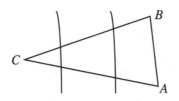

He knows the distance from A to B is 150 feet. He selected a point C and found $m\angle B = 67°$ and $m\angle A = 62°$. Find BC, rounded to the nearest foot.

5-74   Applying the Law of Cosines ★★ (G-SRT.11)

The law of cosines states the following for any $\triangle ABC$:

- $a^2 = b^2 + c^2 - 2bc \cos A$
- $b^2 = a^2 + c^2 - 2ac \cos B$
- $c^2 = a^2 + b^2 - 2ab \cos C$

The law of cosines can be used to find the measure of a side or angle of a triangle if you know the measures of three sides or the lengths of two sides and the angle between them.

Problem: To determine the distance across a lake, a surveyor selected a point B and found AB and BC, as shown on the figure below. $m\angle B = 32.6°$ Find the distance across the lake, rounded to the nearest tenth of a mile.

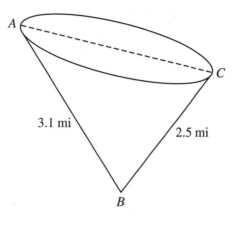

5-75   Identifying Types of Quadrilaterals ★

A quadrilateral is any four-sided polygon. Common types of quadrilaterals are listed below:

- A trapezoid is a quadrilateral that has only one pair of parallel sides.
- A parallelogram is a quadrilateral whose opposite sides are parallel and congruent.
- A rhombus is a parallelogram that has four congruent sides.
- A rectangle is a parallelogram that has four right angles.
- A square is a rectangle that has four congruent sides. A square is a rhombus that has four right angles.

Problem: Six quadrilaterals are pictured below. Choose all the names that apply to each.

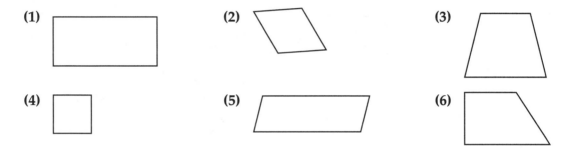

5-76   Classifying Quadrilaterals ★★

Because quadrilaterals can be named in many ways, they are often confused. A working knowledge of the names that apply to quadrilaterals will help to eliminate confusion.

Problem: Decide whether each statement is true or false. If the statement is false, correct it.

    (1) All squares are rectangles.

    (2) Some rhombi are squares.

    (3) All parallelograms are rectangles.

    (4) Some trapezoids are parallelograms.

    (5) All squares are rhombi.

    (6) All rectangles are squares.

5-77   Classifying Quadrilaterals in the Coordinate Plane ★ (G-GPE.4)

You can tell a lot about a quadrilateral by looking at its graph.

Problem: The coordinates of the vertices of quadrilateral $ABCD$ are $A(1,-1)$, $B(5,-1)$, $C(5,-3)$, and $D(1,-3)$. What is the most accurate name for this quadrilateral? Support your answer.

5-78   Parallelograms and Kites ★★

A parallelogram is a quadrilateral in which both pairs of opposite sides are parallel and congruent. In the figure below, $\overline{AB} \parallel \overline{DC}$ and $\overline{AB} \cong \overline{DC}$; $\overline{AD} \parallel \overline{BC}$ and $\overline{AD} \cong \overline{BC}$.

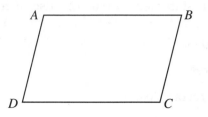

A kite is a quadrilateral that has two pairs of congruent adjacent sides. In the example below, $\overline{GH} \cong \overline{EH}$ and $\overline{GF} \cong \overline{EF}$.

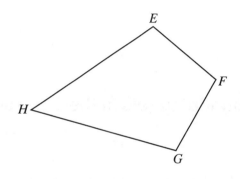

Problem: Are some parallelograms kites? Are all kites parallelograms? Write an explanation of your answers.

5-79   Properties of Quadrilaterals ★★

Parallelograms, rectangles, squares, and rhombi (the plural of rhombus) share some but not all properties.

Problem: The properties of quadrilaterals are listed below. Write the names of the quadrilaterals that have the property. Choose from the following: parallelogram, rectangle, square, and rhombus. (Hint: Some quadrilaterals possess more than one of the properties.)

(1) Opposite sides are parallel.

(2) Opposite angles are congruent.

(3) Opposite sides are congruent.

(4) All angles are right angles.

(5) All sides are congruent.

5-80   Properties of Diagonals of Quadrilaterals ★★

A diagonal of a quadrilateral is a line segment drawn from a vertex to the opposite nonadjacent vertex. Quadrilaterals may be classified by the properties of their diagonals.

Problem: Identify the quadrilaterals whose diagonals have the properties listed below. Choose from among the following: parallelogram, rectangle, square, and rhombus. (Hint: Some quadrilaterals possess more than one of the properties.)

(1) The diagonals bisect each other.

(2) The diagonals are congruent.

(3) The diagonals are perpendicular to each other.

(4) Each diagonal bisects two angles.

5-81   Finding the Equations of Parallel and Perpendicular Lines
★ (G-GPE.5)

Parallel lines never intersect, and perpendicular lines intersect at right angles. Parallel lines have the same slope, while the slope of perpendicular lines are reciprocals and have the opposite sign.

Problem: Use the equation $y = 3x - 4$ to find the equations of the lines described below.

(1) A parallel line that passes through $(-1, 2)$

(2) A perpendicular line that passes through $(-1, 2)$

(3) A parallel line that passes through the origin

(4) A perpendicular line that passes through $(5, 0)$

5-82   Partitioning Line Segments ★★ (G-GPE.6)

If the midpoint C of $\overline{AB}$ partitions $\overline{AB}$ into two congruent segments, $\overline{AC} \cong \overline{BC}$. The ratio of $\dfrac{AC}{AB} = \dfrac{1}{2}$.

But other points on a segment partition the segment into ratios other than $\dfrac{1}{2}$. For example, a point D on $\overline{AB}$ that is $\dfrac{1}{4}$ of the way from A and B partitions $\overline{AB}$ so that $\dfrac{AD}{AB} = \dfrac{1}{4}$. If the end points of $\overline{AB}$ are $(-2, 3)$ and $(6, -1)$, respectively, the coordinates of D are $(0, 2)$.

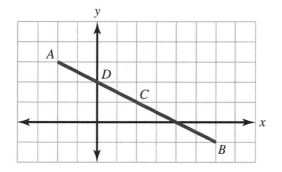

Problem: Consider $\overline{AB}$ pictured above. What are the coordinates of point C that is halfway between A and B? What are the coordinates of the point that is $\dfrac{3}{4}$ of the way from A to B?

5-83   Finding the Area of a Square ★

Each side of a checkerboard measures 40 centimeters. The board contains eight rows of eight squares per row.

Problem: Find the area of each small square on the board.

5-84   Area and Perimeter of Squares ★★★ G

The perimeter of a square is the distance around the square. The area is the space inside the square, measured in square units.

Problem: Statements about squares are listed below. Identify and correct any false statement.

(1) All squares that have the same area have the same perimeter.

(2) If a side of a square is doubled, the perimeter is doubled.

(3) If a side of a square is tripled, the area is 9 times the original area.

(4) The ratio of the area of a square to its perimeter is always greater than or equal to 1.

5-85   Finding the Area of a Rectangle ★

The size of a dollar bill today is smaller than the dollar bills printed before 1929. The dimensions of those bills were 7.42 by 3.13 inches. The bills in circulation today are 6.14 by 2.61 inches.

Problem: Find the area of each bill. How does the area of the larger bill compare with the area of the bills of today?

5-86   Finding the Area of a Rectangle ★★

Roofing shingles are often packaged in groups called "squares." One square covers 100 square feet of a roof.

Problem: The roof of a small bungalow is made of two rectangles, each 13 feet by 36 feet. The rectangles meet to form the peak of the home. How many squares of shingles are needed to cover the roof?

5-87   Finding the Area of a Rectangle by Using Other Figures ★★ (6.G.1)

Celeste's math teacher presented the following figure to the class.

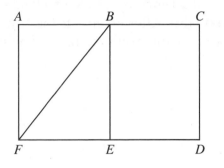

She said that B is the midpoint of $\overline{AC}$ and E is the midpoint of $\overline{FD}$. $\overline{BF}$ is a diagonal of rectangle $ABEF$, and the area of $\triangle ABF$ is 20 square centimeters. She then asked the class to find the area of rectangle $ACDF$. Celeste immediately answered: 80 square centimeters.

Problem: Was Celeste right? If she was, explain how she could have gotten the answer so quickly. If she was wrong, correct her mistake and find the right answer, if possible, with the information provided.

5-88   Finding the Area and Perimeter of a Rectangle ★★ G

The formula for finding the area of a rectangle is $A = l \times w$. A is the area, l is the length of the rectangle, and w is its width.

The formula for finding the perimeter of a rectangle is $P = 2l + 2w$. P is the perimeter, l is the length of the rectangle, and w is its width.

Problem: A rectangle has an area of 12 square inches. Find the smallest perimeter possible if the length and width are whole numbers. Then find the largest perimeter if the length and width are whole numbers.

5-89 Finding the Area of an Irregular Figure ★★ (7.G.6)

A 1-inch by 12-inch rectangle has an area of 12 square inches. A standard sheet of typing paper is $8\frac{1}{2}$ inches by 11 inches and has an area of 93.5 square inches.

Problem: Peter claims he can cut a 1-inch by 12-inch rectangle from a standard sheet of typing paper. Explain how he can do this. After Peter cuts the 1-inch by 12-inch rectangle from the paper, what is the remaining area? (Hint: You may find it helpful to model Peter's method.)

5-90 Finding the Area of an Irregular Figure ★★ G (7.G.6)

Remodeling a house may involve making a room larger or adding a room or rooms.

The Joneses wish to add a family room and a deck to their living room and kitchen. The "before" and "after" plans in a simplified form are shown below. All measurements are in feet.

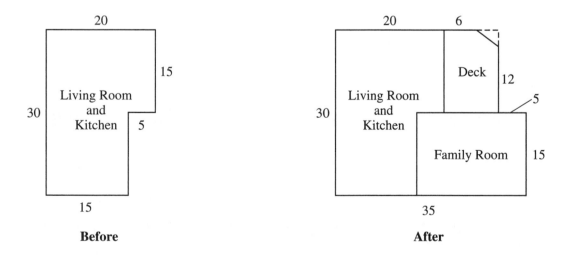

Problem: Find the area of the living room and kitchen, area of the family room, area of the deck, and the total area of the rooms and deck in the "after" plan.

5-91   Area of a Parallelogram ★ (7.G.6)

A parallelogram is a quadrilateral whose opposite sides are parallel and congruent. The area of a parallelogram is found by multiplying the length of its base times its height: $A = b \times h$.

Problem: Write an explanation of how the area of a parallelogram is similar to the area of a rectangle.

5-92   Finding the Area of a Trapezoid ★ (7.G.6)

A trapezoid is a quadrilateral that has only one pair of parallel sides. To find the area of a trapezoid, you can use this formula: $A = \frac{1}{2}(b_1 + b_2)h$.

In this formula, A is the area, b_1 is the length of one parallel side, b_2 is the length of the other parallel side, and h is the height.

Problem: Which trapezoids below have the same area? What are the areas?

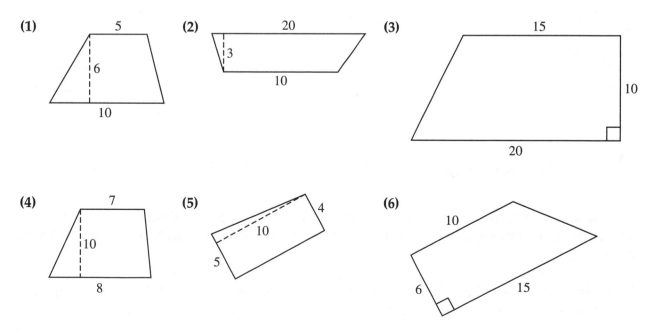

5-93   Using Coordinates to Compute Perimeters and Areas of Figures ★★★ (G-GPE.7)

The area of a geometric figure can be found by using the appropriate formula or by breaking the figure into smaller figures and then using formulas.

To find the length of a side, consider the position of the figure in the coordinate plane:

- If a side is a horizontal segment, find the absolute value of the difference of the x-coordinates.

- If a side is a vertical segment, find the absolute value of the difference of the y-coordinates.

- If a side is neither a horizontal nor vertical segment, use the distance formula: $AB = \sqrt{(x_2 - x_1)^2 + (y_2 - y_1)^2}$, where $A(x_1, y_1)$ and $B(x_2, y_2)$ are points in the coordinate plane.

Problem: Consider the polygons with the following coordinates. Which has the largest perimeter? Which has the largest area?

    (1) Pentagon: $A(-1, 3)$, $B(3, 3)$, $C(2, -1)$, $D(-1, -1)$, $E(-2, 2)$

    (2) Triangle: $F(-3, 4)$, $G(0, -2)$, $H(-5, -2)$

    (3) Rectangle: $I(0, 3)$, $J(6, 0)$, $K(5, -2)$, $L(-1, 1)$

5-94   Circles ★ G

A symbol is something that has meaning beyond itself. Throughout history, circles have always been powerful symbols. Even today, many businesses and organizations use circles in their logos.

Problem: List at least three places a circle is used as a symbol or logo. Why do you think circles are used as symbols and for logos?

5-95   Finding the Diameter and Radius of a Circle ★

The radius of a circle is a line segment drawn from the center of a circle to any point on the circle. The diameter of a circle is a line segment that passes through the center of the circle and has end points on the circle.

Consider rectangle $OABC$ inside the circle below. The center of the circle is O and $AC = 5$.

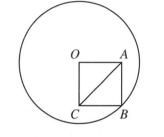

Problem: Find the length of the diameter of the circle. Find the length of the radius. Explain how you arrived at your answers.

5-96   Finding the Circumference of a Circle ★ (7.G.4)

The circumference of a circle is the distance around a circle. To find the circumference, you may use either of two formulas: $C = \pi d$ or $C = 2\pi r$. C is the circumference, d is the length of the diameter, and r is the length of the radius. π is approximately equal to 3.14 or $\frac{22}{7}$.

Problem: Find the circumference of each circle below, given the following information. Use 3.14 for π.

(1) $r = 10$ inches   **(2)** $d = 15$ inches

(3) 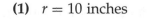 9 mm   **(4)** 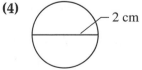 2 cm

5-97   Diameter and Circumference ★★ (7.G.4)

The diameter of a standard basketball rim is 18 inches, and the circumference of a basketball is 30 inches.

Problem: Explain why these dimensions are appropriate to make scoring challenging but not impossible.

5-98   Finding the Area of a Circle ★ (7.G.4)

Area is the space inside a region. The area of a circle is the space inside the circle.

Use the following formula to find the area of a circle: $A = \pi r^2$.

Problem: A beam of light from a lighthouse may be seen for 30 miles in all directions. What is the area in square miles in which the light may be seen? What factors might interfere with the light being seen in this area?

5-99   Finding the Area of a Circle ★★ (7.G.4)

The diameter of an archery target is 48 inches. The diameter of the innermost circle on the target is 9.6 inches.

Problem: How does the area of the smaller circle compare with the area of the target?

5-100   Comparing the Areas of a Square and a Circle ★★ (7.G.4)

The circumference of a circle is equal to the length of its diameter times π. The perimeter of a square is equal to 4 times the length of a side.

Problem: Suppose the circumference of a circle is 31.4 inches, and the perimeter of a square is 31.4 inches. Which figure has the larger area?

5-101   Proving All Circles Are Similar ★★ (G-C.1)

All circles are similar because all circles have the same shape, even though they may not be the same size. The size of the circle depends on the radius.

Problem: Use dilations to explain why all circles are similar.

5-102   Types of Arcs ★★ G

An arc is part of a circle. Arcs are classified as a minor arc, major arc, or semicircle:

- The measure of a minor arc is less than 180°.
- The measure of a major arc is more than 180°.
- The measure of a semicircle is 180°.

The three types of arcs are shown below.

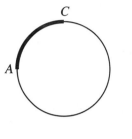

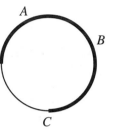

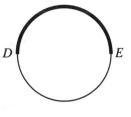

$\overset{\frown}{AC}$ is a minor arc. $\overset{\frown}{ABC}$ is a major arc. $\overset{\frown}{DE}$ is a semicircle.

Problem: A small Ferris wheel is represented below. The cars are labeled with the letters *A-H*. List all minor arcs, major arcs, and semicircles.

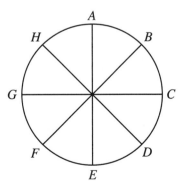

5-103 Central and Inscribed Angles ★★ (G-C.2)

A central angle is an angle whose vertex is at the center of a circle. Its sides are radii. The measure of a central angle is the same as the measure of its intercepted minor arc.

An inscribed angle is an angle whose vertex is on the circle and whose sides are chords. The measure of an inscribed angle is half the measure of its intercepted minor arc.

Problem: Consider the circle below. O is the center, and $m\angle BOC = 60°$. List all of the congruent angles. Then state the measure of each.

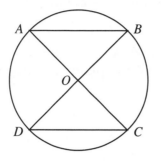

5-104   Arcs and Angles of Circles ★★ (G-C.2)

Circles can be separated into parts called arcs. Following are some facts about arcs:

- The measure of a minor arc is equal to the measure of its central angle.
- A semicircle has a measure of 180°.
- The measure of a major arc is the difference between its related minor arc and 360°.
- The measure of a central angle is equal to the measure of its intercepted minor arc.
- The measure of an inscribed angle is equal to $\frac{1}{2}$ the measure of its intercepted arc.

Problem: Consider circle O. The $m\angle ACB = 60°$ and the $m\overarc{AC} = 120°$. What type of triangle is $\triangle ABC$? What type of triangle is $\triangle AOB$? Explain your reasoning.

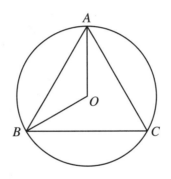

5-105   Secants and Tangents ★

Although a circle is round, many special lines and segments may be associated with it. Diameters, radii, and chords are the most common. Secants and tangents are two others:

- A secant is a line that contains a chord.
- A tangent is a line that meets the circle at one point.

Problem: Consider circle *O*. List all the diameters, radii, chords, secants, or tangents. (Hint: There are a total of nine.)

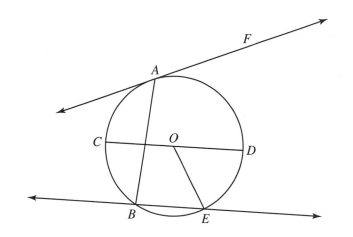

5-106 **Measures of Angles — Chord-Tangent Angle Theorem and Chord-Chord Angle Theorem ★★★ (G-C.2)**

The chord-tangent angle theorem states that the measure of an angle formed by a tangent and a chord drawn from the point of tangency is equal to $\frac{1}{2}$ the measure of the intercepted arc.

The chord-chord angle theorem states that the measure of an angle formed by two chords intersecting in the interior of a circle is equal to $\frac{1}{2}$ the sum of the intercepted arcs.

Problem: Consider circle O. Use the theorems above and facts about semicircles and inscribed angles to find the measure of each arc.

$\overleftrightarrow{DF}$ is tangent to the circle at D.

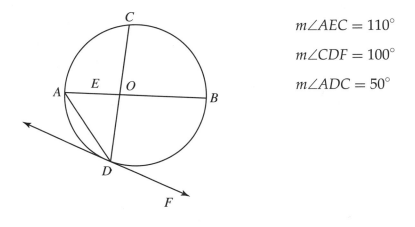

$m\angle AEC = 110°$

$m\angle CDF = 100°$

$m\angle ADC = 50°$

(1) $m\overgroup{AB}$ **(2)** $m\overgroup{CBD}$ **(3)** $m\overgroup{AC}$

(4) $m\overgroup{BD}$ **(5)** $m\overgroup{CB}$ **(6)** $m\overgroup{AD}$

5-107   Measures of Angles Formed by Secants and Tangents Drawn from a Point outside the Circle ★★★

The measure of an angle formed when two secants, two tangents, or a secant and a tangent are drawn from a point outside the circle is equal to $\frac{1}{2}$ the difference of the intercepted arcs.

Problem: Suppose $m\angle BCD = 80°$ and $m\overarc{BD} = 50°$ in each figure below. Find the measure of the intercepted arc in figures 1 and 3. Write an explanation of why it is impossible for two tangents, as pictured in figure 2, to form an 80° angle and intercept an arc of 50°.

(1)

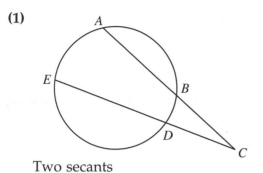

Two secants

$$m\angle BCD = \frac{1}{2}(m\overarc{EA} - m\overarc{DB})$$

(2)

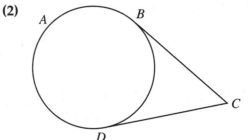

Two tangents

$$m\angle BCD = \frac{1}{2}(m\overarc{DAB} - m\overarc{DB})$$

(3)

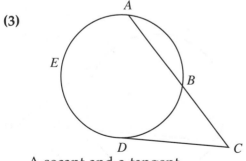

A secant and a tangent

$$m\angle BCD = \frac{1}{2}(m\overarc{AED} - m\overarc{BD})$$

5-108　Lengths of Segments — Chords Intersecting in the Interior of a Circle ★★ (G-C.2)

A chord is a line segment whose end points are on the circle. When two chords intersect in the interior of a circle, the product of the lengths of the segments of one chord equals the product of the lengths of the segments of the other chord.

In the figure, $ab = cd$.

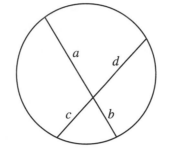

Problem: Consider the figure above. Can you conclude that $a = d$? Write an explanation of your answer, and provide an example to support your reasoning.

5-109　Length of Segments — Secant and Tangent Segments ★★★

The two figures below show the relationship of two segments drawn from an exterior point to the circle.

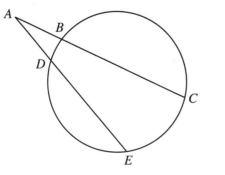　　　　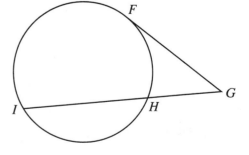

Two secants

$$AC \cdot BA = AE \cdot AD$$

A secant and a tangent

$$FG^2 = GI \cdot HG$$

Problem: Compare and contrast these two relationships.

5-110   Proving Opposite Angles of a Quadrilateral Inscribed in a Circle Are Supplementary ★★ (G-C.3)

A quadrilateral is inscribed in a circle if each vertex of the quadrilateral is on the circle.

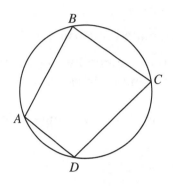

Problem: A proof that the opposite angles of a quadrilateral inscribed in a circle are supplementary is outlined below. Use the figure above to supply the reasons for each step.

(1) Quadrilateral *ABCD* is inscribed in a circle.

(2) $\angle A$, $\angle B$, $\angle C$, and $\angle D$ are inscribed angles.

(3) $\angle A = \frac{1}{2}\overset{\frown}{BCD}$, $\angle B = \frac{1}{2}\overset{\frown}{CDA}$, $\angle C = \frac{1}{2}\overset{\frown}{DAB}$, and $\angle D = \frac{1}{2}\overset{\frown}{ABC}$.

(4) $\overset{\frown}{BCD} = 2\angle A$, $\overset{\frown}{ACD} = 2\angle B$, $\overset{\frown}{DAB} = 2\angle C$, and $\overset{\frown}{ABC} = 2\angle D$.

(5) $\overset{\frown}{BCD} + \overset{\frown}{DAB} = 360°$; $\overset{\frown}{ABC} + \overset{\frown}{CDA} = 360°$.

(6) $2\angle A + 2\angle C = 360°$; $2\angle D + 2\angle B = 360°$.

(7) $\angle A + \angle C = 180°$; $\angle D + \angle B = 180°$.

(8) $\angle A$ and $\angle C$ are supplementary; $\angle D$ and $\angle B$ are supplementary.

5-111   Constructing Tangent Lines to a Circle ★★ (G-C.4) 🖳

Go to http://www.mathopenref.com/consttangents.html, and view a virtual construction of a tangent line through an external point to a circle.

Do the following:

1. Click on "run" to view an animated construction.

2. Scroll down and click on "printable step-by-step instruction sheet" to read about how to construct two possible tangent lines from a point to a given circle.

Problem: Follow the instructions and draw two tangent lines to the circle on your paper.

5-112   Arc Lengths ★★

The measure of a minor arc of a circle is the same as the measure of its central angle. The length of an arc is a portion of the circumference of the circle.

If $m\overarc{AB} = x$, the length of $AB = \dfrac{x}{360} \cdot 2\pi r$, where r is the radius of the circle.

Problem: Using the relationship above, explain how all three arcs below are part of the same circle. (Hint: They are, even if they do not look like they are.)

5-113   Area of a Sector ★★ (G-C.5)

A sector of a circle is the part of a circle bounded by two radii and the intercepted arc. For example, a slice of pizza is a sector of the circular pie.

$A = \dfrac{x}{360} \cdot \pi r^2$ is the formula for finding the area of a sector of a circle. In this formula, A is the area of the sector, x is the measure of the central angle, and r is the length of the radius.

Problem: Two pizzas have a 12-inch diameter. One pie is cut into 8 equal slices, and the other is cut into 6 equal slices. How does the area of a slice of pizza from the 8-slice pie compare to the area of a slice of pizza from the 6-slice pie?

5-114   Deriving the Formula for Finding the Area of a Sector ★★ (G-C.5)

A sector is a part of a circle bounded by two radii and the intercepted arc. For example, a pie graph, also known as a circle graph, has pie-shaped parts, which are examples of sector.

Problem: Gabriella knows that the formula for finding the area of a circle is $A = \pi r^2$, and the formula for finding the area of a sector is $A = \dfrac{x}{360} \pi r^2$. Explain what $\dfrac{x}{360}$ represents and why this is multiplied by the area of the circle to find the area of the sector.

5-115   **Deriving the Equation of a Circle ★★ (G-GPE.1)**

The equation of a circle with center (h, k) and radius r is $(x - h)^2 + (y - k)^2 = r^2$. It can be derived from the Pythagorean theorem, $a^2 + b^2 = c^2$, where c is the length of the hypotenuse and a and b are the lengths of the legs.

Problem: Kevin started to derive the equation of a circle by using the Pythagorean theorem. He used the sketch below but was unable to derive the equation. Amy suggested that he find the coordinates of the right angle, find the length of each leg, and then substitute the length of each leg into the Pythagorean theorem. Derive the equation using Amy's suggestions.

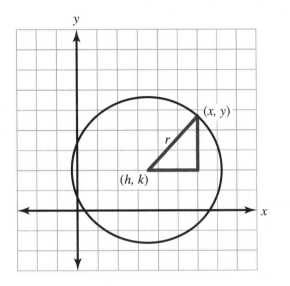

5-116   Deriving the Equation of a Parabola ★★★ (G-GPE.2)

A parabola is the set of all points that are equidistant from a fixed line and a fixed point not on the line. The fixed line is called the directrix, and the fixed point is the focus.

Problem: Roland wants to find the equation of the parabola sketched below. He knows that if $P(x, y)$ is any point on the parabola, and $F(4, -1)$ is the focus, and $y = 3$ is the directrix, then $PF = PD$. But he is unsure of how to continue. Explain how Roland could use the distance formula, $D = \sqrt{(x_2 - x_1)^2 + (y_2 - y_1)^2}$, to find the equation of the parabola.

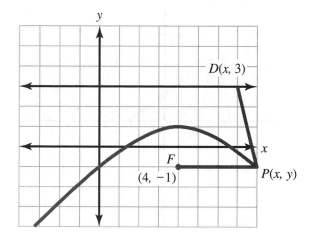

5-117   Deriving the Equation of an Ellipse ★★★ (G-GPE.3)

An ellipse is the set of all points P in a plane, such that the sum of the distances from P to the foci (plural of focus) is constant.

Problem: Use the distance formula, $D = \sqrt{(x_2 - x_1)^2 + (y_2 - y_1)^2}$, to find the equation of an ellipse whose foci are $F_1(-3,0)$ and $F_2(3,0)$, and the sum of the distances from each point on the ellipse to the foci are 10.

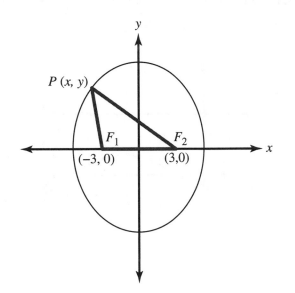

To get you started, the first steps are provided.

(1) $PF_1 = \sqrt{(x+3)^2 + y^2}$

(2) $PF_2 = \sqrt{(x-3)^2 + y^2}$

(3) $PF_1 + PF_2 = 10$

You should get an equation of the form $\dfrac{x^2}{a^2} + \dfrac{y^2}{b^2} = 1$. Solve for a^2 and b^2.

5-118   Slicing Three-Dimensional Figures ★★ (7.G.3) 🖳

When you slice a three-dimensional figure, the cross section forms a two-dimensional figure. To virtually slice a cube, go to http://www.learner.org/courses/learningmath/geometry/session9/part_c/index.html#cl.

Here is what to do:

1. Read about the cross-sections and interactive activity.

2. Scroll down to view the interactive activity that displays the cube. This is the beginning of Problem C1.

3. Think about how you would slice the cube so that the cross section forms a square.

4. Click on "Start."

5. Click on "Rotate." Keep rotating until you think you can form a square by cutting a cross section; then click on "Cut." (The figure formed by slicing the figure is shaded.)

6. Repeat step 5 and try to make an equilateral triangle. Try to make the other cross sections listed in c–i.

Problem: State which two-dimensional figures result from slicing a cube.

5-119   **Identifying Three-Dimensional Objects Generated by Rotations of Two-Dimensional Objects ★★★ G (G-GMD.4)**

When a two-dimensional object is rotated, a three-dimensional object is formed. The three-dimensional object that is formed depends on which two-dimensional figure is rotated and the line about which it is rotated.

Problem: A cylinder, sphere, or cone may be generated when some of the figures below are rotated. Consider the figures and lines described below. State which three-dimensional figures are generated, if possible. (Hint: You may want to sketch the figures.)

(1) A semicircle rotated about its diameter

(2) A right triangle rotated about its leg

(3) A rectangle rotated about a line of symmetry

(4) A rectangle rotated about its diagonal

(5) A right triangle rotated about its hypotenuse

(6) A circle rotated about its diameter

(7) A rectangle rotated about its side

(8) An isosceles triangle rotated about its line of symmetry

5-120   **Using Geometric Shapes to Describe Objects ★★ G (G-MG.1)**

Some shapes that we see every day resemble, but are not true, geometric figures. For example, a starfish suggests a pentagon; a car tire is shaped like a cylinder.

Problem: Identify five objects and the geometric shapes that they resemble.

5-121   Finding the Volume of a Rectangular Prism ★★ (6.G.2)

To find the volume of a rectangular prism, use the formula $V = l \times w \times h$. V is the volume, l is the length, w is the width, and h is the height.

Problem: Find the volumes of the rectangular prisms with the following dimensions. (Hint: Remember that the units of measurement must be the same.)

(1) Length = 24 inches; width = 1.5 feet; height = 18 inches

(2) Length = $2\frac{3}{4}$ feet; width = $2\frac{1}{2}$ feet; height = 5 feet

(3) Length = 16 meters; width = 28.5 meters; height = 30 meters

(4) Length = 1.5 feet; width = 15 inches; height = 2.5 feet

5-122   Finding the Volume of a Rectangle Prism ★★★ G (6.G.2)

The volume of a rectangular prism is found by multiplying its length by its width by its height. You can use the formula $V = l \times w \times h$, where V is the volume, l is the length, w is the width, and h is the height.

Problem: A shoe box measures 6.5 inches by 3.5 inches by 12 inches. Pete is packing the box with 0.5-inch cubes. He figures that the bottom of the box will hold 91 cubes (13 by 7) and that he can pack 24 rows for a total of 2,184 cubes. But the volume of the shoe box, according to the formula, is 273 cubic inches. Where did Pete make an error in his reasoning?

5-123   **Using Nets to Find the Surface Area of a Three-Dimensional Figure ★★ (6.G.4)**

A net is a two-dimensional pattern that can be used to make a model of a three-dimensional figure.

Problem: If the net shown below was cut out and then folded along the dark lines, it would form a triangular prism. The two bases are triangles and the faces are rectangles. Use this net to find the surface area of the triangular prism.

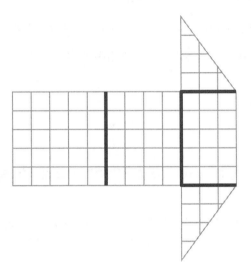

5-124   **Finding the Surface Area of a Rectangular Prism ★★ (7.G.6)**

Cheralyn baked cookies to give as holiday gifts. She plans to place the same number of cookies in six identical boxes and wrap the boxes with the same amount of wrapping paper.

Problem: Cheralyn has a partially used roll of wrapping paper. The paper is 24 inches by 7 feet. The dimensions of each of the six boxes she wants to wrap are 12 inches by 9 inches by 2.5 inches. Will she have enough paper to wrap the six boxes? If she does not have enough wrapping paper, how much more paper will she need?

5-125   Finding the Surface Area of a Rectangular Prism
★★★ (7.G.6)

The surface area of a three-dimensional figure is the sum of the areas of all the faces and the bases of the figure.

Dice are cubes, which are a special type of rectangular prism. Each side of a die is a face, and each die, because it is a cube, has six faces. To find the surface area of the die, you must find the area of each face by multiplying length times width, and then add the areas of the faces. (Because the area of each face is the same, you can simply multiply the area of one face by six instead of adding the areas of the faces.)

Problem: Twelve $\frac{3}{4}$-inch dice are stacked in two layers. Each layer has two rows with three dice per row. (Six dice are in each layer.) Find the surface area of the box.

5-126   Finding the Volume and Surface Area of Pyramids
★★★ (7.G.6)

A pyramid is a three-dimensional figure whose base is a regular polygon and whose other faces are congruent triangles.

The formula for finding the volume of a pyramid is $V = \frac{Bh}{3}$, where V is the volume, B is the area of the base, and h is the height of the pyramid.

The formula for finding the surface area is $SA = B + \frac{1}{2}ps$. In this formula, SA is the surface area, B is the area of the base, p is the perimeter of the base, and s is the slant height of the triangular faces.

Problem: The Great Pyramid near Cairo, Egypt, was originally 481 feet in height. (Age and erosion have since reduced its size.) The square base measured 756 feet on each side, and the slant height was 612 feet. Find the original volume and surface area of the Great Pyramid.

5-127   Finding the Volume of Cones ★★ (8.G.9)

Some fancy ice cream dishes are shaped like a cone. Many restaurants serve ice cream sundaes in a variety of cone-shaped dishes.

To find the volume of a cone, use the formula $V = \frac{1}{3}\pi r^2 h$, where V is the volume, r is the length of the radius, and h is the height.

Problem: Two cone-shaped dishes are pictured below. Which has the greater volume?

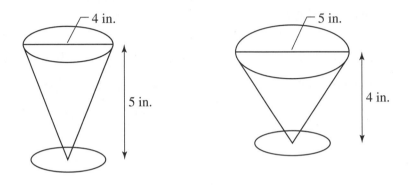

5-128   Finding the Volume of Spheres ★★★ (8.G.9)

A sphere may be defined as a hollow or solid figure enclosed by a surface where every point is equidistant from the center. A baseball, basketball, and globe are examples of spheres.

To find the volume of a sphere, use the formula $V = \frac{4}{3}\pi r^3$, where V is the volume and r is the length of the radius.

Problem: The radius of a basketball is 4.75 inches. The circumference of a soccer ball is 28 inches. Find the volumes. Use 3.14 for π. Round your answers to the nearest tenth.

5-129   Using Various Volume Formulas ★★ (G-GMD.3)

Crystal says that there is one case when the volume of a cone is equal to the volume of a sphere that has the same radius as the cone.

Problem: Do you agree with her? Explain your answer.

5-130   Providing an Informal Argument for the Area of a Circle ★★ (G-GMD.1)

Logan is an inquisitive student and wonders how formulas are derived. In particular, he finds the formula for finding the area of a circle puzzling.

His teacher sketched the following figures for him. Each semicircle is cut into sectors and the sectors are rearranged to form a parallelogram.

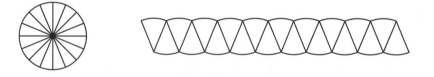

Problem: Explain how these figures may be used to show how the formula for finding the area of a circle, $A = \pi r^2$, is derived.

5-131   Cavalieri's Principle and the Volume of a Sphere ★★★ (G-GMD.2) 🖥

Go to http://www.cut-the-knot.org/Curriculum/Calculus/Cavalieri.shtml to learn about Cavalieri's principle and its application for finding the volume of a sphere.

Here is what to do:

1. Read about Cavalieri's principle.
2. Study the figures and examples.
3. Pay particular attention to the relationships between a cylinder, cone, and sphere.

Problem: Jillian can follow most of the information on this website about how the volumes of cylinders, cones, and spheres are related according to Cavalieri's principle. But she does not understand how the Pythagorean theorem is applied to the sphere. Explain how the Pythagorean theorem is used to clarify the explanation on the website.

5-132   Density in Modeling ★★★ (G-MG.2)

The population of New York City in 2010 was 8,175,133. The area of the city is 302.64 square miles. According to a 2011 estimate, the population of Tokyo, Japan, was 13,189,000. The area of Tokyo is 2,188 square kilometers.

Problem: Given the facts above, which city is more densely populated? (Hint: 1 square mile is about 2.59 square kilometers and 1 square kilometer is about 0.39 square miles.)

5-133 Solving Design Problems ★★ (G-MG.3)

On a recent trip to a sporting goods store, Roberto noticed that tennis balls are packed in a cylinder, three balls per cylinder. He thought that this was odd because the tennis balls must be displayed upright on a circular base. He believes that the containers of tennis balls would be easier to stack if they were rectangular prisms rather than cylinders.

Problem: Why do you think tennis balls are packaged in a cylinder rather than in a rectangular box?

5-134 A Quotation about Geometry ★★

Plato (429–347 BC) was a Greek philosopher who believed that knowledge of mathematics, and particularly geometry, was essential to sound thinking.

Among the vast achievements of Plato was his founding of his Academy in Athens, which became a center of learning. Above the door of Plato's Academy was placed the following statement: "Let no one ignorant of geometry enter here."

Problem: Why might Plato have felt so strongly about the importance of the study of geometry? Do you agree with him? Why or why not?

Section 6

Statistics, Probability, and Data Analysis

6-1 Statistical and Nonstatistical Questions ★ G (6.SP.1)

A statistical question is a question that anticipates a variety of answers. For example, if a group of students were asked to identify their favorite baseball team, a number of answers are possible: Yankees, Red Sox, Mets, Phillies, Cubs, Rangers, Tigers, Dodgers, Giants, and so on.

Unlike a statistical question, a nonstatistical question typically has only one correct answer. For example, which team won the World Series last year?

Problem: Write one statistical question and one nonstatistical question. For the statistical question, provide at least three possible answers. For the nonstatistical question, provide the answer.

6-2 Distribution of Data ★ (6.SP.2)

The person who is asking a statistical question expects a variety of answers. The answers have an average and a range, and the graph of the answers has a specific shape.

Problem: To complete a part of his math homework about statistical questions, Ahmed asked several of his friends how much they spent for lunch yesterday. Because the price of the school lunch is always the same, his friends had the same response: $1.75. By looking at the data, which had an average of $1.75, a range of 0, and a graph that was a point, Ahmed realized that something was wrong. What had happened?

6-3   Finding the Mean of a Set of Numbers ★

Mean is another word for *average*, which comes from the Arabic word *awariyah*, meaning "damaged goods." The word was originally associated with trade. If any goods of a merchant were damaged during transportation or trade, the merchant and any partners would share the losses equally. The losses were averaged among the investors.

Problem:

(1) What is the mean of the first five prime numbers? Round your answer to the nearest whole number.

(2) What is the mean of the first five composite numbers? Round your answer to the nearest whole number.

6-4   Finding the Weighted Mean ★★

To find the mean, or average, of a set of numbers, add the numbers and divide by the amount of numbers in the set.

A weighted mean takes into account the importance of each quantity.

Suppose you have two test grades: 85 and 90. But you also have a midterm exam grade of 88, which is twice as important as a single test grade. To find the weighted mean of these scores, add 85, 90, 88 and 88, and then divide by 4. The weighted mean is 87.75.

Problem: Carterville's recreation center needs a new TV. Because the recreation department does not have enough money in its budget to buy a new TV, several people have offered to donate money for its purchase. Using your knowledge of weighted means, find the average donation toward the purchase of a wide-screen TV for Carterville's recreation center.

6 people each donated $10   5 people each donated $25
2 people each donated $100   3 people each donated $75
1 person donated $200   8 people each donated $50

6-5   Finding the Mode ★

The mode is the number that occurs most often in a set of data. Depending on the set of data, there can be one mode, many modes, or no mode.

Problem: Count the number of times each letter appears in the first sentence of the introduction to this problem. Then find the mode, or modes.

6-6   The Median ★

The median is the middle number when a set of data is arranged in numerical order. When there are two middle numbers, the median is their average.

Problem: When may the median of a set of data not be a member of the set of the data? Explain your answer, and provide an example.

6-7   Finding the Median and the Mode ★★

Whereas the median is the middle number when a set of data is arranged in ascending or descending order, the mode is the number that appears most often.

Problem: Consider the perfect squares from 1 to 25 inclusive. List the number of factors of each perfect square; then find the median. How does the median compare to the mode?

6-8   Finding the Mean, Median, and Mode ★★ (6.SP.3)

Consider the following western states (in the contiguous United States) and their record high temperatures (Fahrenheit):

Arizona: 128°

California: 134°

Colorado: 118°

Idaho: 118°

Montana: 117°

Nevada: 125°

Oregon: 119°

Utah: 117°

Washington: 118°

Wyoming: 115°

Problem: Find the mean, median, and mode.

6-9   Using the Measures of Center and Measure of Variation ★★ (6.SP.3)

The measures of center—mean, median, and mode—summarize all of the data with a single number.

The measure of variation—the range (the difference between the largest and smallest values)—describes how the values vary with a single number.

Problem: Carlo wants a smart phone. He checked ads and found that most of the phones he preferred cost about $199. Carlo doubted that he could afford a phone of this price. His mother pointed out that there is a price range of about $50 for the models of phones he is interested in. What measure was Carlo using? What measure was his mother using? Which measure could be used to show that Carlo might be able to afford a smart phone?

6-10   Making a Histogram ★★ (6.SP.4)

A frequency table consists of a category, tally marks, and frequency, which is the number of tally marks. Frequency tables show the number of times an item occurs in a set of data.

A histogram is a bar graph that shows the data in a frequency table.

Problem: The time it takes a planet to rotate (turn) on its axis is called a day. The Earth takes 23.9 hours to rotate, which makes our day about 24 hours long. Because the rotation rates of planets vary, the lengths of days on the other planets in our solar system are not usually as long as a day on Earth. Following are the rotation rates of the planets of our solar system, expressed in Earth time:

Mercury: 58.7 days   Jupiter: 9.9 hours
Venus: 243.0 days   Saturn: 10.7 hours
Earth: 23.9 hours   Uranus: 17.2 hours
Mars: 24.6 hours   Neptune: 17.0 hours

Complete a frequency table for the rotation of the planets. (Hint: For rotation time use 0–24 hours, 1–10 days, and more than 10 days.) Then make a histogram.

6-11   Making a Bar Graph ★

A bar graph uses the lengths of bars to compare data. Bars are usually separated by spaces. Bar graphs are one of the most common types of graphs.

Problem: Following are the maximum speeds of some animals for short distances (a quarter of a mile or less) in miles per hour. Make a bar graph to illustrate their speeds. Be sure to title your graph and label the scale. (Hint: Before labeling your graph, consider what the best values for the units would be.)

cat (domestic): 30 mph   giraffe: 32 mph
coyote: 43 mph   lion: 50 mph
elephant: 25 mph   rabbit: 35 mph

6-12   Using Stem-and-Leaf Plots ★★

A stem-and-leaf plot is used to condense a set of data. The greatest place value of the data forms the stem. The next greatest place value forms the leaves. Stem-and-leaf plots may be used to show various types of data.

In the case of the number of votes per state in the electoral college, 0|3 means 3 votes. A stem-and-leaf plot is a shorter way of representing the number of electoral votes by state than listing each state individually.

For example, the New England states have the following electoral votes for president of the United States:

| Maine, 4 | New Hampshire, 4 | Vermont, 3 |
| Massachusetts, 11 | Rhode Island, 4 | Connecticut, 7 |

Here is a stem-and-leaf plot of that information.

$$
\begin{array}{c|ccccc}
0 & 3 & 4 & 4 & 4 & 7 \\
1 & 1
\end{array}
$$

Problem: Construct a stem-and-leaf plot to represent the number of electoral votes of the Mid-Atlantic states.

New York, 29	New Jersey, 14
Pennsylvania, 20	Delaware, 3
Maryland, 10	

6-13   Completing a Circle Graph ★

Circle graphs, also known as pie graphs, represent data expressed as parts of a whole. The circle equals 100%. Each part of the circle representing data is called a sector.

Problem: Ricardo is an athlete who realizes the importance of a healthy diet. He eats sensibly and carefully plans his meals. His meals yesterday included the following servings from different food groups:

Fats, oils, sweets: 1

Milk, yogurt, cheese: 3

Meat, poultry, fish, dry beans, eggs, and nuts: 3

Vegetables: 5

Fruits: 4

Bread, cereal, rice, and pasta: 8

Using the data above, complete the circle graph below.

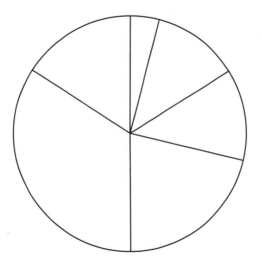

6-14   **Summarizing Numerical Data ★★ (6.SP.5)**

Data may be presented in a variety of ways, including tables, charts, and graphs.

Problem: Caitlyn's mother attended a parent-teacher conference and was concerned that Caitlyn got an 80 on a data analysis test in math. The teacher showed Caitlyn's mother the printout that follows. Should Caitlyn's mother be concerned with Caitlyn's grade? Explain your answer.

Results of the Data Analysis Test

Grade	Number of Students
95–100	1
90–94	5
85–89	3
80–84	9
75–79	2
70–74	3
65–69	1
0–64	0

6-15   Obtaining Information about a Population ★ (7.SP.1)

A population is a whole group. It may be a relatively small group or a very large group.

A sample population is a part of the group. The sample must be representative of the overall group in order to draw valid conclusions about the group.

Problem: Anthony was assigned a math project in which he had to find a sample that represented a population of his choice. For his population, he chose the vehicles—cars, pickup trucks, minivans, and SUVs—that people in his town drove. He decided that a good method for obtaining information about his population would be to record the types of vehicles that parents drove when they dropped off their children at Anthony's school. This would be his sample population.

The next morning, Anthony recorded the number and kinds of different vehicles parents used when driving their children to school. He found that more parents drove minivans and SUVs than other vehicles. Do you think the sample that Anthony recorded is representative of his population? Why or why not?

6-16   Using Data from Random Samples to Draw Inferences about a Population ★★★ (7.SP.2)

Samuel Morse (1791–1872) was the inventor of the Morse code, a series of dots and dashes assigned to a letter. When he was developing the code, Morse realized that he needed to know which letters of the alphabet were used most frequently. He could then assign the simplest codes to the letters used most often.

To find these letters, Morse counted the number of letters in sets of printers' type, which was used at that time to print letters and sentences on paper, for example, in newspapers. From these samples, Morse found that E and T were the two most frequently used letters, and he assigned a dot to E and a dash to T. Other letters were assigned more complicated codes based on their frequency of use.

Problem: Do you think that this was a good way to make an inference about the entire population (of letters in the alphabet)? Explain your answer.

6-17   **Assessing Numerical Data Distributions ★★ G (7.SP.3)**

The mean of a set of data can be found by adding the numbers of the set and dividing the sum by the number of data.

The mean absolute deviation can be found by finding the mean, then finding the distance between each number and the mean, finding the sum of the distances, and dividing the sum by the number of data.

Problem: The weights in pounds of ten 1-year-old female and male golden retrievers are listed below.

    Females: 63.5, 62, 63.5, 61, 62.5, 63, 65, 60, 61.5, 63
    Males: 73, 70, 74.5, 74, 75.5, 74, 71, 73.5, 74.5, 70

Using the data, find the mean and mean absolute deviation of the weights of the female and male golden retrievers.

6-18   **Drawing Comparative Inferences about Two Populations ★★ (7.SP.4)**

Mona loves to wear designer jeans. She often shops at Jennifer's Jeans, a clothing store at the mall. Her friend Liza prefers to shop at the Jennifer's Jeans outlet instead. One day the girls randomly priced thirty pairs of jeans at each place and recorded the jeans and their prices. The results are summarized below.

Jennifer's Jeans Store

Cost	Tally
$89.99	4
$79.99	4
$69.99	3
$59.99	4
$49.99	4
$39.99	8
$29.99	3

Jennifer's Jeans Outlet

Cost	Tally
$49.99	3
$39.99	6
$29.99	11
$19.99	9
$9.99	1

Problem: According to the prices above, which place, the store at the mall or the outlet, has less expensive jeans? Explain your answer.

6-19   The Probability of Impossible and Certain Events
★★ G (7.SP.5)

When it is impossible for an event to occur, the probability of this event is 0. When it is certain that an event will occur, the probability of this event is 1.

Problem: Is it possible for the probability of an event occurring to be greater than 1 or less than 0? Explain your reasoning. List three events that have a probability of 0. List three events that have a probability of 1.

6-20   Finding Simple Probability ★ G

If a day is chosen at random from the month of March, there are 31 possible outcomes. Each outcome is equally likely.

Suppose a date that contains a 3 is picked. This selection is now called a favorable outcome. The likelihood, or probability, that a day in March contains the number 3 is 5 out of 31 possible days or $\frac{5}{31}$. This is written $P(3) = \frac{5}{31}$.

To find the probability of an event when all outcomes are equally likely, use the following formula.

$$P = \text{number of favorable outcomes} \div \text{number of possible events}$$

Problem: Refer to the calendar here. State the probability of choosing each of the following.

(1) A Saturday or a Sunday

(2) St. Patrick's Day

(3) A prime number

(4) A palindrome

(5) A number that has exactly three factors

(6) A perfect square

March						
S	**M**	**T**	**W**	**T**	**F**	**S**
	1	2	3	4	5	6
7	8	9	10	11	12	13
14	15	16	17	18	19	20
21	22	23	24	25	26	27
28	29	30	31			

6-21   Approximating the Probability of a Chance Event
★★ (7.SP.6)

All 200 seventh-grade students at Munroe Middle School attended a school dance. Upon entering, each student placed a ticket in a box with his or her name on it. At the end of the dance, 20 tickets were randomly drawn, and 20 prizes were awarded.

The next day, Kirk noted that 4 out of the 20 students in his math class had won a prize at the dance. He thought that the probability of this was amazing. He had not thought that so many students in one class would have won.

Problem: Based on the number of prizes and the number of students who attended the dance, how many students in a class of 20 would you expect to have won a prize? How might the high number of students winning a prize in Kirk's class be explained?

6-22   Predicting Relative Frequency ★★★ (7.SP.6)

A fast-food restaurant is trying to increase its business by sponsoring a drawing so that each customer receives a card offering a free soft drink, a free sandwich, or $0.50 off the next purchase. There are also cards that say "Sorry, try again." The restaurant will order 2,000 cards to be printed.

Problem: If $P(\$0.50 \text{ off the next purchase}) = \frac{1}{2}$, $P(\text{free soft drink}) = \frac{1}{10}$, and $P(\text{free sandwich}) = \frac{1}{20}$, find the number of cards that must be printed for each prize. How many cards that say "Sorry, try again" should be printed?

6-23   Developing a Probability Model ★ G (7.SP.7)

A member of the glee club sings the national anthem at the beginning of each home sporting event at River Town High School. Because all members of the glee club are excellent singers, the director cannot decide whom he should select to sing the national anthem at the school's first home football game of the season.

Problem: What method could he use to randomly select a student? Using this method, what is the probability that Miguel Sanchez, a member of the glee club, will be selected from the 32 glee club members?

6-24   Spinners as Probability Models ★ (7.SP.7)

Spinners are often used with board games. The area they spin over is usually circular and divided into equal parts called sectors. This makes each outcome equally likely. If the sectors are various sizes, the probability of the events will differ.

Problem: Draw a spinner that has only the numbers 1, 2, and 3 and the probabilities shown below.

$$P(1) = \frac{1}{4} \qquad\qquad P(2) = \frac{1}{4} \qquad\qquad P(3) = \frac{1}{2}$$

6-25   Representing the Sample Spaces of Compound Events ★★ (7.SP.8)

An event is the set of one or more outcomes in a sample space. For example, tossing a penny is an event.

A compound event is the set of two or more outcomes in a sample space. For example, tossing a penny and a dime is a compound event.

A sample space is the set of all possible outcomes of an experiment. If a penny is tossed, there are two outcomes: Ph, which means the penny lands heads up, or Pt, which means the penny lands tails up. If a penny and a dime are tossed, there are four possible outcomes: PhDh, PhDt, PtDh, and PtDt.

The outcomes of tossing a penny and a dime can be represented in the tree diagram.

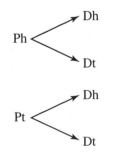

Problem: A penny, a dime, and a quarter are tossed. Draw a tree diagram to show the possible outcomes. Then use your tree diagram to find the probability of getting 3 tails, 2 heads and a tail, 2 tails and a head, and 3 heads.

6-26   Constructing a Scatter Plot ★★ G (8.SP.1)

Mrs. Sosa believes that there is a relationship between the amount of time students study and their math exam grades. At the end of her students' final exam, she included this question: "How long did you study for this exam?" Her students' answers, along with their exam grades, are summarized in this table.

Study Time (in hours)	Exam Grade	Study Time (in hours)	Exam Grade	Study Time (in hours)	Exam Grade
0	75	0.75	82	1.75	70
0	50	1	88	1.75	82
0	85	1	92	1.75	87
0.25	75	1	85	1.75	98
0.25	80	1	95	1.75	68
0.5	75	1.5	95	1.75	94
0.5	72	1.5	98	2	75
0.5	65	1.5	70	2	90
0.75	60	1.5	85	2	98
0.75	75	1.5	95	2	87

Problem: Make a scatter plot of the data, placing the study time on the horizontal axis and the exam grade on the vertical axis. Use your scatter plot to determine if there is a relationship between the study time and exam grades. Explain your conclusions.

6-27   Using Scatter Plots ★★ (8.SP.2)

A scatter plot, also called a scattergram, suggests whether two sets of data are related. To make a scatter plot, you must graph sets of data as ordered pairs.

To determine if the data in a scatter plot are related, imagine that a line is drawn so that about half the points in the scatter plot are above the line and about half are below. If the line between the points slants up and to the right, there is a positive relationship. If the line slants downward and to the right, there is a negative relationship. If no line is apparent, there is no relationship.

Problem: Three scatter plots are shown below. Match each scatter plot with the statement that describes it. Which scatter plot suggests a linear association?

(1) Field goals attempted and field goals made

(2) A person's weight and the number of pets he owns

(3) The outside temperature and heating costs

6-28   Positive, Negative, and No Relationship ★★

Data may be graphed along the horizontal and vertical axes in a bar or broken-line graph. The data may be related in a positive manner, a negative manner, or not related at all:

- When data are related in a positive manner, both the horizontal and vertical values increase.

- When data are related in a negative manner, the horizontal values increase as the vertical values decrease.

- When there is no relationship, there will be no pattern between the horizontal and vertical values.

Problem: Determine which events have a positive relationship, a negative relationship, or no relationship.

(1) Age and value of antiques

(2) Age and the value of a new car

(3) School attendance and grades

(4) Watching the news and the scores on a current events quiz

(5) Practicing basketball and the ability to play well

(6) Taking a school bus and completing homework

6-29   Representing the Slope and Y-Intercept ★ (8.SP.3)

Ellie recently did an experiment based on information she found in *The Old Farmer's Almanac* regarding cricket chirps and temperature. Each evening over the course of one month, she counted the number of times a cricket chirped in 14 seconds and then recorded the temperature in degrees Fahrenheit. She made a scatter plot and found the equation of the line of best fit, $F = n + 40$, where n is the number of times the cricket chirps in 14 seconds and F is the temperature in degrees Fahrenheit.

Problem: What do the slope and *y*-intercept represent in this experiment?

6-30   Using Two-Way Tables ★ (8.SP.4)

Mr. Harper asked the 25 students in his seventh-period math class if they owned a smart phone and if they owned a laptop. The results are summarized in this two-way table.

Own a smart phone?

		Yes	No	
Own a laptop?	Yes	8	1	Total 9
	No	12	4	Total 16
		Total 20	Total 5	Total 25

Problem: According to the data, do most of the students who own smart phones also own laptops?

6-31   Representing Data with a Box-and-Whisker Plot ★ (S-ID.1)

Alton is interested in buying a used book for a college course from an online book store. Twenty-four people were selling the book he was interested in. The cost of each of the 24 books, including the $3.99 shipping fee, is shown below.

$11.95, $12.00, $14.38, $14.88, $15.99, $16.85

$16.87, $18.41, $18.43, $19.00, $20.00, $20.75

$22.71, $23.00, $23.00, $23.74, $26.16, $29.79

$34.33, $39.35, $48.75, $48.98, $56.63, $72.36

Problem: Represent the costs of these books on a box-and-whisker plot.

6-32 Comparing the Center and Spread of Two Sets of Data ★★ (S-ID.2)

Kelli is a real-estate agent. Because she receives a commission for each house she sells, she tries to sell as many houses as she can each month. She knows that being aware of the real estate market helps to make her a good salesperson. The selling prices of homes in Harmony Village and Valley Town for last month are listed below.

Harmony Village	Valley Town
$310,000	$490,000
$325,000	$299,000
$350,000	$380,000
$280,000	$425,000
$200,000	$650,000
$360,000	$545,000
$245,000	$395,000
$390,000	$410,000
$225,000	
$600,000	

Problem: What is the median selling price in Harmony Village? What is the median selling price in Valley Town? How else do the data sets vary?

6-33 Accounting for Outliers ★ (S-ID.3)

James is a good math student who is very concerned about his grades. This marking period, his quiz grades were 100, 90, 85, 94, 40, 85, 90, and 86.

James found the median of the grades to be 88, the first quartile to be 85, and the third quartile to be 92. His average was 83.75. He asked his teacher to drop the grade of 40 because he was absent before that quiz and the grade was inconsistent with his other quiz grades.

Problem: How would dropping this score affect the median, the first quartile, the third quartile, and his quiz average? Should James's teacher drop the 40? Why or why not?

6-34 Using the Mean and Standard Deviation of a Data Set ★ (S-ID.4)

Matt is a very busy student who enjoys running. He wants to run a 5-kilometer race next month. But because of his schedule, he finds it hard to run a consistent length of time each day.

For his 10 most recent runs, he had various times (in minutes): 45, 45, 40, 55, 30, 60, 25, 60, 65, and 40.

Problem: How many of these runs are within one standard deviation of the mean?

6-35 Summarizing Categorical Data ★ (S-ID.5)

Chloe was the president of the glee club at Roosevelt High School. She was disappointed to learn that the activities director at the school planned an assembly that required the glee club to perform on the same day and time that a marching band competition was to be held. Several members of the glee club also belonged to the marching band.

Chloe presented the band director with the table below that summarized students' participation in the glee club and marching band. She said that if the assembly was held, about a third of the marching band members would not be able to attend the band competition. If the students who were in marching band were excused from the assembly, two-thirds of the glee club would not be present at the assembly.

In the marching band?

		Yes	No	
In the glee club?	Yes	60	30	Total 90
	No	115	605	Total 720
		Total 175	Total 635	Total 810

Problem: According to the table, was Chloe correct? Explain how she may have arrived at her figures.

6-36 Describing How Variables Are Related ★★ (S-ID.6)

At every freshman basketball game, Shawn's class conducts a raffle for a $100 gift card to a local restaurant. The money the school earns from the raffle is donated to the athletic department. Since the school is small and attendance at the games is poor, the class advisor wants to determine if the raffle is cost-effective. The class treasurer tabulated the following figures.

Attendance	Money Collected for Raffle
90	$189
94	$194
108	$245
106	$240
119	$250
125	$260

Attendance	Money Collected for Raffle
96	$200
94	$191
115	$259
110	$250
100	$205
128	$270

Problem: What is the relationship between the number of people attending the game and the amount of money collected for the raffle? Write a function to express this relationship.

6-37 Interpreting the Slope and Y-Intercept ★★ (S-ID.7)

The drama club sold tickets for the spring play. The tickets cost $3.00 each if purchased in advance and $6.00 each if purchased at the door. After the play, the total amount of money received for tickets for the play (both presales and at the door) totaled $630.00. If x represents the number of $6.00 tickets sold and y is the number of $3.00 tickets sold, the ticket sales can be represented by $6x + 3y = 630$ or $y = -2x + 210$.

Problem: Identify the slope and y-intercept. Explain their meaning in the context of the problem.

6-38   Interpreting the Correlation Coefficient of a Linear Fit ★ (S-ID.8)

For his math homework, Leon used his graphing calculator to make a scatter plot. He then found the equation of the line of best fit and r, the correlation coefficient.

Problem: Leon noticed that most of the points in the scatter plot were on the line. Because there was a strong correlation between x and y, he expected that r should be very close to 1. But instead he noted that $r = -0.9998$. How might this be?

6-39   Distinguishing between Correlation and Causation ★ (S-ID.9)

A group of high school girls started an exercise program. They danced to an exercise video three times per week. At the end of every week, each girl recorded her weight. After a few months, they noticed that everyone in the group had lost weight. They believed that this was a result of their exercise and concluded that exercise results in weight loss.

Problem: Do you agree with their conclusion? Explain your reasoning.

6-40   Understanding the Value of Statistics ★ G (S-IC.1)

Sam listened to the results of an election poll conducted by phone. According to the poll, the incumbent governor of his state was leading his opponent among likely voters, 48% to 45% with 7% undecided.

Problem: What factors can affect the validity of polls?

6-41   Deciding If Results Are Consistent ★ (S-IC.2)

Molly's math teacher had an incentive program to reward students who consistently hand in their work on time. She kept accurate records and at the end of the week placed the names of all students who completed their work on time in a box. She then randomly selected the name of one student each week. That student received two free movie passes. The program lasted ten weeks.

Problem: Molly says that this program was not fair, because she handed her work in on time each week for ten weeks but never won. Her two best friends each won twice. Was the incentive program fair? Explain your reasoning.

6-42   Recognizing Sample Surveys, Observational Studies, and Experiments ★★ (S-IC.3)

Sample surveys, observational studies, experimental studies, and statistical experiments can provide information about problems or issues. Each method has its own attributes.

Problem: The attributes of sample surveys, observational studies, experimental studies, and statistical experiments are described below. Match each description with its name.

(1) The researcher observes what is happening.

(2) The researcher tries to obtain information about a population by measuring samples of the population.

(3) The researcher manipulates one of the variables and sees how that manipulation affects other variables.

(4) The researcher knows each possible outcome in advance.

6-43   Using Data from a Sample Survey ★★ (S-IC.4)

For the upcoming election for student council president, Carl surveyed 20 out of the 100 students in his class. He asked them who they were most likely to vote for: Serena Martinez or Jacob Wilson. The results of his sample survey indicated that 11 students intended to vote for Serena and 9 intended to vote for Jacob.

Based on his sample, Carl concluded that Serena would win the upcoming election with 55% of the vote with a margin of error of plus or minus 2.5. He found the margin of error by assuming that 5 students would be absent on election day and therefore would not vote. Because he could not know how these 5 students would vote if they were in school, he divided the 5 votes by the two candidates, which resulted in the margin of error of 2.5.

Problem: Are Carl's conclusions valid? Explain your reasoning.

6-44   Data and Simulations ★★ (S-IC.5)

A simulation is a means by which to model random events. The outcomes of properly conducted simulations can closely mirror real-world outcomes.

Natalie and her class recently learned about simulations and the steps necessary for conducting a useful simulation. For one of the lessons, Natalie's teacher conducted a randomized survey among her students asking if homework is necessary for achievement in school. The survey, based on 50 students, is shown below. The teacher presented the results of the survey to her students.

	Yes	No	Total
Girls	12	10	22
Boys	10	18	28
Total	22	28	50

Problem: Natalie's teacher asked the class to list the steps necessary to produce a useful simulation for the information above. Natalie wrote the following steps, but two steps are out of order. Which steps are out of order?

(A)   Describe the possible outcomes.

(B)   Select one or more random numbers for each outcome.

(C)   Select a source of random numbers.

(D)   Based on the random number, record the simulated outcome.

(E)   Select a random number.

(F)   Keep selecting random numbers and recording the simulated outcomes until a pattern appears.

6-45   Evaluating Reports Based on Data ★★ (S-IC.6)

Every year, the Board of Education in Potterville publishes a report about the town's public schools. The report contains information and statistics on enrollment, attendance, number of teachers, and so on.

Problem: Andrew's father read the report and noted that the student–faculty ratio at Andrew's high school was 12 to 1. He concluded that this must be wrong, because in each of Andrew's classes, there are at least 20 other students. This was also the case for several of Andrew's friends: each of them had 20 or more students in every class. Andrew's father felt that the information in the report was wrong. Do you agree or disagree? Explain your reasoning.

6-46   Describing Events as Subsets of a Sample Space ★ (S-CP.1)

Janelle listed all of the possible outcomes of spinning the spinners shown below.

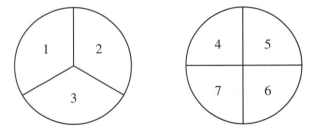

(1, 4), (1, 5), (1, 6), (1, 7)
(2, 4), (2, 5), (2, 6), (2, 7)
(3, 4), (3, 5), (3, 6), (3, 7)

Problem: List the subsets of the sample space that have the attributes described below.

(1) Both numbers are prime numbers.

(2) Both numbers are even.

(3) The sum of the numbers is at least 8.

(4) The sum of the numbers is not a multiple of 2.

6-47   **The Probability of Independent Events ★ (S-CP.2)**

Independent events are two or more events in which the outcome of one event does not affect the outcome of the other event or events.

To find the probability of two independent events, multiply the probability of the first event by the probability of the second event. Use this formula: $P(A \text{ and } B) = P(A) \times P(B)$.

Problem: Tony's mother purchased two bags of bagels. One bag contains eight plain bagels and four cinnamon-raisin bagels. The other contains two blueberry, four banana-nut, and six apple-nut bagels. What is the probability of Tony's randomly selecting the following?

   (1) One plain and one banana-nut bagel

   (2) One plain and one apple-nut bagel

   (3) One cinnamon-raisin and one blueberry bagel

   (4) One onion and one apple-nut bagel

6-48   The Probability of Independent Events ★★ G (S-CP.2)

In most games of chance that have spinners, the spinner lands on numbers. In some, however, spinners may land on names or symbols, such as hearts, diamonds, clubs, spades, or geometric shapes.

Problem: Fill in the spinners below with the correct geometric shapes so that all of the statements are correct.

  (1) Spinner A contains only triangles. No two are congruent or similar.

  (2) Spinner B contains only quadrilaterals. No two are congruent or similar.

  (3) P(each figure has no congruent sides) $= \dfrac{1}{12}$.

  (4) P(equilateral figures) $= \dfrac{1}{6}$.

  (5) P(2 figures that have at least one right angle) $= \dfrac{1}{6}$.

  (6) P(2 figures, each of which has at least 1 pair of congruent sides) $= \dfrac{1}{2}$.

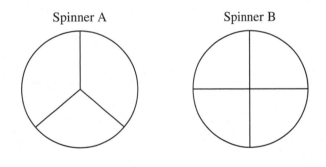

Spinner A   Spinner B

6-49   Understanding Conditional Probability ★★ (S-CP.3)

Alexander read that the conditional probability of A given B is the same as the probability of A and B, divided by the probability of B.

Stated algebraically, $P(A|B) = \dfrac{P(A \text{ and } B)}{P(B)}$, where $P(A|B)$ means the probability of A given B. But he needs an example to illustrate this concept.

Problem: Show that the conditional probability equation above is true using the following two events. $P(A)$ is the probability of tossing a die and it comes up as 3. $P(B)$ is the probability of tossing a coin and it lands heads up.

6-50   Interpreting a Two-Way Frequency Table ★ (S-CP.4)

Lakeside High School students were randomly surveyed and asked to select their favorite TV show from three types of popular shows. The results of the survey are shown in the table.

Favorite TV Shows of Lakeside High School

Grade Level	Reality	Situation Comedy	Crime Drama
9	8	3	1
10	7	4	2
11	7	2	4
12	6	3	3

Problem: Based on the survey, answer the following questions.

   (1) How many students were surveyed?

   (2) What would be a reasonable estimate of the probability that of the three types of TV shows in the survey, reality TV will be the favorite show of a randomly selected Lakeside High School eleventh grader?

   (3) What would be a reasonable estimate of the probability that of the three types of TV shows in the survey, situation comedy will be the favorite show of a randomly selected Lakeside High School ninth grader?

   (4) What would be a reasonable estimate of the probability that of the three types of TV shows in the survey, crime drama will be the favorite show of a Lakeside High School student?

6-51   Conditional Probability ★★ G (S-CP.5)

Conditional probability is the probability that an event B occurs given that event A has already occurred. Conditional probability can be applied to real-world events. Following is an example of a real-world situation to which conditional probability can be applied.

Heart disease is among the greatest killers of Americans. Millions of Americans suffer from some form of heart disease, which can include high blood pressure, cardiovascular disease, stroke, chest pain (angina), heart attacks, and heart defects. Heart disease has been linked to diet, particularly diets high in saturated fats.

Problem: Explain the concepts of conditional probability and independence in terms of heart disease and diet. Compare the chance of a person having heart disease if he consumes foods high in saturated fats to the chance of a person consuming foods high in saturated fats if he has heart disease.

6-52   Finding Conditional Probability ★★ (S-CP.6)

Paulo used a deck of playing cards to investigate conditional probability. He drew a red card from the deck and wanted to find the probability that the card is also a heart. He used the following formula:

$$P(A|B) = \frac{P(A \text{ and } B)}{P(B)}$$

$$P(B) = P(\text{red}) = \frac{26}{52} = \frac{1}{2}$$

$$P(A \text{ and } B) = P(\text{red heart}) = \frac{13}{52} = \frac{1}{4}$$

$$P(A|B) = P(\text{heart}|\text{red}) = \frac{\frac{1}{4}}{\frac{1}{2}} = \frac{1}{2}$$

Paulo noted that if a red card is picked, the probability that it is also a heart is $\frac{1}{2}$. He said that this is the same as the fraction of red cards that are also hearts.

Problem: Do you agree? Explain your reasoning.

6-53   Applying the Addition Rules for Finding Probability ★ (S-CP.7)

There are two addition rules for finding probability:

- Rule I is used when A and B are mutually exclusive probabilities: $P(A \text{ or } B) = P(A) + P(B)$.
- Rule II is used when A and B are not mutually exclusive: $P(A \text{ or } B) = P(A) + P(B) - P(A \text{ and } B)$. Note that $P(A \text{ and } B)$ is the probability of the overlap and must be subtracted so that an event is not counted twice.

Problem: A deck of 52 cards is shuffled, and a card is randomly selected. What is the probability that it is an ace or a diamond?

6-54   Applying the General Multiplication Rule ★ (S-CP.8)

The multiplication rule for finding probability is $P(A \text{ and } B) = P(A)P(B|A)$.

Fifty percent of the students at Green Oaks High School attended the homecoming dance. Of those students attending, the probability of winning a prize was 25%.

Problem: Use the multiplication rule to find the probability that a randomly selected high school student had attended the homecoming dance and won a prize.

6-55   Using the Factorial Counting Rule ★

The factorial counting rule states that different items may be arranged in order $n!$ different ways.

$n!$ is the product of all the counting numbers beginning with n and counting down to 1. You may use the formula $n! = n \times (n - 1) \times (n - 2) \times \ldots \times 1$.

For example, $6! = 6 \times 5 \times 4 \times 3 \times 2 \times 1 = 720$. By definition $0! = 1$ and $1! = 1$.

Problem: A candidate for governor wants to visit the county seat of each of the 21 counties in his state. Assuming he travels from one county seat to another, how many different ways may his visits to the county seats be arranged?

6-56   Using the Permutations Rule ★★ (S-CP.9)

Permutations are arrangements of things in a particular order. The factorial counting rule is used to determine the way a number of items can be arranged in some type of ordered sequence. If only some items (not all items) are to be included, the permutations rule can be used.

The number of permutations (or arrangements) of n items taken r at a time can be shown by this formula: $_nP_r = \dfrac{n!}{(n-r)!}$

Problem: Find the number of possible permutations for the following.

(1) A teacher must display five papers on the bulletin board. He has eight papers from which to choose.

(2) A security system with nine buttons can be disarmed when three different buttons are pressed. (No digit is used twice.)

(3) A building inspector has time to visit only seven of ten buildings or offices on her list of inspection sites.

6-57   Using the Combinations Rule ★★ (S-CP.9)

Combinations are a grouping of items without regard to order. The number of combinations of n items taken r at a time can be found with the following formula: $_nC_r = \dfrac{n!}{(n-r)!r!}$

Problem: Find the number of possible combinations for the following.

(1) Three students are chosen from a group of six to form a committee.

(2) Four numbers are chosen from a group of 36 numbers.

(3) A roving reporter selects five people from twelve people who are available for an interview.

6-58   **Defining a Random Variable ★ (S-MD.1)**

Alicia is spinning two spinners as shown below. She is interested in finding the sum of the outcomes.

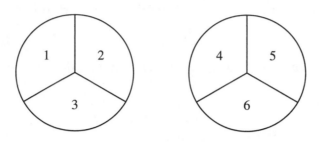

Problem: Let x be the random variable that represents the sum of the outcomes. Let $P(x)$ be the probability distribution. Complete the table below.

x	$P(x)$
5	
6	
7	
8	
9	

6-59   Calculating the Expected Value of a Random Variable ★ (S-MD.2)

George is a biologist whose duties include keeping track of the numbers of animals that inhabit a protected forest. Lately there has been growing concern that the populations of some birds are decreasing, sparrows in particular.

To begin his research into the sparrow population, George decided to conduct a somewhat unscientific but useful observation. He would walk through the forest and record the number of sparrows he saw. He would then compare his findings to a previous survey of sparrows that can be shown by a probability distribution $f(x)$, where x is the number of sparrows that was encountered during a similar walk through the forest five years ago.

x	$f(x)$
0	0.31
1	0.23
2	0.20
3	0.16
4	0.10

Problem: Use the probability distribution above to find the number of sparrows George expects to see on his walk if the sparrow population has not declined since the last survey.

6-60   Developing a Probability Distribution ★★ (S-MD.3)

For his math homework in probability, Joshua had to develop a probability distribution for a random variable and calculate its theoretical probabilities. The problem he developed follows.

A series of raffles is being held at his school to raise funds for a class trip. For each raffle, 100 tickets are to be sold, and the prize is a gift basket worth $300. According to Joshua, the theoretical probability of winning is 1 out of 100. The theoretical probability of losing is 99 out of 100. He said that if the raffle were conducted many times, the expected value of the random variable would be $0.01(\$300) + 0.99(0) = \$3.00$.

Problem: Are Joshua's example and calculations valid? Explain your reasoning.

6-61   A Probability Distribution Using Empirical Data ★★ (S-MD.4)

As technology advances, new products are invented and new terms that name and describe this technology come into common use. In the early 2000s, the term *smart phone* was not part of the everyday vocabulary. By 2012 smart phones were common, though not everyone understood the term.

In 2012, 2,250 cell phone owners were asked: "Is your cell phone a smart phone?" 33% answered "yes," 53% answered "no," and 14% answered "not sure."

Problem: Develop a probability distribution for a random variable in this survey using the random variable X to represent the responses to the survey. Suppose this survey was conducted this year. How many people would you predict would answer yes that their cell phone is a smart phone?

6-62   Evaluating a Flood Insurance Plan ★★★ G (S-MD.5)

Deena is a high school senior who has a great mind for math. Recently her grandfather spoke with Deena about the small home he owns along the coast in a flood zone. During severe storms, such as a hurricane, the land around the house may flood. A severe flood could damage the house extensively, or possibly destroy it completely.

Nevertheless, Deena's grandfather is thinking of cancelling his flood insurance policy because of its high cost and what he feels is the unlikelihood of a flood damaging his house. He cites the following facts:

- The cost of his flood insurance policy is $2,000 per year. The policy insures the house for $150,000. But the policy has a $2,500 deductible, which means that before the insurance company makes any payment for flood damage, Deena's grandfather must pay $2,500 to repair the damage.

- The policy pays only for damage directly caused by flood waters. For example, if flood damage to the house was $4,500, the policy would pay only $2,000 because of the deductible of $2,500.

- Deena's grandfather has owned the house for 10 years and has already paid several thousand dollars in premiums for the insurance policy.

- There has been no major flood in this area for 50 years. During that flood 50 years ago, the house suffered significant damage. Prior to that, the last major flood was in 1915, before the house was built.

- Deena's grandfather points out that if he pays $2,000 for flood insurance for the next 10 years (assuming that the cost does not increase, which is unlikely), he will pay $20,000 for flood insurance. He says that he can instead save this money, which he can then use if he suffers any flood damages. He also says that he is sorry that he has paid for flood insurance for the past ten years when he did not need it.

Problem: Deena advised her grandfather not to cancel the policy. Do you agree or disagree with her? Explain your reasoning. (Hint: Consider the chances that a major flood will occur and damage Deena's grandfather's home. Also consider the cost of the policy and its possible payouts in the case of flood damage to the home.)

6-63   Using Probabilities to Make Fair Decisions ★★★ G (S-MD.6)

The science department at Ocean View High School planned a trip to a local planetarium. Based on student interest, it was decided that two buses, each able to accommodate 48 students, would be needed. But there was a mix-up in ordering two buses, and only one bus was available for the trip.

Unfortunately, 94 students had signed up for the trip. Since only 48 could go, it was decided that the fairest way to select those 48 students out of the 94 who had signed up for the trip would be to assign a number from 1 to 94 to each student. A random number generator would then be used to randomly select 48 numbers. (Numbers were assigned to the students in the order that they signed up for the trip.) The probability of each student being chosen for the trip was assumed to be 1 out of 94.

There was another problem, though. Because no allowance was made for duplicate entries of the random generator, some numbers were generated more than once. For example, the numbers 23 and 54 were generated twice, and the numbers 7, 19, and 82 were generated three times.

Rather than discarding these numbers and then having the number generator select new numbers, it was decided that the students holding the numbers selected more than once could choose a friend (who had signed up for the trip) to go on the trip.

Some students protested this decision, saying it was unfair. But others felt that it was fair. These students said that it would have been unfair to run the random number generator more than 48 times, which would be necessary to select other numbers. They assumed that this would change the original probability of being chosen.

Problem: Do you feel that the decision to allow students whose numbers were randomly selected multiple times to choose friends to go on the trip was fair? Or rather, do you feel that it would have been fair to run the random number generator more than 48 times? Would this change the probability that a student's number would be selected? Explain your reasoning.

6-64   Basing Decisions on Probability ★★★ G (S-MD.7)

The Jefferson High School Panthers and Washington High School Lions are playing each other for the conference football championship. There are 2 minutes left in the game. The Panthers have just scored a touchdown (6 points) and now trail the Lions 22 to 21.

Coach Smith of the Panthers has a hard decision to make.

He may decide to have his team kick for the extra point, which, if successful, would tie the game at 22. But the Lions then would have the ball with 2 minutes remaining. If the Lions are unable to score, the game will go into overtime. Either team could then win.

Or Coach Smith could decide to have his team go for a two-point conversion, which, if successful, would give the Panthers the lead, 23 to 22. The Lions would get the ball back, but they would be behind. If the Lions are unable to score in the final 2 minutes of the game, the Panthers will be the champions of the conference. But if the two-point conversion fails, it is likely that the Lions will be the champions.

Before he decides what to do, Coach Smith has some important probabilities to consider:

- Based on past performance, the probability that his kicker makes the extra point is 95%.
- The probability that the Panthers will be able to make the two-point conversion is 45%.
- After the Lions get the ball back, they will need to move the ball at least to the Panthers' 20-yard line to give their field goal kicker a 50% chance to kick a winning field goal.
- The Lions have been averaging nearly 4 yards per play from scrimmage throughout this game. It takes them about 22 seconds to huddle and run a play.
- The Lions have averaged 25 yards in running the ball back after a kickoff throughout this game.

Problem: If you were Coach Smith, what would you do? Explain your answer in terms of probability.

6-65   A Quotation about Statistics ★★

Statistics are used in providing, comparing, and analyzing information. Statistics are often the foundation of decision making.

Problem: Explain this anonymous quote: "Some men use statistics as a tired man uses a lamppost for support rather than illumination."

Number and Quantity

7-1 Using Rational Exponents ★ (N-RN.1)

The properties of exponents can be extended to include rational exponents. If $a > 0$ and m and n are integers with $n > 0$, then $a^{\frac{m}{n}} = \left(\sqrt[n]{a}\right)^m$ and $a^{\frac{m}{n}} = \sqrt[n]{a^m}$.

Problem: Explain how $9^{\frac{1}{2}}$ can be expressed as a radical, using the property listed above.

7-2 Rewriting Expressions Using Radicals and Rational Exponents ★★ (N-RN.2)

There are limitless ways to apply the properties of exponents where the exponents are rational numbers. Here are a few examples:

- $64^{\frac{2}{3}} = \left(\sqrt[3]{64}\right)^2 = 4^2 = 16$

- $27^{-\frac{1}{3}} = \frac{1}{27^{\frac{1}{3}}} = \frac{1}{\sqrt[3]{27}} = \frac{1}{3}$

- $7^{\frac{1}{2}} \cdot 7^{\frac{3}{2}} = 7^{\frac{4}{2}} = 7^2 = 49$

- $\left(\sqrt{10}\right)^3 = \left(10^{\frac{1}{2}}\right)^3 = 10^{\frac{3}{2}}$

Problem: Rewrite each expression. Identify which expressions are equivalent.

(1) $8^{-\frac{2}{3}}$ **(2)** $16^{\frac{1}{4}}$ **(3)** $16^{-\frac{1}{2}}$ **(4)** $4^{\frac{3}{2}}$ **(5)** $25^{-\frac{1}{2}}$ **(6)** $8^{\frac{1}{3}}$

7-3   Explaining Products and Sums ★ (N-RN.3)

Kyle said that $\dfrac{a}{b} \cdot \dfrac{c}{d} = \dfrac{ac}{bd}$, where $b \neq 0$ and $d \neq 0$, shows that the product of two rational numbers is rational. He also said that $\dfrac{a}{b} + \dfrac{c}{d} = \dfrac{ad + cb}{bd}$, where $b \neq 0$ and $d \neq 0$, shows that the sum of two rational numbers is rational.

Problem: Kyle has trouble understanding why the sum of a rational number and an irrational number is irrational, and the product of a nonzero rational number and an irrational number is irrational. How would you explain this to him?

7-4   Using Units as a Way to Understand Problems ★★ (N-Q.1) 🖥

Albert Einstein (1875–1955) was the physicist who found that energy equals mass times the speed of light squared, which can be stated algebraically as $E = mc^2$. E stands for energy, m for mass, and c^2 for the speed of light squared.

To interpret the units in this formula, go to http://www.1728.org/einstein.htm. Read the information about the formula and study the example.

Problem: Based on the information and example, what is a joule (J)? What does a joule equal?

7-5   Defining Appropriate Quantities ★★ (N-Q.2)

Maria, who hopes to be a meteorologist someday, wants to measure the rainfall rate during a heavy rainstorm.

Problem: How might she do this?

7-6   Levels of Accuracy ★★ (N-Q.3)

When you work with measurements in the real world, the numbers always carry some degree of inaccuracy. No ruler, for example, is perfectly straight.

Roland's mother asked him and his brother to dig a new flower bed in the front yard. Roland used a yardstick to mark off the dimensions of a rectangular flowerbed: 10 feet by 8.5 feet. When he announced that the area of the flower bed would be 85 square feet, his brother, who had recently learned about levels of accuracy and measurement in his math class, said that Roland's statement about the area of the flower bed was inaccurate. Roland retorted that the math was clear: the area of a rectangle is found by multiplying length times width. 10 feet $\times$ 8.5 feet = 85 square feet.

Problem: What might Roland's brother have meant? Explain your reasoning.

7-7   Using Imaginary Numbers ★★★ (N-CN.1)

Sometimes problems cannot be solved if only real numbers are used. For example, $x^2 = -25$ has no solution in the set of real numbers. Equations like this fall into the realm of complex numbers.

A complex number is a number of the form $a + bi$ where a and b are real numbers. a is called the real part, and b is called the imaginary part. The imaginary unit i is defined as the square root of -1. Following are two examples:

$$i = \sqrt{-1} \qquad i^2 = -1$$

The solution to the equation $x^2 = -25$ is $x = \pm 5i$. Generally if $x > 0$, then $\sqrt{-x} = i\sqrt{x}$.

Problem: Simplify each of the following expressions.

(1) $\sqrt{-18}$ (2) $-\sqrt{-9}$ (3) $(3i)^2$ (4) $(i\sqrt{7})^2$

7-8   Using Powers of *i* ★★★

Some interesting patterns emerge for the powers of *i* as the exponent increases, as these examples show:

$$i = \sqrt{-1}$$
$$i^2 = -1$$
$$i^3 = i^2 \cdot i = -i$$
$$i^4 = i^2 \cdot i^2 = 1$$
$$i^5 = i \cdot i^4 = i$$
$$i^6 = i^3 \cdot i^3 = -1$$
$$i^7 = i^3 \cdot i^4 = -i$$

Problem: After studying the pattern above, complete the following statement. (Hint: Your choices for answers should include real and imaginary numbers.)

Any positive integer power of *i* that is greater than 1 equals _____, _____, _____, or _____.

7-9   Adding, Subtracting, and Multiplying Complex Numbers ★★ (N-CN.2)

The imaginary number *i* is equal to the square root of −1. Numbers of the form $a + bi$, where *a* and *b* are real numbers, are called complex numbers. They can be added, subtracted, and multiplied.

When computing with complex numbers, treat *i* as a constant but substitute −1 for i^2 if possible.

Problem: Consider the following complex numbers: $5 + 6i$, $1 - 2i$, $3 + 4i$, and $5 + 2i$. Which two numbers satisfy the following?

(1) The sum is $4 + 2i$.

(2) The difference is $2 + 2i$.

(3) The product is $11 - 2i$.

(4) The product is $9 - 8i$.

7-10   Finding Quotients of Complex Numbers ★ (N-CN.3)

The numbers $a + bi$ and $a - bi$ are complex conjugates. Their product is $a^2 - b^2i^2$ or $a^2 + b^2$.

To simplify the quotient of two imaginary numbers, multiply the numerator and denominator by the conjugate of the denominator.

Problem: Simplify each of the following quotients.

$$(1)\ \ \frac{4 + i}{4 - i} \qquad\qquad (2)\ \ \frac{6 - i}{2 + 3i} \qquad\qquad (3)\ \ \frac{8 - 3i}{2 - i}$$

7-11   Using an Argand Diagram ★ (N-CN.4)

An Argand diagram, named after Jean-Robert Argand (1768–1822), represents complex numbers. The diagram is similar to a graph in the coordinate plane, but the y-axis represents the imaginary part. The x-axis represents the real part. Note the figure below.

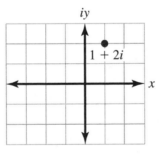

The point (1, 2) represents the complex number $(1 + 2i)$.

Problem: Graph the points that represent the following complex numbers. Then connect the points in the order you have graphed them, 1 to 2, 2 to 3, and so on. The first point is graphed for you in the above figure. What symbol have you drawn?

(1) $1 + 2i$ (2) $2 + 3i$ (3) $3 + 0i$ (4) $4 + 4i$ (5) $6 + 4i$

7-12   **Representing Operations with Complex Numbers in the Complex Plane** ★★ **(N-CN.5)**

Just as complex numbers can be graphed in the complex plane, so can their sums, differences, opposites, and conjugates.

Problem: Consider the complex numbers $w = 1 - 3i$ and $z = 2 + i$.

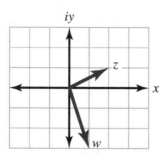

Identify the following points in the above figure.

    (1) $w + z$

    (2) $-z$

    (3) $w - z$

    (4) $\bar{z}$, the conjugate of z

7-13   Finding the Distance between Numbers in the Complex Plane ★★ (N-CN.6)

The modulus (or absolute value) of a complex number, $z = a + bi$, is $|z| = \sqrt{a^2 + b^2}$.

The distance between two numbers, z and w, in the complex plane is $|z - w|$.

Problem: Caryn is trying to find the distance between $(1 + 4i)$ and $(9 + 10i)$. She said that $|1 + 4i| = \sqrt{17}$ and $|9 + 10i| = \sqrt{181}$. She found the absolute value of $\sqrt{181} - \sqrt{17}$ and said that the distance between the numbers is about 9.3 units. Melanie said that the distance between $(9 + 10i)$ and $(1 + 4i)$ is the side of a right triangle whose vertex is at $(9 + 4i)$. By using the Pythagorean theorem, she finds that the distance between $(9 + 10i)$ and $(1 + 4i)$ is 10. Who is correct? Explain your answer.

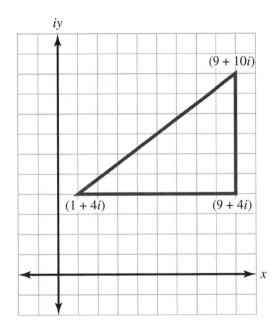

7-14 **Solving Quadratic Equations by Using the Quadratic Formula — Complex Solutions ★★ (N-CN.7)**

Mary Ann prefers to use the quadratic formula to solve quadratic equations because she can tell whether the roots are real or imaginary by looking at the discriminate.

Problem: Use the discriminate to determine if the roots of each quadratic equation are real or imaginary. Then solve the equations.

      (1) $3x^2 - 7x + 5 = 0$ **(2)** $x^2 - 3x - 1 = 0$ **(3)** $x^2 - 4x = -5$

7-15 **Extending Polynomial Identities to the Complex Numbers ★★ (N-CN.8)**

Sue learned that the difference of squares such as $x^2 - 16$ can be factored as $(x - 4)(x + 4)$. She could verify the product of $x - 4$ and $x + 4$ by multiplying the binomials.

Problem: Now that Sue knows about complex numbers, she can factor $x^2 + 16$, the sum of two squares. How could she do this? Check your answer by multiplying the complex numbers.

7-16 **The Fundamental Theorem of Algebra ★★★ (N-CN.9)**

Karl Friedrich Gauss (1777–1855) proved the fundamental theorem of algebra, which states that any polynomial of degree n has n roots.

Problem: Fernando says that all quadratic polynomials have either two real roots or two complex roots. Is he correct? Explain your reasoning.

7-17   **Vector Quantities ★ (N-VM.1)**

A vector is represented by a single letter written in bold. **v** represents vector **v**.

The norm of **v**, denoted by ‖**v**‖, is the length of the vector. It is also called the magnitude of the vector.

Problem: Use the figure below to answer the questions.

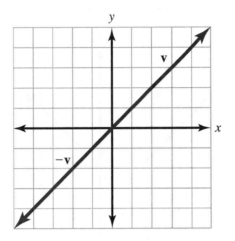

(1) What is ‖**v**‖?

(2) What is ‖−**v**‖?

(3) Are **v** and −**v** the same? Explain your reasoning.

7-18   The Components of Vectors ★ (N-VM.2)

The components of $\overrightarrow{AB}$ can be found by subtracting the coordinates of point B from point A. $\overrightarrow{AB} = (x_2 - x_1, y_2 - y_1)$ where (x_1, y_1) are the coordinates of A and (x_2, y_2) are the coordinates of B.

To find the components of any vector, subtract the coordinates of the initial point from the coordinates of the terminal point.

Problem: State the component form of each vector in the figure below.

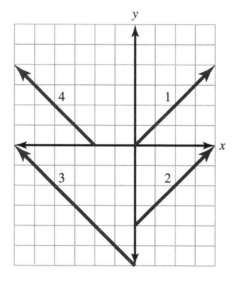

7-19   Using Vectors to Find a Plane's Ground Speed and True Course ★★★ (N-VM.3)

Lisa's father owns a small plane and has his pilot's license. Recently he and Lisa were flying at 152 mph (air speed) at a heading of 150°. A wind of 25 mph was blowing from 30°. Lisa's father explained that because of the wind and its direction, the plane's air speed and heading were not the same as its ground speed (speed relative to the ground) and its true course.

Problem: Find the plane's ground speed and true course.

7-20   Using the Parallelogram Rule ★ (N-VM.4)

Daniel knows that vectors can be translated to form a parallelogram. The diagonal is the sum of the two adjacent vectors. This sum is called the resultant.

His friend Eliot said that he knew of a case where vectors can be used to form a rectangle and the diagonal is the resultant of two adjacent vectors.

Problem: Which vectors was Eliot describing?

7-21   Multiplying a Vector by a Scalar ★ (N-VM.5)

A scalar is a real number. To multiply the vector **v** by a scalar, multiply the length of **v** by the absolute value of the scalar. If the scalar is less than zero, change the direction of the vector.

Problem: Kaleen said that multiplying a vector by a scalar reminds her of dilating a function. Do you agree with her? Explain your reasoning.

7-22   Using Matrices to Represent Data ★ (N-VM.6)

A matrix uses rows and columns to represent data. This makes the data easy to interpret.

Problem: There were three popular events at field day last week: an obstacle course, a relay race, and a bean bag toss. Team 1 scored 18 points for the obstacle course, 12 points for the relay race, and 20 points for the bean bag toss. Team 2 scored the following points for the events above, in the same order: 18, 18, and 12. Team 3 scored the following points for the same events, in the same order: 10, 20, and 18. Use a matrix to represent this data. (Hint: Let each row represent a team score and each column represent an event.)

7-23   Multiplying Matrices by a Scalar ★ (N-VM.7)

To multiply a matrix by a scalar, multiply every element in the matrix by the number. The product, called the scalar product, has the same number of rows and columns as the original matrix.

Problem: The number of students enrolled in Madison High School is represented by the matrix below. Use this matrix to find the matrices described.

$$\begin{array}{cccc} \text{Grades} & 9 & 10 & 11 & 12 \end{array}$$
$$A = \begin{bmatrix} 204 & 288 & 192 & 300 \\ 256 & 284 & 248 & 200 \end{bmatrix} \begin{array}{l} \text{girls} \\ \text{boys} \end{array}$$

(1) $\frac{1}{4}$ of the students will be on a field trip and will not be in school. Find the matrix $\frac{3}{4}A$, which represents the number of students who will be in school.

(2) Next year the enrollment at Madison High School is projected to be 10% more than this year. Find $1.1A$, the projected enrollment for next year. Round each entry to the nearest whole number, if necessary.

7-24   Adding and Subtracting Matrices ★ (N-VM.8)

A matrix is a rectangular array of numbers or letters. The dimensions of a matrix are the number of rows and columns. If a matrix has m rows and n columns, it is an m by n matrix.

Matrices (the plural of matrix) can be added and subtracted by adding and subtracting corresponding elements (the numbers or letters of the matrix). Only matrices of the same dimensions can be added or subtracted.

Problem: Solve for x, y, and z.

(1) $\begin{bmatrix} 1 \\ 3 \\ 8 \end{bmatrix} + \begin{bmatrix} 2 \\ 4 \\ 1 \end{bmatrix} = \begin{bmatrix} x \\ y \\ z \end{bmatrix}$

(2) $\begin{bmatrix} 1 & 0 \\ 3 & x \end{bmatrix} - \begin{bmatrix} y & 1 \\ 4 & 5 \end{bmatrix} = \begin{bmatrix} 5 & 1 \\ z & 6 \end{bmatrix}$

(3) $\begin{bmatrix} 2 & 3 & x \\ 1 & 8 & 4 \end{bmatrix} + \begin{bmatrix} y & 1 & 3 \\ 2 & 0 & 4 \end{bmatrix} = \begin{bmatrix} 8 & 4 & 5 \\ 3 & z & 8 \end{bmatrix}$

7-25   Multiplying Matrices ★★ (N-VM.8)

In order to multiply two matrices, the number of columns in the first matrix must be the same as the number of rows in the second matrix. You can then multiply the elements of a row in the first matrix by the elements of a column in the second matrix. The product is a matrix that has the same number of rows as the first matrix and the same number of columns as the second matrix.

Problem: Find the products, if the matrices can be multiplied.

(1) $\begin{bmatrix} 3 & 2 \end{bmatrix} \begin{bmatrix} 4 & 6 & 1 \\ 0 & -1 & 3 \end{bmatrix}$

(2) $\begin{bmatrix} -1 & 4 \\ 8 & 0 \end{bmatrix} \begin{bmatrix} 3 & -1 \\ 1 & 2 \end{bmatrix}$

(3) $\begin{bmatrix} 0 & -1 & 3 \\ -2 & -1 & 1 \end{bmatrix} \begin{bmatrix} -8 & 0 & -3 \\ -1 & 0 & 7 \end{bmatrix}$

(4) $\begin{bmatrix} 1 & 2 & -1 \\ -1 & 0 & 2 \end{bmatrix} \begin{bmatrix} 1 & -1 \\ 2 & 0 \\ -1 & 2 \end{bmatrix}$

7-26   Proving the Properties of Matrix Multiplication for Square Matrices ★★★ (N-VM.9)

Ben is trying to convince his friend Tony that the associative and distributive properties apply to matrix multiplication. (Tony knows that the commutative property does not apply to matrix multiplication.) Ben started to prove the associative property. $(AB)(C) = A(BC)$

$$A = \begin{bmatrix} a & b \\ c & d \end{bmatrix} \quad B = \begin{bmatrix} e & f \\ g & h \end{bmatrix} \quad C = \begin{bmatrix} i & j \\ k & l \end{bmatrix}$$

He multiplied to find the following products:

$$AB = \begin{bmatrix} ae + bg & af + bh \\ ce + dg & cf + dh \end{bmatrix} \quad BC = \begin{bmatrix} ei + fk & ei + fl \\ gi + hk & gj + hl \end{bmatrix}$$

$$(AB)C = \begin{bmatrix} (ae + bg)i + (af + bh)k & (ae + bg)j + (af + bh)l \\ (ce + dg)i + (cf + dh)k & (ce + dg)j + (cf + dh)l \end{bmatrix}$$

$$A(BC) = \begin{bmatrix} a(ei + fk) + b(gi + hk) & a(ej + fl) + b(gj + hl) \\ c(ei + fk) + d(gi + hk) & c(ej + fl) + d(gj + hl) \end{bmatrix}$$

Problem: Tony thanked Ben for helping him start on the proof of the associative property for matrix multiplication. Due to Ben's help, Tony now knows how to prove the distributive property for matrices. $A(B + C) = AB + AC$ What work did Tony do to prove the associative property, and how could he prove the distributive property for matrices?

7-27 Using the Zero Matrix and the Identity Matrix ★★★ (N-VM.10)

The zero matrix, O, is a matrix whose elements are all zero. $\begin{bmatrix} 0 & 0 \\ 0 & 0 \end{bmatrix} = 0$

The identity matrix, I, is a matrix whose elements in the main diagonal of the matrix (from upper left to lower right) are 1 and the other elements are zero. $\begin{bmatrix} 1 & 0 \\ 0 & 1 \end{bmatrix} = I$

Problem: Explain how the zero matrix and the identity matrix are similar to how 0 and 1 are used in addition and multiplication with real numbers. Provide examples to support your reasoning.

7-28 Translations and Vectors ★

A translation is a transformation in which a shape "slides" or "glides" without turning. Every point moves in the same direction.

Suppose a triangle has vertices at (1, 2), (3, 2), and (4, 5), and it should be moved 5 units to the left and 4 units up. This movement can be expressed by the vector $\begin{pmatrix} -5 \\ 4 \end{pmatrix}$. To find the vertices of the resulting triangle, add $\begin{pmatrix} -5 \\ 4 \end{pmatrix}$ to each vertex. The first vertex is found for you: $\begin{pmatrix} 1 \\ 2 \end{pmatrix} + \begin{pmatrix} -5 \\ 4 \end{pmatrix} = \begin{pmatrix} -4 \\ 6 \end{pmatrix}$

Problem: Find the other two vertices of the triangle. Then sketch the original triangle and its translation to verify your results.

7-29   Using Transformation Matrices: Reflection ★★ (N-VM.11)

A transformation can be represented by a 2 × 2 matrix. A point (x, y) is transformed to a point (x_1, y_1) by multiplying $\begin{bmatrix} x \\ y \end{bmatrix}$ by the appropriate matrix.

The transformation matrix that produces a reflection in the x-axis is $\begin{bmatrix} 1 & 0 \\ 0 & -1 \end{bmatrix}$.

Suppose you wanted to reflect the quadrilateral whose vertices are (0, 4), (3, 5), (2, 8), and (0, 5) in the x-axis. Find the product of $\begin{bmatrix} 1 & 0 \\ 0 & -1 \end{bmatrix}$ and each ordered pair expressed as $\begin{bmatrix} x \\ y \end{bmatrix}$.

The first point is found for you: $\begin{bmatrix} 1 & 0 \\ 0 & -1 \end{bmatrix} \times \begin{bmatrix} 0 \\ 4 \end{bmatrix} = \begin{bmatrix} 0 \\ -4 \end{bmatrix}$

Problem: Find the other three vertices of the quadrilateral. Then sketch the original quadrilateral and its reflection to verify your results.

7-30   Using Transformation Matrices: Enlargement ★★ (N-VM.11)

An enlargement matrix is $\begin{bmatrix} k & 0 \\ 0 & k \end{bmatrix}$ where k is the linear scale factor and k^2 is the area scale factor.

Problem: Suppose each side of a square is to be three times as large as the original. What matrix would be used? How does the area of the new square compare with the original?

7-31   **Using the Determinate to Find Area ★★ (N-VM.12)**

Consider $\triangle PQR$ with vertices (1, 5), (3, 4), and (6, 7).

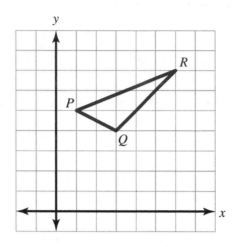

$\overrightarrow{PQ}$, expressed in component form, is (2, −1).

$\overrightarrow{PR}$, expressed in component form, is (5, 2).

Problem: Use the determinate to find the area of $\triangle PQR$.

7-32   **A Quotation about the Boundaries of Mathematics**

David Hilbert (1862–1943), a German mathematician, said: "Mathematics knows no races or geographic boundaries; for mathematics, the cultural world is one country."

Problem: What do you think Hilbert meant?

Potpourri

8-1   Emirps ★

An emirp ("*prime*" spelled backward) is a prime number that remains a prime when its digits are reversed. For example, 13 is an emirp because it is a prime number as 13, and it is also a prime number when reversed as 31.

Problem: List three emirps (other than 13 and 31) that are less than 100.

8-2   Deficient Numbers ★

The ancient Greeks considered a number to be deficient if the sum of its factors, excluding the number itself, is less than the number. For example, 8 is a deficient number because the sum of its factors $(1 + 2 + 4) = 7$. (Remember, the number 8 cannot be used as a factor itself.)

Problem: Which of the following are deficient numbers?

(1) 36   **(2)** 40   **(3)** 41   **(4)** 50

8-3   Perfect Numbers ★

According to the ancient Greeks, a perfect number is a number that equals the sum of its factors, excluding the number itself. For example, 6 is a perfect number because the sum of the factors $(1 + 2 + 3) = 6$. (Remember, the sum of the factors does not include the number itself.)

Problem: Which of the following are perfect numbers?

(1) 24   **(2)** 28   **(3)** 32   **(4)** 44

8-4   Abundant Numbers ★

The ancient Greeks defined an abundant number as a number whose factors, excluding the number itself, add up to a sum that is more than the number. For example, 12 is an abundant number because the sum of its factors $(1 + 2 + 3 + 4 + 6) = 16$. (Remember, 12 is excluded as a factor.)

Problem: There is one abundant number between 45 and 50. What is it? Show the sum of its factors.

8-5   Deficient, Abundant, and Perfect Numbers ★★ G

The ancient Greeks enjoyed mathematics and classified all natural numbers as deficient, abundant, or perfect. To do this, they found the sum of the factors of a number but did not include the number in the sum:

- If the sum of the factors (excluding the number itself) is less than the number, the number is deficient.
- If the sum of the factors (excluding the number itself) is greater than the number, the number is abundant.
- If the sum of the factors (excluding the number itself) is equal to the number, the number is perfect.

Problem: Consider the numbers 20 through 30. Classify each as deficient, abundant, or perfect.

8-6   Linear Measurement — The Customary System ★

The word *mile* comes from the Latin *mille passum*, which means 1,000 paces. During the days of the Roman Empire, a Roman pace was the distance covered by two strides.

Problem: How many strides were in a Roman "mile"? Is this an accurate measurement? Write an explanation of your answer.

8-7   Linear Measurement — The Customary System ★★

King Kong was a giant Hollywood gorilla who starred in a 1933 movie classic of the same name.

Problem: Use the clues below to determine the length of King Kong's arm, leg, ear, chest, nose, and height:

The distance around his chest is 10 feet more than his height.

His nose is $\frac{1}{25}$ the length of his height.

His ear is $\frac{1}{2}$ the length of his nose.

His leg is 15 times the length of his ear.

His arm is 2 feet less than half of his height.

His face is 7 feet long. This is $3\frac{1}{2}$ times the length of his nose.

8-8   Linear Measurement — The Metric System ★★

When most people think of dinosaurs, they think of huge, frightening creatures. But not all dinosaurs were big. The compsognathus, for example, was only a little bigger than a chicken and was about 600 millimeters in length. A brachiosaur was about 26 meters from its nose to its tail.

Problem: Convert the length of the compsognathus and brachiosaur to centimeters. The length of the brachiosaur is about how many times the length of the compsognathus?

8-9   Linear Measurement — The Customary and Metric Systems ★★

Below are some approximations to help you compare units of length of the customary system to units of length of the metric system:

1 inch ≈ 2.54 centimeters   1 centimeter ≈ 0.375 inch

1 foot ≈ 30 centimeters   1 meter ≈ 39.37 inches

Problem: A large American flag measures 64 by 125 meters. Express the dimensions of this flag rounded to the nearest foot.

8-10   Linear Measurement — Obsolete Units ★★

Ancient societies did not use the systems of measurement we use today. The ancient Egyptians, for example, used parts of their arms to measure length.

Following are some units of Egyptian measurement for length:

4 digits (fingers) ≈ 1 palm (the width of a hand)

2 palms ≈ 1 span (the width of an outstretched palm from the tip of the pinkie to the tip of the thumb)

2 spans ≈ 1 cubit (the length of a forearm)

Problem: How many digits equal 1 cubit?

8-11   Linear Measurement — Obsolete Units ★★

Some measurements found in the Bible are in cubits and spans. A cubit was the length of a forearm, which is approximately 18 inches. A span was the diagonal measure of an outstretched hand from the tip of the pinkie to the tip of the thumb, which is about 8 inches. Using body parts for measurement was troublesome, however, because people are different and one person's "span" frequently did not equal another's.

Problem: In the Bible, Goliath was described as being 6 cubits and 1 span in height. Approximately how tall was he? Round your answer to the nearest foot.

8-12   Measurement — Quotation ★★

The following words have been used in regard to the Special Olympics: "How far is far? How high is high? You'll never know until you try."

Problem: Explain these words.

8-13   Weight — The Customary System ★

In the customary system of measurement, ounces, pounds, and tons are three common units of measurement for weight:

16 ounces (oz) = 1 pound (lb)

2,000 pounds = 1 ton (T)

Problem: Arrange the nine weights below in order from least to greatest.

1 pound	2,000 pounds	30,000 ounces
32 ounces	1 pound 5 ounces	0.75 tons
1.5 pounds	200 pounds	1.25 pounds

8-14   Weight — The Metric System ★★

Some dinosaurs were big, but their brains were small. The weight of a stegosaurus's brain was about 80 grams, which was about 0.00258% of the stegosaurus's weight.

Problem: Find the weight of the stegosaurus in kilograms.

8-15   Weight — Using Balances ★

The ancient Egyptians used balance scales for weighing things as early as 3000 BC. Objects of known weight were placed on one side of the scale, and objects of unknown weight could be placed on the other. Weights could then be added to or taken away from either side until the two sides balanced.

Problem: Suppose only three weights are available. One of the weights equals 1 gram, another equals 2 grams, and the third equals 5 grams. What amounts could be weighed? (Hint: You may wish to make a table or chart to help you organize your information.)

8-16   Capacity — The Customary System ★★

A 10-gallon hat is the name for the large hat that many cowboys of the Old West wore. Although this hat was big, it held only about $\frac{3}{4}$ of a gallon.

Problem: How many quarts did the so-called 10-gallon hat actually hold? What percent of a 10-gallon container would that fill?

8-17   Capacity — The Metric System ★

Three common units of capacity in the metric system are the kiloliter, the liter, and the milliliter:

   1 kiloliter (kL) = 1,000 liters (L)
   1 liter = 1,000 milliliters (mL)

Problem: The numbers on the left of the equal signs are correct, but some decimal points and/or zeros are incorrect in the numbers to the right of the equal signs. Correct the decimal points and/or zeros to make each statement true.

   (1) 3.6 L = 0.00036 kL   **(2)** 0.13 mL = 0.0013 L
   (3) 400 L = 4 kL   **(4)** 23 L = 0.00023 mL
   (5) 6 mL = 600 L   **(6)** 7.3 kL = 73,000,000 mL

8-18 Time and the Calculation of *Pi* ★

The symbol π (*pi*) is a special one in mathematics. In most texts, *pi* is written as a decimal and rounded to 3.14. Actually *pi* goes on forever without repeating or terminating. In 1987, a Japanese man recited from memory the value of *pi* to 40,000 places. According to the *Guinness Book of World Records*, it took him 17 hours and 21 minutes, including four 15-minute breaks!

Problem: How many hours and minutes was he actually reciting?

8-19 Interpreting Time ★★

Some problems found in math texts are not always entirely accurate in the real world. Following is an example of a problem that might appear in a math text.

Suppose Sam runs a lap around the high school track in 2.5 minutes. How long will it take him to run 6.5 laps? The answer would be 16.25 minutes.

Problem: In real life, this answer is possible but unlikely. Why would Sam's time probably not be 16.25 minutes? Explain your reasoning.

8-20 Time — A Tricky Problem ★★

Can you figure out the following tricky time problem?

Problem: It occurs once in a minute, twice in a moment, not at all in a thousand years, but begins and ends a millennium. What is it?

8-21   Temperature ★

Even without knowing the specific temperature of things, most people can describe them as being hot, cold, or lukewarm.

Problem: Without using any math, arrange the items below from hottest to coldest, based on their temperatures.

- **(A)** A normal human body temperature
- **(B)** A hot oven
- **(C)** Normal room temperature
- **(D)** A "cool" fall day
- **(E)** A pot of boiling water
- **(F)** Ice water
- **(G)** Frozen yogurt

8-22   Converting Temperatures — Fahrenheit and Celsius ★★

Because the degrees on Fahrenheit and Celsius thermometers are not equivalent, you must use a formula to convert the temperatures of one to the other:

- To convert from Celsius to Fahrenheit: $F = \dfrac{9}{5}C + 32$

- To convert from Fahrenheit to Celsius: $C = \dfrac{5}{9}(F - 32)$

Problem: Convert the temperatures in Celsius to Fahrenheit and the temperatures in Fahrenheit to Celsius.

- **(1)** A high fever, $40°C$
- **(2)** Hot soup, $176°F$
- **(3)** A snowy day, $-11°C$
- **(4)** Ice water, $33°F$

8-23   Measurement — Light-Years ★ G

A light-year is the distance light travels in one Earth year. The speed of light is about 186,000 miles per second. In one year, light travels about 5,878,000,000,000 miles.

Problem: After our sun, the nearest star to the Earth is Proxima Centauri, which is about 25,000,000,000,000 miles away. About how many light-years is this?

8-24   Babylonians and Angles in a Circle ★

Thousands of years ago, the Babylonians, a people living in a region of the Middle East known as Mesopotamia, counted things in groups of 60. We still use this number system when we measure time. There are 60 seconds in a minute and 60 minutes in an hour.

The Babylonians were fine mathematicians and enjoyed geometry. They divided the circle into 360 equal parts. We use this system today too, and call each part a degree. A quarter of a circle contains 90°, and a semicircle contains 180°.

Problem: Write an explanation of the relationship between 360° in a circle and the number of seconds in an hour. (Hint: Think of a circular clock.)

8-25 Platonic Solids and Euler's Formula ★★

Regular polyhedra are solid figures bounded by regular polygons in a manner such that the same number of faces meet at each vertex. There are only five regular polyhedra, which are also called Platonic solids.

Euler's formula states that $V - E + F = 2$, when V is the number of vertices, E is the number of edges, and F is the number of faces. The formula applies to Platonic solids as well as other polyhedra.

Problem: Use Euler's formula to complete the chart.

Name	Faces	Edges	Vertices
Regular Tetrahedron	4		4
Regular Hexahedron or Cube	6	12	
Regular Octahedron		12	6
Regular Dodecahedron	12		20
Regular Icosahedron	20	30	

8-26 Squares on a Checkerboard ★★ G

A checkerboard contains eight squares along the sides of the board and eight squares along the top and bottom. Each of these squares is 1 by 1. The total number of 1 by 1 squares is 64.

Problem: Find the total number of squares on a checkerboard. Include 2 by 2 squares, 3 by 3 squares, and so on.

8-27   Rectangles on a Checkerboard ★★ G

A checkerboard has 64 small squares.

Problem: How many different-sized rectangles are there on a checkerboard? (Remember, a square is a rectangle.) List the dimensions of the different-sized rectangles. Keep in mind that a 1×2 rectangle is the same as a 2×1 rectangle.

8-28   Finding the Area of a Rectangular Chicken Coop ★

The 1897 *Farmer's Almanac* included some good advice for chicken farmers regarding the specifications for building a chicken coop: "Ten feet is wide enough and every ten feet in length will afford space for fifteen hens."

Problem: According to the specifications in the *Farmer's Almanac*, find the area of a coop that could accommodate 60 hens.

8-29   Edward I and the Area of a Rectangle ★★

Before the reign of England's Edward I (c. 943–975), an acre was the amount of land a yoke of oxen could plow in a day. Because the performance of oxen varied greatly, Edward fixed an acre at an area of 40 rods long and 4 rods wide. That measurement has not changed.

Problem: If a rod is 16.5 feet long, express an acre in terms of square yards.

8-30   Finding the Area of a Triangle Using Hero's Formula ★★★

In the first century AD, Hero of Alexandria devised a formula for finding the area of a triangle. It is aptly called Hero's formula and is stated below:

$$A = \sqrt{s(s-a)(s-b)(s-c)}$$

A stands for the area; s is half of the perimeter; and a, b, and c are the lengths of the sides.

Problem: Using Hero's formula, find the area of a triangle whose sides have lengths of 8, 10, and 12 units. Round your answer to the nearest hundredth.

8-31   An Ancient Palestinian Formula for Finding the Area of a Circle ★★★

Ancient Palestinians used the formula $A = \dfrac{11d^2}{14}$ for finding the area of a circle, where A is the area and d is the diameter of the circle.

Problem: Using this formula, find the area of a circle whose diameter is 10 inches. Then find the area of the same circle using the formula $A = \pi r^2$. Compare the answers. Explain why they might be different.

8-32   Palindromes ★

Palindromes are numbers, words, phrases, or sentences that are read the same from left to right as from right to left. Following are some examples of palindromes:

- *Words*: mom; dad; radar; wow
- *Phrase*: A man, a plan, a canal, Panama
- *Sentence*: Madam, I'm Adam.
- *Numbers*: 22; 303; 1991

Problem: Find two palindromes whose sum is a palindrome. Find two palindromes whose difference is a palindrome. Do you think it is always true that if the sum of two palindromes is a palindrome, their difference is also a palindrome? Explain your answer.

8-33   Palindromes ★★ G

Mathematical palindromes can be both interesting and fun.

Sometimes the product of two 2-digit palindromes is also a palindrome. For example, $11 \times 11 = 121$. Here is another, $11 \times 33 = 363$.

A product of a 2-digit palindrome and a 3-digit palindrome may also be a palindrome. For example, $22 \times 313 = 6,886$, and $11 \times 121 = 1,331$.

Problem: Using numbers other than those provided in the examples, find the product of two 2-digit palindromes that is also a palindrome; and then find the product of a 2- and 3-digit palindrome that is also a palindrome.

8-34 Using Cryptarithms ★★

A cryptarithm is a sum in which letters have been substituted for numbers. The digits 0 to 9 with different letters for different digits are used. Following is an example:

```
 TWO          928
+TWO         +928
-----        -----
FOUR         1856
```

In the above cryptarithm, T = 9, W = 2, O = 8, F = 1, U = 5, R = 6.

Problem: Solve the following cryptarithm to find the value of each letter below.

```
 ONE
+ONE
-----
 TWO
```

8-35 Number Ciphers ★★ G

A cipher is a secret system of writing in which every letter is replaced with a symbol. For example, a cipher might use the code A = 1, B = 2 , and so on. Another example of a cipher is A = 26, B = 25, and so on. (Not all ciphers use numbers in order to stand for letters. Of course, such ciphers can be difficult to figure out.)

Problem: Decipher this cipher.

20–23–15   9–19   20–8–5   15–14–12–25   5–22–5–14   16–18–9–13–5.

8-36   Number Ciphers ★★★

Number ciphers enable a person to write a message in code. In a number cipher, a number takes the place of a letter. For example, A = 1, B = 2, and so on, or A = 5, B = 6, and so on. You can select any number to replace a letter, but the numbers and letters must remain consistent in the message.

Problem: Write a short message using a number cipher. Exchange your message for the message of a partner and try to decipher each other's messages.

8-37   Using Number-Box Ciphers ★

A number-box cipher consists of five rows and five columns that make 25 boxes as in this example:

	1	2	3	4	5
1	A	B	C	D	E
2	F	G	H	I	J
3	K	L	M	N	O
4	P	Q	R	S	T
5	U	V	W	XY	Z

Because there are 26 letters in the alphabet, one box must contain two letters. Since x is not used very often in English words, x and y may be placed in the same box. The boxes are numbered from 1 to 5 across and down.

The numbers obtained from the rows and columns represent the letters. For example, 11 (row 1, column 1) stands for A, 32 (row 3, column 2) stands for L, and 43 (row 4, column 3) stands for R.

Problem: Using the number-box cipher above, decipher the following message.

35–34–15   24–44   11   41–15–43–21–15–13–45   44–42–51–11–43–15.

8-38   Roman Numerals ★★ G

The Romans, conquerors of the ancient Mediterranean world, along with much of Britain, Germany, and Asia Minor, were well known for their engineering skills. Some Roman roads are still in use today. However, the Romans never developed a practical number system. It is likely that Roman numerals were as confusing to Roman students as they are to students today.

Following are some examples of Roman numerals:

I = 1	X = 10
II = 2	L = 50
III = 3	C = 100
IV = 4	D = 500
V = 5	M = 1,000

Roman numerals are read from left to right. When a symbol of lesser value comes before a symbol of greater value, subtract the lesser from the greater. For example, IV = 4, which is 1 taken from 5. When a symbol of lesser value follows a symbol of greater value, the two values are added. VI = 6, or 5 + 1. There was no symbol for 0 in Roman numerals.

Although many of the lands that had once been part of the Roman Empire continued to use the Roman number system after Rome fell, eventually the Western world came to adopt the number system developed by Arabs in the Middle East. We continue to use the Arabic system today.

Problem: Make up at least four math problems using Roman numerals. Exchange your problems with the problems created by another group and solve each other's problems. Be sure to make a key for your answers.

8-39   Symbols (Infinity) ★★

Sometimes symbols and numbers are confusing. A teacher explained that division by 0 is impossible. It is not defined. To show this, she used $\frac{8}{0} = \infty$ as an example.

Later she gave the class some problems to work out. One of the problems was $\frac{5}{0} = $ _____. Some students responded that $\frac{5}{0} = \infty$.

Problem: Explain how these students misunderstood what the teacher had tried to explain. What concept did they misunderstand?

8-40   Figural Analogies ★★

Figural analogies are relationships between figures. Sometimes the figures may appear quite different, but they are related in some way. Following is an example of a figural analogy.

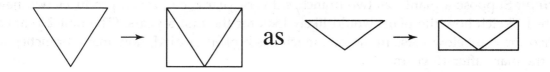

Problem: Complete the figural analogies.

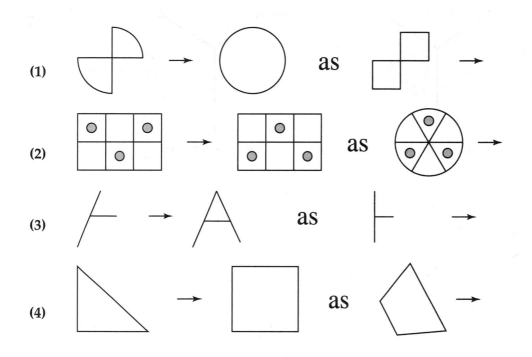

8-41   Fractals ★

A fractal is a figure that results from iterations (repetitions) in which each new part of the figure is similar to the previous figure.

Problem: Suppose a plant has two branches. Every year each branch produces two new branches. Sketch how the plant would likely look for the first 5 years. (The first 2 years are sketched for you below.) Assuming no branch has broken or died, how many branches would be on the plant after 10 years?

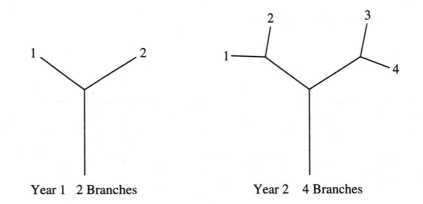

Year 1   2 Branches   Year 2   4 Branches

| 8-42 | **Fractals — Using the Sierpinski Triangle ★★** |

A fractal is a geometric shape that can be repeated by following the same process over and over.

Waclaw Sierpinski (1882–1969), a Polish mathematician, introduced the Sierpinski triangle, also called the Sierpinski gasket, which illustrates the concept of fractals. To use the Sierpinski triangle, follow the steps below.

Stage 0: Start with an equilateral triangle.

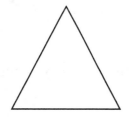

Stage 1: Find the midpoint of each side and connect the midpoints, forming a "new" triangle. Shade this triangle.

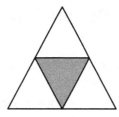

Stage 2: Find the midpoint of each unshaded triangle and connect these midpoints, forming "new" triangles. Shade these new triangles.

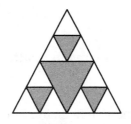

The process repeats with each new figure being similar to the original.

Problem: How many unshaded triangles are in stage 4 of Sierpinski's triangle?

8-43   **Figurate Numbers — Square Numbers ★**

Figurate numbers are numbers that can be represented by geometric figures.

One type of figurate number is a square number, which is a number that can be represented by dots in such a way that the number of dots on each side of the square is the same. The first three square numbers are shown below.

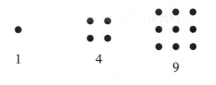

1   4

9

Problem: What is the tenth square number? What is another name for square numbers?

8-44   **Figurate Numbers — Square Numbers ★★**

A figurate number is a number that can be represented by a geometric figure. A square number is a figurate number that can be represented by the same number of dots on each side of the square. The first three square numbers are shown below.

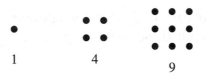

1   4

9

When square numbers are added, some interesting patterns emerge. One pattern relates square numbers to the sum of odd numbers.

Problem: Fill in the blanks in 1–3. Then answer the question.

   (1) The first square number = 1 = the first _____ number.

   (2) The second square number = 4 = sum of the first and second _____ numbers.

   (3) The third square number = 9 = sum of the _____, _____, and third _____ numbers.

   (4) How could you express the seventh square number as the sum of odd numbers?

8-45   **Figurate Numbers — Rectangular Numbers ★**

Rectangular numbers are figurate numbers that can be represented by a rectangle that has at least two rows and two columns. Some examples are shown below.

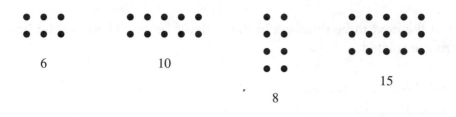

Problem: Draw a rectangular grouping of dots. Then count the dots and write the rectangular number.

8-46   **Figurate Numbers — Rectangular Numbers ★★**

A rectangular number can be represented as dots in a rectangular grouping of numbers. The rectangle must have at least two rows and two columns.

Sometimes the same rectangular number may be pictured by several rectangles. Each of the rectangular groups of dots below represents the number 12.

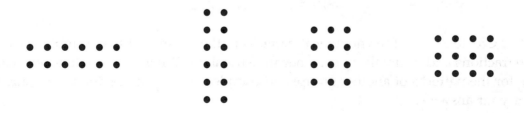

Problem: How many ways can 18 dots be arranged? Are there any numbers, other than 1, that are not rectangular? If so, what types of numbers are they?

8-47   Numerical Patterns ★

A pattern is a plan, diagram, or model to be followed. By finding a relationship between the items that make up the pattern, you can determine the next items in the pattern. Understanding patterns can be helpful in making predictions.

Problem: Find the next three numbers in the patterns below. Then explain how the numbers in each pattern are related.

   (1) 1, 2, 4, 8, 16, _____, _____, _____

   (2) 1, 4, 9, 16, 25, _____, _____, _____

   (3) 100, 50, 25, 12.5, _____, _____, _____

   (4) 2, 1, 4, 3, 6, 5, _____, _____, _____

8-48   Numerical Patterns ★★ G

If you understand the sequence of a mathematical pattern, predicting what numbers come next is relatively easy.

For example, the even numbers make a simple pattern. Once you recognize that the first four numbers are even, you can easily predict the next three numbers:

$$2, 4, 6, 8, \_\_\_\_\_, \_\_\_\_\_, \_\_\_\_\_$$

Problem: Create at least four numerical patterns in the manner of the example above. You may use fractions and decimals, or even negative numbers. When you are done, exchange your patterns for the patterns of another group, and complete each other's patterns. Be sure to make a key for your answers.

8-49   Line Symmetry ★

Line symmetry is a type of symmetry where one half of a given shape covers the other half exactly. This is also called reflexive symmetry, because if a mirror was placed on the line of symmetry the total shape would result.

Problem: Five letters of the words LINE SYMMETRY have line symmetry. Which are they? Provide an example of a word and a number that have line symmetry.

8-50   Lines of Symmetry ★★

A line of symmetry divides a figure into two congruent parts that are mirror images of each other.

Problem: Consider the regular polygons below. Draw the lines of symmetry in each. Then make a conjecture about the number of lines of symmetry of a regular *n*-gon.

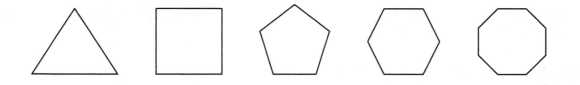

8-51   Networks ★

A network is any diagram of connected lines. Networks have three main features:

- The lines of the diagram, called arcs
- The points at which the lines meet, called nodes
- The areas for which the lines form a boundary, called regions

A node is odd if the number of paths leaving the node is odd. A node is even if the number of paths leaving the node is even.

Problem: Classify each node in the diagrams below as even or odd.

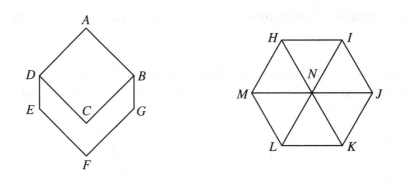

8-52   **Traceable Networks ★★ G**

A network is traceable if it can be drawn without taking the pen (or pencil) off the paper or going over the same line twice.

Problem: Which networks below *cannot* be traced?

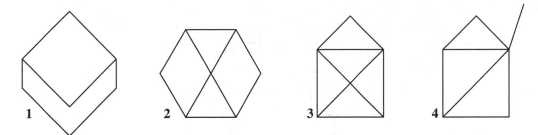

Count the number of odd and even nodes in each network. Then make a conjecture. A network is traceable if either there are only _____ _____ nodes, or there are all _____ nodes.

8-53   **Using Digraphs ★**

A digraph is a graph with arrows that represent a certain relationship.

Problem: The towns in the diagram are joined by a bus line. In the digraph, the bus travels in the direction of the arrow, meaning the arrow between Spotswood and South River indicates that a bus travels from Spotswood to South River. Use the digraph to list all of the bus routes between the towns.

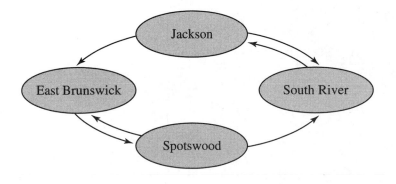

8-54   **Using Digraphs** ★★

A digraph is a graph that uses arrows to indicate how certain things are related.

Below are six softball teams, labeled A, B, C, D, E, and F. $A \rightarrow B$ means that team A defeated team B.

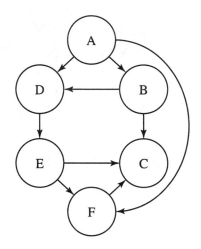

Problem: Use the digraph to answer the following questions.

    (1) How many games were played?

    (2) What was the outcome of each game?

    (3) Which team won the most games?

    (4) Which team did not win any games?

8-55　　Using Digraphs ★★ G

Although digraphs can show relationships, they have limitations just as other graphs do.

Consider the case of four girls—Elle, Lauren, Hallie, and Carla—who were making calls to plan a time to leave for a movie. In the digraph below, $E \rightarrow H$ means that Elle called Hallie.

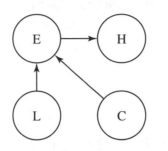

Problem: Was each girl aware of the plans? (Hint: Several answers are possible.) Explain your answer.

8-56　　Symbols and Letters in Math ★★

Mathematicians often use symbols and letters as a type of shorthand when writing mathematical expressions. Although using symbols and letters makes it easier to write expressions, the symbols and letters can sometimes be confusing.

Problem: Following are some symbols and letters commonly used in math. Identify what each means.

    (1) L in the metric system

    (2) l in geometric figures

    (3) P in geometric figures

    (4) P in number theory

    (5) P as in $P(A)$ in probability

    (6) C in a temperature formula

    (7) c in right triangles

    (8) C in a geometry formula

8-57   Quotation about Mathematics ★★

Galileo Galilei (1564–1642), an Italian mathematician, physicist, and astronomer, was one of the foremost thinkers of his time. Although he was not a pure mathematician, his inquiries of the natural world paved the way for applied mathematics.

Problem: Write an explanation of this quote by Galileo: "Mathematics is the pen with which God has written the universe."

8-58   A Personal Quotation about Mathematics ★

Although you are still in school, you have, over the years, learned much about mathematics.

Problem: Consider your knowledge of math, and especially why mathematics is important. Write a statement—a personal quote—that you would like to pass down to younger students about mathematics.

Answer Key

Section 1: Whole Numbers and Integers: Theory and Operations

1-1   Answers will vary. A few include "on cloud nine," "40 winks," and "the chances are a million to one."

1-2   (1) 3   (2) 6   (3) 10   (4) 15   (5) 21
     Answers will vary. One pattern is that the sum of the first n numbers is n more than the sum of the first $n-1$ numbers. For example, if $n=5$, the sum of the first 5 numbers is 5 more than the sum of the first 4 numbers.

1-3   S, S, E. The letters are the first letter of "six," "seven," and "eight."

1-4   Answers will vary. A possible answer is that 0 serves as a placeholder. Without 0, it would be impossible to distinguish numbers such as 68 from 608 or 680. Mathematically, 0 shows that a place (in place value) has nothing in it.

1-5   1947

1-6   1954

1-7   Explanations will vary. A possible answer is that because computers only "compute" or "calculate," results are based on data provided by the user.

1-8   Answers will vary. A few possible answers include: all together, sum; product, multiplication; twice, two times; quotient, division.

1-9   2 and 4 are correct. (1) 9,638   (3) 5,414

1-10   Explanations and examples will vary. A possible answer follows. Write the larger number, then write the smaller number beneath it. Line up the numbers according to place value. For example, to subtract 39 from 56, regroup 1 ten from the tens digit in 56, leaving 4 tens. Add 1 ten to the 6 ones for a total of 16. Subtract 9 ones from 16 to find 7, and subtract 3 tens from 4 tens to find 1 ten. The answer is 17.

1-11   (1) $\begin{array}{r} 6{,}763 \\ -3{,}929 \\ \hline 2{,}834 \end{array}$ (2) $\begin{array}{r} 71{,}146 \\ -4{,}876 \\ \hline 66{,}270 \end{array}$

1-12   9,222. Explanations will vary. A possible answer follows: Multiply 318 by the ones digit, 9, to find 2,862. Multiply 318 by the tens digit, 20, to find 6,360. Add these partial products to find the product, 9,222.

1-13 $431 \times 52 = 22{,}412$

1-14   1, 2, and 3 are correct. The correct quotient for 4 is 71 R40.

1-15   Explanations will vary. A possible explanation follows. Estimate to find how many groups of the divisor can be formed from the dividend. Write this number in the quotient in the correct place. Multiply this number by the divisor. Subtract this product from the dividend. Compare the difference with the divisor. If it is more than or equal to the divisor, your estimate was too small. Try a larger estimate and repeat the previous steps. If the difference is less than the divisor, bring down the next number and repeat the process.

1-16 10 complete teams (with two players left over).

1-17 Two answers are possible. The first is one person, meaning the narrator, because "met" may mean that the other group of people and animals were coming from St. Ives. If they were all going in the same direction, the answer is 2,753 which equals 1 narrator + 1 man + 7 wives + 343 cats + 2,401 kits.

1-18 1

1-19 Student problems will vary, but should demonstrate the use of compatible numbers in estimation.

1-20 2, 3, and 5

1-21 (1) Divisible by 2   (2) Divisible by 2   (3) Divisible by 2, 4, 8
(4) Divisible by 2, 4, 8

1-22 (1) Divisible by 3, 6   (2) Divisible by 3, 9   (3) Divisible by 3, 9
(4) Divisible by 3, 6, 9, 12

1-23 10, 5, 5, 10. Examples will vary. A possible example is 30, which is divisible by 10 and 5. Another example is 55, which is divisible by 5 but not 10.

1-24 144 dozen; 1,728 items

1-25 24 (or a multiple of 24)

1-26 2, 3, and 4 are correct. 1 is incorrect. GCF = 10

1-27 $208\overline{)464}$ 2 R48 $48\overline{)208}$ 4 R16 $16\overline{)48}$ 3   GCF = 16

1-28 First five multiples of 5 are 5, 10, 15, 20, 25. First five multiples of 9 are 9, 18, 27, 36, 45. First five multiples of 12 are 12, 24, 36, 48, 60. First five multiples of 15 are 15, 30, 45, 60, 75.

1-29 5,500 miles

1-30 (3) 6 and 12

1-31 (1) 60   (2) 50   (3) 63   (4) 493

1-32 Numbers will vary. The sum has no common factor other than 1 because each of the original numbers was divided by the GCF.

1-33 2, 3, 5, 7, 11, 13, 17, 19, 23, 29, 31, 37, 41, 43, 47

1-34 Explanations will vary. A possible answer is that 1 has only one factor.

1-35 10, 4 factors; 12, 6 factors; 14, 4 factors; 15, 4 factors; 16, 5 factors; 18, 6 factors; 20, 6 factors.

1-36 Explanations will vary but should note that all composite numbers in the grid are multiples of 2, 3, 5, 7, 11, 13, 17, or 19.

1-37 1, 4, 9, 16, 25, 36, 49, 64, 81, 100

1-38 7 red stripes; 6 white stripes; 50 stars

1-39 1 and 3 have the same value. (1) 19   (2) 35   (3) 19   (4) 16

1-40 There are many possible answers. Some answers include: $(2 + 1) - (4 - 3) = 2$; $(4 - 3) + (2 \times 1) = 3$; $(4 + 3) - (2 + 1) = 4$; $(4 + 3) - (2 \times 1) = 5$;

$(4 \times 3) \div (2 \times 1) = 6; (4 + 3) \times (2 - 1) = 7; 2(3 - 1) + 4 = 8; 1 \times (4 + 3 + 2) = 9;$
$4 + 3 + 2 + 1 = 10$

1-41 $64 = 4^3 = 8^2$

1-42   (1) $7 \times (6 - 4) \times 4$ (2) $(18 - 8) \times 5 + 6$ (3) $8^2 - 1 \times 2^3$
(4) $(2^2 + 3) \times (9 - 1)$

1-43   40 feet

1-44   451. *Fahrenheit 451* is the title of a novel written by Ray Bradbury. The novel depicts a future when book burning is common. According to Bradbury, 451 °F is the temperature at which book paper auto-combusts.

1-45   (1) $4^2 = 16$ (2) $2^2 - 3 = 1$ (3) $6 + 12 = 18$ (4) $1 + 5^2 = 26$
(5) $3 \times 5^3 = 375$ (6) $6^2 \div 3^2 = 4$

1-46   (A) $5, 8$ (B) 1 (C) $3, 7$ (D) $2, 4, 8$ (E) $4, 8$ (F) 6

1-47   20 seconds; blastoff $= 0$

1-48   Explanations will vary. A possible explanation is that a debt represents a negative number. To cancel a debt is the same as subtracting a negative number, which makes the number positive. For example, because a gift is a gain, it may be thought of as being a positive. Suppose your brother owes you $5. If you tell him he does not have to pay you back, your brother has, in theory, $5 more than he would have had if he paid you back.

1-49   Students should disagree. Explanations will vary. A possible explanation is that on the Fahrenheit scale, 32° is the freezing point. While −10° is "really cold," most people would also consider 10° to be "really cold." Opposites do not necessarily represent opposite extremes.

1-50   (1) E   (2) F, G, H, I   (3) F   (4) B

1-51   Browning

1-52   Students should disagree. For example, $|0| = 0$ and $|2.5| = 2.5$, which are not positive integers.

1-53   Answers will vary. A possible answer is that the debt represents money Samantha must pay to her sister. When she pays it, she will have $25 less. This amount can be represented as −$25. To her sister, however, the debt simply is $25. There is no loss to her sister. Her sister will gain $25 when Samantha repays the loan.

1-54   (1) 0 or 1; $\{-3, -2, 0, 1, 7\}$ (2) 0; $\{-7, -6, -5, -4, 0\}$
(3) −8 or −9; $\{-9, -8, -7, -6, -5\}$ (4) 6 or 8; $\{-4, 2, 4, 6, 8\}$

1-55   Explanations will vary. A possible answer is that the fast-forward symbol resembles the greater-than symbol because fast forwarding moves the program in a forward, or positive, direction, which implies larger numbers. The rewind symbol represents the less-than symbol because rewinding moves the program back, or in a negative direction, which implies smaller numbers.

1-56   (1) $<$ (2) $>$ (3) $>$ (4) $<, >$ (5) $>, <$

1-57   Answers will vary, but should note that Mike confused the placement of integers with absolute value. His map was correct, but he should have used absolute value to make conclusions about distances. $|-4| = |4| = 4$. This supports the fact that both houses are the same distance from the school.

1-58   1, 2, and 3 are false. Statements may vary. Possible answers follow.
(1) The point is always in the first or fourth quadrant.
(2) The point is on the x-axis.
(3) The point is always in the first or third quadrant.
(4) True

1-59   Explanations will vary. A possible answer is that the row number can be interpreted as the y-axis and the seat number as the x-axis.

1-60   Two rectangles have sides that are 4 units wide and 8 units long. The vertices of these rectangles are $(-3, -1)$, $(1, -1)$, $(1, 7)$, $(-3, 7)$ and $(-3, -1)$, $(1, -1)$, $(1, -9)$ $(-3, -9)$. Two rectangles have sides that are 2 units wide and 4 units long. The vertices of these rectangles are $(-3, -1)$, $(1, -1)$, $(1, 1)$, $(-3, 1)$ and $(-3, -1)$, $(1, -1)$, $(1, -3)$, $(-3, -3)$.

1-61   First magic square: -15. Second magic square, missing numbers: first row, -2; second row, 3, 1; third row, -3, 4.

1-62   Explanations will vary. A possible answer is that adding a negative integer to a positive integer is the same as subtracting. Suppose you were paid \$8 for babysitting and owed your father \$5. After paying your father \$5, you are left with \$3.

1-63   (1) -5 (2) -8 (3) -39 (4) -7

1-64   Student problems will vary.

1-65   (1) Positive   (2) Cannot be determined   (3) 0   (4) Negative
(5) Cannot be determined

1-66   Subtracting a negative number is the same as adding its opposite. $-1 - (-3)$ is the same as $-1 + 3$ and is modeled the same way.

1-67   (1) -16 (2) -8 (3) 0   (4) 8   (5) 16   (6) 24
Pattern: $-16, -8, 0, 8, 16, 24$. Each answer is 8 more than the previous answer.

1-68   Explanations will vary.

1-69   (1) c) $-6 \times (-3) \times (-2) \times (-7)$ is the only product that is positive. (2) a) $-3 \times (-4) \times 0$ is the only product that is 0. (3) d) $-5 \times (-3) \times 9$ is the only product that is not divisible by 2.

1-70   1, 3, 6, 7, 8, and 9 are correct. Corrections may vary. Possible corrections follow.
(2) $-21 \div (-7) = 3$ (4) $-156 \div (-12) = 13$ (5) $-20 \div 0$ is undefined.

1-71   There are two numbers with different signs that have the same quotient even if the quotient is a negative number. For example, $45 \div (-5) = -9$ and $-45 \div 5 = -9$. There is an infinite number of divisors that have 0 as a quotient. $0 \div 5 = 0$ and $0 \div (-5) = 0$ are just two examples. 0 divided by any number except 0 equals 0.

1-72   (1) -14 (2) 17   (3) -24 (4) -10

1-73   Problems will vary.

1-74   (1) 10; -10 (2) Two; 8 correct with 2 unanswered and 9 correct with 1 incorrect   (3) -10 (4) -1

1-75   Highest. $20 \times 10 - (-4) + (-2) \div (-1) = 206$. Lowest: $-4 \times 20 + 10 \div (-1) - (-2) = -88$

1-76   (1) 25   (2) -25 (3) 21   (4) 2,401   (5) -135 (6) $-3,375$

1-77 $1 \times 10^{100}; 1 \times 10^{10^{100}}$

1-78   (1) Jupiter   (2) Mars   (3) Neptune   (4) Uranus

1-79   (1) 1,392,000 miles   (2) 9,461,000,000,000 kilometers
          (3) 546,000,000,000   (4) 4,326,000,000,000,000

1-80   Answers will vary. A possible answer is that a person who does not think will never attempt to analyze or solve problems, particularly challenging problems.

Section 2: Rational Numbers: Fractions, Decimals, and Percents

2-1   (1) 15   (2) 36   (3) 12   (4) 42

2-2   The simplified fractions are $\dfrac{13}{14}, \dfrac{29}{37}, \dfrac{47}{63}$, and $\dfrac{2}{9}$. Those that must be simplified are

$\dfrac{21}{49} = \dfrac{3}{7}; \dfrac{15}{21} = \dfrac{5}{7}; \dfrac{19}{38} = \dfrac{1}{2}; \dfrac{12}{18} = \dfrac{2}{3}; \dfrac{10}{45} = \dfrac{2}{9}.$

2-3   Fractions equivalent to $\dfrac{14}{18}$ are $\dfrac{21}{27}, \dfrac{63}{81}$, and $\dfrac{77}{99}$. Fractions that cannot be

simplified are $\dfrac{20}{21}, \dfrac{9}{11}$ and $\dfrac{3}{14} \cdot \dfrac{7}{9}$ is in the part of the circles that overlap.

2-4   2, 3, and 4 are correct. (1) $\dfrac{32}{7} = 4\dfrac{4}{7}$

2-5   (1) 37   (2) 67   (3) 47   (4) 58

2-6   Explanations will vary but should note that fractions with lesser values are graphed to the left of fractions with greater values; or fractions with greater values are graphed to the right of fractions with lesser values.

2-7   The equivalent fractions are $\dfrac{2}{3} = \dfrac{50}{75}, \dfrac{3}{5} = \dfrac{45}{75}, \dfrac{2}{5} = \dfrac{30}{75}$, and $\dfrac{21}{25} = \dfrac{63}{75}$. The correct

order is $\dfrac{2}{5}, \dfrac{33}{75}, \dfrac{3}{5}, \dfrac{2}{3}$, and $\dfrac{21}{25}$.

2-8
(1) $\begin{aligned} \dfrac{3}{7} &= \dfrac{15}{35} \\ +\dfrac{4}{5} &= \dfrac{28}{35} \\ \hline \dfrac{43}{35} &= 1\dfrac{8}{35} \end{aligned}$

(2) $\begin{aligned} \dfrac{5}{6} &= \dfrac{10}{12} \\ +\dfrac{3}{4} &= \dfrac{9}{12} \\ \hline \dfrac{19}{12} &= 1\dfrac{7}{12} \end{aligned}$

2-9 $1\dfrac{7}{8}$ miles

2-10
(1) $\begin{aligned} 8\dfrac{7}{12} &= 8\dfrac{7}{12} \\ +6\dfrac{3}{4} &= 6\dfrac{9}{12} \\ \hline 14\dfrac{16}{12} &= 15\dfrac{1}{3} \end{aligned}$

(2) $\begin{aligned} 7\dfrac{5}{6} &= 7\dfrac{15}{18} \\ +2\dfrac{1}{9} &= 2\dfrac{2}{18} \\ \hline 9\dfrac{17}{18} \end{aligned}$

2-11   1 and 3 are correct.   (2) $13\dfrac{1}{20}$ (4) $9\dfrac{5}{24}$

2-12   (1) $\dfrac{1}{18}$ (2) $\dfrac{2}{15}$ (3) $\dfrac{2}{21}$ (4) $\dfrac{17}{40}$

2-13 $\frac{1}{12}$ cup

2-14   2 and 3 are correct. (1) $13\frac{1}{4}$ (4) $4\frac{1}{2}$

2-15   Explanations and student examples will vary. Possible answers should note that the first mixed number should be renamed in terms of the common denominator. Then the steps for subtracting fractions and whole numbers should be followed. Student examples will vary.

2-16 $1\frac{3}{4}$ feet

2-17   5 pounds

2-18 $\frac{1}{9}$; $\frac{1}{36}$

2-19   2 is correct. (1) $\frac{1}{6}$ (3) $1\frac{5}{6}$

2-20   1 is the only problem that is equal to 12.   (2) $11\frac{1}{3}$ (3) $12\frac{3}{8}$ (4) 14

2-21   12. Explanations will vary but should note that $2\frac{3}{4}$ can be rounded up to 3 and $4\frac{1}{3}$ can be rounded to 4. $3 \times 4 = 12$

2-22   Each square represents 1 egg. Therefore, the grid represents 24 eggs. To find $\frac{3}{4}$ of the eggs, divide the grid into four equal parts and lightly shade three of the parts. (The first three rows of the grid represent the 18 eggs that were decorated.) To find $\frac{1}{2}$ of the eggs she kept, divide the three rows into two equal groups and darken one group, which represents the 9 eggs she kept. The remaining 9 lightly shaded squares represent the eggs she gave away.

2-23   20 gifts

2-24 $\frac{7}{9} \div \frac{11}{2} = \frac{14}{99}$; $\frac{7}{11} \div \frac{9}{2} = \frac{14}{99}$; $\frac{2}{11} \div \frac{9}{7} = \frac{14}{99}$; $\frac{2}{9} \div \frac{11}{7} = \frac{14}{99}$

2-25   2 is correct. (1) $5\frac{1}{5}$ (3) $2\frac{1}{4}$

2-26   There is enough ribbon to tie $12\frac{2}{5}$ goodie bags, which means Mariana has enough ribbon for 12 bags.

2-27 $1\frac{1}{4}$. Lists of the steps will vary but should include the following points. Change the mixed numbers to improper fractions. Change the division sign to a multiplication sign. Multiply by the reciprocal of the divisor. Simplify the quotient.

2-28   No. He needs at least $2\frac{1}{4}$-inch nails.

2-29 $12.90

2-30   Explanations will vary. A possible explanation is that a dime is equal to 10 cents, or 0.10 of a dollar. Our number system is based on 10.

2-31   Sullivan, 26.83; Burgess, 22.583; Webb, 21.25; Tiraboschi, 16.55.

2-32   (1) 0.01, 0.0638, 0.12, 2.03, 5.1   (2) Correct
(3) 101.2, 10.21, 6.04, 0.75, 0.468   (4) 2.5, 1, 0.92, 0.565, 0.103

2-33   146.5 meters

2-34   Answers will vary. Possible answers include $\frac{1}{10} = 0.1$, $\frac{1}{2} = 0.5$, and $\frac{1}{8} = 0.125$.

2-35   (1) $2\frac{3}{5}$ (2) $\frac{3}{4}$ (3) $14\frac{19}{20}$ (4) $1\frac{1}{250}$

2-36 $0.1\frac{1}{9} = \frac{1}{9}$; $0.6\frac{1}{3} = \frac{19}{30}$; $0.7\frac{1}{7} = \frac{5}{7}$; $0.33\frac{1}{3} = \frac{1}{3}$; $0.83\frac{1}{3} = \frac{5}{6}$

2-37 $\frac{1}{7} = 0.\overline{142857}$; $\frac{1}{9} = 0.\overline{1}$

2-38 $\frac{1}{3} = 0.\overline{3}$; $\frac{5}{6} = 0.8\overline{3}$; $\frac{2}{9} = 0.\overline{2}$; $\frac{7}{11} = 0.\overline{63}$; $\frac{13}{15} = 0.8\overline{6}$

2-39   (2) $\frac{7}{16} = 0.4375$ which is closest to 0.425, without being too small.

2-40   Yes. Her estimate was $5.00, and she has $5.00. No. The actual cost of her food is $5.17. Explanations will vary. A possible explanation is that two of Maria's estimates were each $0.29 less than the cost of the items and one estimate was $0.41 more than the cost of the item. This resulted in her overall estimate being slightly lower than the actual cost of her lunch.

2-41   Whole numbers: (1) 1   (2) 3   (3) 3   (4) 0
Tenths: (1) 0.9   (2) 2.8   (3) 3.1   (4) 0.4
Hundredths: (1) 0.94   (2) 2.76   (3) 3.06   (4) 0.44
Thousandths: (1) 0.938   (2) 2.764   (3) 3.059   (4) 0.444

2-42   (1) $1.00   (2) $1.34   (3) $1.12   (4) $0.29

2-43   (1) 32.95   (2) 53.885   (3) 89.346   (4) 28.078

2-44 $14.75

2-45   (1) 0.92   (2) 351.4174   (3) 3.51   (4) 0.03548

2-46   (1) $4.11: 4 one-dollar bills, 1 dime, 1 penny.   (2) $2.41: 2 one-dollar bills, 1 quarter, 1 dime, 1 nickel, 1 penny.   (3) $7.00: 1 five-dollar bill, 2 one-dollar bills.   (4) $12.40: 1 ten-dollar bill, 2 one-dollar bills, 1 quarter, 1 dime, 1 nickel.

2-47   (1) 3.6×54; 36×5.4 (2) 0.78×0.21 (3) 324×6.5; 32.4×65
(4) 0.00007×3; 0.0007×0.3; 0.007×0.03; 0.07×0.003; 0.7×0.0003; 7×0.00003. Explanations will vary. A possible explanation is that in each case, the sum of the decimal places in the factors must equal the number of decimal places in the product.

2-48   4 is correct. (1) 0.14336   (2) 1.296   (3) 6.04064

2-49 $7.25

2-50   680; explanations will vary. A possible explanation follows. Multiply the divisor and dividend by 100, and move the decimal point in the divisor and dividend two places to the right. Add a placeholder in the dividend. Write a decimal point in the quotient directly above the decimal point in the dividend and divide as you would divide whole numbers.

2-51   None are correct. (1) 7.5   (2) 0.0743   (3) 85.9   (4) 0.0085

2-52   The average length of the arm (the humerus and ulna) is 25.45 inches. The average length of the leg (the femur and tibia) is 36.82 inches. The average length of the leg is longer.

2-53 A 12-ounce box is $0.25 per ounce. The cereal offered by the online store costs about $0.26 per ounce. The 12-ounce box is the slightly better buy.

2-54 $470.60

2-55 "Buy one, get one free" is the better buy because each roll costs about $0.17. The price per roll with the coupon is about $0.19.

2-56 $17.48

2-57 $320

2-58 10,018.8 miles

2-59 27.12

2-60 0.126

2-61 $13.68 \div 3.8 + 5.2 \times (2.4 - 1.7) = 7.24$

2-62 Answers will vary depending on the month and number of school days. Answers should note the three ways of writing ratios: as a fraction, with the word "to," and with a colon.

2-63 (1) 151:42   (2) 42:16 or 21:8   (3) 16:8 or 2:1

2-64 He received the higher score on the first quiz. Explanations will vary. A possible explanation is that the ratios of correct answers to the number of questions correct can be written as fractions, $\frac{24}{30}$ and $\frac{15}{20}$. Compare the fractions by finding common denominators. $\frac{24}{30} = \frac{48}{60}$ is larger than $\frac{15}{20} = \frac{45}{60}$.

2-65 1 and 3 are proportions.   (2) $\frac{5}{7} = \frac{25}{35}$ or $\frac{5}{7} = \frac{35}{49}$ (4) $\frac{10}{9} = \frac{30}{27}$ or $\frac{10}{1} = \frac{30}{3}$

2-66 Missing denominators: (1) 21   (2) 14   (3) 7   (4) 3.5. Explanations will vary. A possible explanation is that as the numerator of the fractions whose denominator is 7 increases, the denominator of an equivalent fraction whose numerator is 6 decreases.

2-67 $1\frac{2}{3}$ inches; explanations will vary. Possible explanations should note that you need to know where Washington is in relation to Jackson before you can determine the distance between Washington and Lincoln.

2-68 Row 1: 1, 12, 110. Row 2: 3, 3, 330. Row 3: 6, 72, 660. Row 4: 10, 10, 120.

2-69 Row 1: $2. Row 2: $4. Row 3: 5. Row 4: $32. Row 5: 25. Students should plot the points (1, 2), (2, 4), and (5, 10). The ratio of the total cost to the number of students is $2 to 1. The ratio of y to x is $2 to 1.

2-70 Another class with the same number of students and 100% attendance joined Mrs. Smith's class.

2-71 Explanations will vary, but should note that it is impossible to offer 110% off the price of auto services because that would be more than the cost of the service. According to the sign, Fred would pay people so that he (Fred) could fix their cars. Fred must delete the "110% off" and make it clear that only one discount may be applied to each service.

2-72 $\frac{1}{10}$, 0.1, 10%; $\frac{3}{4}$, 0.75, 75%; $\frac{1}{2}$, 0.5, 50%; $\frac{1}{8}$, 0.125, 12.5%; $\frac{2}{5}$, 0.4, 40%; 1, 1.0, 100%

2-73   0.25, 25%; 0.375, 37.5%; 0.50, 50%; 0.625, 62.5%; 0.75, 75%; 0.875, 87.5%. Explanations will vary, but should note that each increment of $\frac{1}{8}$ equals an increment of 0.125 or 12.5%.

2-74   66.$\bar{6}$% replaces 66%. $\frac{3}{8}$ replaces $\frac{3}{27}$. 10% replaces 1%. $\frac{5}{6}$ replaces $\frac{3}{8}$. 0.$\bar{5}$ replaces 0.55.

2-75   No. Explanations and examples will vary but should note that all unit fractions whose denominators are multiples of 3 will repeat.
$\frac{1}{3} = 0.\bar{3} = 33.\bar{3}\%$; $\frac{1}{6} = 0.1\bar{6} = 16.\bar{6}\%$; $\frac{1}{9} = 0.\bar{1} = 11.\bar{1}\%$; $\frac{1}{12} = 0.08\bar{3} = 8.\bar{3}\%$

2-76   4 is correct. (1) 4,901.52   (2) 294.84   (3) 800.4

2-77   12; dozen

2-78   Savings, $24; recreation and entertainment, $19; extras for lunch, $14; clothing, $29; miscellaneous expenses, $10

2-79   Explanations will vary. A possible explanation is that any percent less than 100% is a part of a number. Multiplying by a fraction that is less than 1 gives a product that is less than the number that is being multiplied.

2-80   (1) $\frac{n}{238} = \frac{40}{100} = 95.2$ (2) $\frac{n}{240} = \frac{34}{100} = 81.6$

(3) $\frac{n}{150} = \frac{110}{100} = 165$ (4) $\frac{n}{100} = \frac{68}{100} = 68$

2-81   36 feet

2-82   (1) $\frac{24}{n} = \frac{30}{100}, n = 80$ (2) $\frac{6}{n} = \frac{5}{100}, n = 120$ (3) $\frac{42}{n} = \frac{150}{150}, n = 28$

2-83   (1) 80%   (2) 80%   (3) 87.5%   (4) 80%   (5) 72%

2-84   (1) $n = 40$; 40% of 70 is 28.   (2) $n = 36.\bar{6}$; $36\frac{2}{3}$% of 60 is 22.   (3) $n = 200$; 200% of 7 is 14.   (4) $n = 0.5$; 0.5% of 1,800 is 9.

2-85   (1) $\frac{n}{100} = \frac{49}{56}, n = 87.5$ or 87.5%   (2) $\frac{7}{100} = \frac{n}{56}, n = 3.92 \approx 4$

(3) $\frac{7}{100} = \frac{56}{n}, n = 800$

2-86   Both are correct. Reasons will vary, depending on the individual student.

2-87   Explanations will vary, but should note that multiples of 10% are easy to calculate. A possible explanation is that $33\frac{1}{3}$% off is exactly $\frac{1}{3}$ off the original price.

2-88   No. Examples will vary. If the cost of a $200 item is reduced 40%, the reduced price would be $120. If this is reduced another 10%, the cost of the item would be $108. This is not the same as a 50% discount of a $200 item, which would cost $100 after the discount.

2-89 $18

2-90   The cost per person is $10.99 when rounded to the nearest cent. It would be more practical for each person to pay $11.00.

2-91   18,567%

2-92   66%

2-93 (1) $-3\frac{6}{7} + \left(-1\frac{2}{21}\right) = -4\frac{20}{21}$ (2) $-12\frac{5}{8} + 6\frac{3}{5} = -6\frac{1}{40}$

(3) $8\frac{3}{4} + \left(-2\frac{1}{2}\right) = 6\frac{1}{4}$ (4) $-3\frac{1}{2} + 3\frac{1}{2} = 0$

2-94 $-8\frac{7}{9} + 6\frac{1}{3} = -2\frac{4}{9}$ or $6\frac{1}{3} + \left(-8\frac{7}{9}\right) = -2\frac{4}{9}$

2-95 1 and 3 are correct.   (2) $-9\frac{1}{2}$ (4) $1\frac{1}{4}$

2-96 They are both correct. Explanations will vary. A possible explanation is that when you subtract a number, you are adding its opposite.

2-97 $\frac{-7}{2} \times \left(\frac{-5}{3}\right) = \frac{35}{6} = 5\frac{5}{6}$ or $\frac{-7}{3} \times \left(\frac{-5}{2}\right) = \frac{35}{6} = 5\frac{5}{6}$

2-98 Problems will vary. Explanations will vary but should note that dividing $-7\frac{2}{3}$ by a positive mixed number will result in a number that when multiplied by the divisor will result in a product of $-7\frac{2}{3}$.

2-99 (1) $-5\frac{5}{6} \div 3\frac{1}{3} = -1\frac{3}{4}$ (2) $3 \div \left(-\frac{3}{4}\right) = -4$ or $-3 \div \frac{3}{4} = -4$

(3) $7\frac{1}{3} \div 2\frac{1}{5} = 3\frac{1}{3}$ or $-7\frac{1}{3} \div \left(-2\frac{1}{5}\right) = 3\frac{1}{3}$ (4) $-11\frac{1}{4} \div \left(-1\frac{4}{5}\right) = 6\frac{1}{4}$

2-100 $8\frac{3}{4} \div \left(-3\frac{1}{2}\right) = -2\frac{1}{2}$

2-101 $\frac{1}{2} \times \left(-\frac{3}{4}\right) \div \frac{3}{8} + \frac{3}{4} - \left(-\frac{1}{4}\right) = 0$

2-102 Answers will vary. One explanation is that he copied the problem incorrectly. He wrote the numerator of the complex fraction as 5, but it should have been $\frac{5}{7}$.

2-103 1 and 4 equal $3\frac{1}{2}$.   2 and 3 equal $3\frac{1}{3}$.

2-104 (1) 1.622   (2) -279.37 (3) 24.06   (4) -2.532

2-105 2 and 4. (1) -13.723 (3) 1.612

2-106 Answers will vary. Dividing -97.52 by a positive number will result in a quotient that when multiplied by the divisor will result in a product of -97.52.

2-107 (1) C   (2) D   (3) A   (4) B

2-108 (1) $2.8 + (-0.8) = 2$ or $-0.8 + 2.8 = 2$ (2) $-1.4 - 2.8 = -4.2$
(3) $2.8 \times (-1.4) = -3.92$ or $-1.4 \times 2.8 = -3.92$ (4) $-1.4 \div (-0.8) = 1.75$

2-109 Answers will vary, but should conclude that Alicia is incorrect. All of the numbers, including $\sqrt{4}$, are rational. $\sqrt{4} = 2$, which can be expressed as $\frac{2}{1}$. All square roots of numbers whose radicands are perfect squares are rational numbers.

2-110 Danielle's conjecture is correct. Explanations will vary. A possible explanation is to let n equal the decimal. In the first case, multiply the equation by 10 and subtract n from it. $9n$ is equal to the digit that repeats. Using the first example, $n = 0.\overline{2}$, $10n = 2.\overline{2}$, $9n = 2$, $n = \frac{2}{9}$. In the second case, multiply the equation by

100 and subtract n from it. $99n$ will equal the two digits that repeat. Using the example, $n = 0.\overline{42}$, $100n = 42.\overline{42}$, $99n = 42$, $n = \dfrac{42}{99} = \dfrac{14}{33}$.

2-111   He should have said $10n = 4.16\overline{6}$ and found $9n = 3.75$, or, multiplying by 100, $900n = 375$; $n = \dfrac{375}{900}$ or $\dfrac{5}{12}$.

2-112   (1) $\sqrt{5}, \sqrt{6}, \sqrt{7}, \sqrt{8}$ (2) $\sqrt{5}, \sqrt{6}$ (3) $\sqrt{3}, \sqrt{5}, \sqrt{6}$ (4) $\sqrt{2}$

2-113   (1) $\dfrac{1}{5}$ or 5^{-1} (2) 2^{-2} or $\dfrac{1}{4}$ or $\dfrac{1}{2^2}$ (3) -1 or $\dfrac{-8}{8}$ (4) $\dfrac{1}{5^4}$ or $\dfrac{1}{625}$

2-114   The expression that has a different value is written first. (1) $2^5 = 32$ The other expressions equal 64.   (2) $\dfrac{3^4}{3^{-1}} = 3^5$ or 243   The other expressions equal 27. (3) $\dfrac{1}{5^{-1}} = 5$ The others equal $\dfrac{1}{5}$.   (4) $\dfrac{1}{4^0} = 1$ The others equal $\dfrac{1}{4}$.

2-115   (1) 4   (2) 64   (3) 729   (4) 1,000

2-116   Explanations will vary. A possible explanation follows. Write 0.000081. Then move the decimal point in the original number five places to the right so that it is to the right of 8. Write 8.1. Because moving the decimal point 5 places to the right is the same as multiplying by 0.00001, the exponent is -5. The final answer is 8.1×10^{-5}.

2-117   (1) 2.5×10^{13} miles   (2) 1.27×10^7 meters   (3) 9×10^{-28} grams   (4) 2.5×10^{-5} centimeters

2-118   (1) $(4.8 \times 10^2) + (1.6 \times 10^2) = 6.4 \times 10^2$
(2) $(4.8 \times 10^2) - (1.6 \times 10^2) = 3.2 \times 10^2$
(3) $(1.6 \times 10^3) \times (3.2 \times 10^{-2}) = 5.12 \times 10^1$
(4) $(1.6 \times 10^3) \div (3.2 \times 10^{-2}) = 5 \times 10^4$

2-119   (1) 100,000 hairs   (2) 0.00000000000000000000002 gram
(3) 4,500,000,000 kilometers   (4) 0.0000000319 centimeter

2-120   Explanations will vary. A possible explanation is that Einstein was working with extremely complex mathematics in his quest to understand the physical universe.

Section 3: Algebra and Beyond

3-1   100, although this number varies with specific orchestras. Comparisons will vary.

3-2   1877

3-3 $163.84

3-4   Answers will vary and may include equal, =; negative, −; and multiplication, ×.

3-5   (1) B   (2) D   (3) E   (4) A

3-6   (1) $0.62   (2) $0.72   (3) $0.20   (4) $0.13.   Explanations will vary but should note that because of inflation, the dollar had greater "worth" in the past.

3-7   1958

3-8   (1) 19 miles per second   (2) 125 miles per second
(3) 200 million years   (4) 430 light-years

3-9   (1) $4x$ (2) $6x$ (3) $7, 4y$ (4) x, x

3-10 $4(5x - 25); 5(4x - 20); 10(2x - 10); 20(x - 5)$

3-11 $16x - 24 = 8(2x-3); 16x - 40 = 8(2x - 5); 3x + 2x = 5x = 8x - 3x;$
$5(x - 8) = 5x - 40$

3-12   Tara is incorrect. Explanations will vary but should note that equivalent expressions must have the same value no matter what values are substituted for x. $20x - 4x = 4x(5x - 1)$, only when $x = 0$ and when $x = 1$.

3-13   (1) $x = \dfrac{1}{3}$ (2) $x = 0$ (3) $x = 3$ (4) $x = 3$ (5) $x = 0$ (6) No solution because division by zero is undefined.

3-14   Answers will vary but should note that Sarah does not understand the meaning of the inequality symbols. She is interpreting $\geq$ as $>$ and $\leq$ as $<$.

3-15   Answers will vary but should note that a variable can stand for many different values.

3-16   (1) $6s$ (2) $s \div 20$ (3) $s \div 4$ (4) $2(s \div 4)$ or $s \div 2$

3-17   Problems will vary. A possible problem follows. Of all the members of our school's jazz band, 7 were home sick with the flu and only 8 attended yesterday's practice. How many students are members of the jazz band? Add 7 to both sides of the equation. $x = 15$

3-18   All of the problems can be solved by using subtraction, except number 5, which can be solved by using addition.   (1) $x = 5$ (2) $x = 1$ (3) $x = 45$ (4) $x = 0$ (5) $x = 26$ (6) $x = 15$

3-19   Problems 1 and 5 can be solved by adding 8 to both sides. Problems 2, 3, 4, and 6 can be solved by subtracting 8 from both sides.   (1) $x = 23$ (2) $x = 19$ (3) $x = 2$ (4) $x = 16$ (5) $x = 18$ (6) $x = 8$

3-20   Explanations will vary. A possible explanation follows. Multiply $\dfrac{1}{4}x$ by $\dfrac{4}{1}$ so that x is on the left side of the equation. When you multiply the left side of the equation by 4, you must multiply the right side of the equation by 4. $20 \times 4 = 80$. Therefore, $x = 80$.

3-21   (1) $x = 16$ (2) $x = 8$ (3) $x = 4$ (4) $x = 192$ (5) $x = 96$ (6) $x = 128$

3-22   (1) $3, \dfrac{1}{3}, 5$ (2) $\dfrac{1}{3}, 3, 45$

3-23   (1) $n \geq 4$ (2) $t > 96°\,\text{F}$ (3) $e > 30$ (4) $h \leq 4$

3-24 $\dfrac{1}{2}(80 + x) \geq 95$, where x is the score needed on the next test. Solving the inequality results in $x \geq 110$. Unless the test contains extra credit and Marco gets the entire test and extra credit correct, it is impossible for him to earn an average of 95. The inequality he wrote is correct, but the conclusion he drew from it is unreasonable.

3-25   (1) \$37.50   (2) \$75   (3) \$56.25   (4) \$22.50 $s = r - \dfrac{1}{4}r$ or $s = \dfrac{3}{4}r$

3-26 $b =$ number of test booklets; $t =$ number of teacher's manuals.
(1) $58b + t + 42b + 3t = 100b + 4t$ (2) $100b + 4t - 10b - t = 90b + 3t$
(3) $90b + 3t = 3(30b + t)$

3-27 Answers will vary. If t = tip and s = sales tax = 7% of bill, possible expressions are $t \approx 2s$ or $t = 2\frac{1}{7}s$.

3-28 The solution to 1 and 3 is -2. The solution to 2 and 4 is -7.

3-29 Problems will vary. A possible problem follows. Sue works part-time at a beauty salon and earns $112 each week. If she shampoos a client's hair, she earns an extra $2. How many people must she shampoo in order to earn a total of $136 for the week? x = the number of people whose hair she shampoos. $2x + \$112 = \$136; x = 12$

3-30 Both equations are correct. Joanna used mental math and multiplied 30 by 2 and l by 2 before writing her equation.

3-31 (1) $s = 10$; rational   (2) $e = 6$; rational   (3) $s = \sqrt{8}$; irrational
(4) $e = 2$; rational   (5) $e = 10$; rational   (6) $s = 1$; rational

3-32 Beans (no salt): $C = 20s$; vegetables in butter sauce: $C = 90s$; veggie medley: $C = 60s$; mixed vegetables: $C = 45s$ Students should graph the second equation, $C = 90s$, as a line through the origin that has a slope of 90.

3-33 Explanations will vary. A possible explanation follows. Since AB is the ratio of $\frac{BC}{AC}$ and AD is the ratio of $\frac{DE}{AE}$, AD is a multiple of AB. Graphically, line segment AD is found by extending line segment AB, and D is a point on the segment. If additional triangles that are similar to $\triangle ABC$ and $\triangle ADF$ were drawn on the figure, the slope of the hypotenuse would be the same.

3-34 (1) $(-5, 15)$ (2) $(0, 1)$ (3) $(6, -1)$

3-35 Explanations will vary. A possible explanation follows. If the points (x_1, y_1) and (x_2, y_2) lie on a horizontal line, $y_1 = y_2$. Therefore, $y_2 - y_1 = 0$. 0 divided by any number equals 0. If the points (x_1, y_1) and (x_2, y_2) lie on a vertical line, $x_2 = x_1$. Therefore, $x_2 - x_1 = 0$. Because division by 0 is undefined, the slope of a vertical line is undefined.

3-36 Since half of the span is equal to 12 and the rise is 10, the pitch $= \frac{10}{12}$ or $\frac{5}{6}$. Slope $= \frac{\text{rise}}{\text{run}} = \frac{10}{12} = \frac{5}{6}$. The pitch and the slope are the same.

3-37 Problems 1 and 4 contain like terms. (2) $7x^3, 4x^3$ or $7x^2, 4x^2$.   (3) $8y^2, 8y^2$ or $8y, 8y$

3-38 (1) $15x + 7y$ (2) $4x - 3y + 10$ (3) $4x - 3y + 10$ (4) $5x + 7y$
(5) $-x + y + 10$ 2 and 3 are equivalent expressions.

3-39 (1) $-2a, 3$ (2) $4a, 20b, 6$ (3) $a, c, 2b$ (4) $5a, 8$

3-40 (1) $2a + 3b - 12c - 6; -61$ (2) $5a - 9b + 4c - 10; -27$
(3) $-4a - 3b - 4c; -21$ (4) $-4a + 8b + 3c + 10; 57$
The values are increasing.

3-41 $40, 30, -12, -1$

3-42 Both equations are correct.

3-43 1, 2, and 3 have solutions that are even numbers. The solution to 4 is odd.
(1) $n = 8$ (2) $n = 12$ (3) $n = 4$ (4) $n = 15$

3-44 2, 3, and 4 have no solution. 1, 5, and 6 are true for all real numbers.

3-45   Carrie is correct. Explanations will vary. Two possible explanations are that if you substitute 3 for x in both equations, $y = 7$, or students may explain that a solution of a system of equations is the point where the graphs intersect.

3-46 $x \approx -2$ and $y \approx -1\frac{1}{2}$

3-47   (1) $x = -2.5$; $y = -2.5$ (2) The lines are parallel. There is no solution.
(3) The lines coincide. There are an infinite number of solutions.
(4) $x = -2.4$; $y = -2.2$

3-48   (1) First equation y; second equation x or y; $x = 2$; $y = 10$ (2) Second equation y; $x = 5$; $y = 1$ (3) First equation y; $x = -4$; $y = -3$

3-49   Explanations will vary but should note the following. 2 is partially correct; he needs to also solve for x. $x = 27$. 4 is partially correct; x should equal $5\frac{3}{4}$. Since there were eight answers (two answers for each problem) and he got 6 out of 8 correct, his score should be 75%.

3-50   Preferences will vary, but most will probably prefer John's method because only one equation is multiplied. $x = 0$; $y = \dfrac{-17}{3}$

3-51   (1) $x = 0$; $y = 0$ (2) $x = -1$; $y = 3$ (3) $x = 6$; $y = -8$
(4) $x = 2$; $y = 1$

3-52   (1) $15a^8$, two errors   (2) $18x^6$, one error   (3) $6c^2$, two errors
(4) Correct   (5) $-8c^5$, one error   (6) $-30r^6s^7$, one error

3-53 $2\pi r^3 = \dfrac{4}{3}\pi r^3 + \dfrac{2}{3}\pi r^3$

3-54   (1) a^5 (2) $8a^7$ (3) $9a^2$ (4) $4a^6b^8$

3-55   The volume of the larger cube is 27 times the volume of the smaller cube.

3-56   (1) $(2x)^3$ (2) $(2x^3)^2$ (3) $(5x^4)^2$ (4) $(4x^6)^2$ (5) $(3x^2)^3$
(6) $(9x^5)^2$ (7) $(5x)^3$ (8) $(6x^2)^2$

3-57   Explanations will vary. A possible answer follows. If the bases are the same, subtract the exponents. In the first example, subtract 2 from 5 to get 3. The quotient is a^3. In the second example, subtract 8 from 9. The quotient is $\dfrac{1}{a}$. In the third example, the exponents are equal and their difference is 0. The quotient is a^0 or 1.

3-58   1,000 times

3-59   3 is incorrect. The quotient is $3a^4$.

3-60   (1) $4s$; $2(l + w)$ (2) $(l + w)$; $2a + b$ (3) $2(l + w)$; $2a + b$ (4) $2(l + w)$

3-61   (1) D   (2) F   (3) A   (4) B   (5) E   (6) C

3-62   33; student polynomials will vary. A possible polynomial is a team score in football, $3t + e + 2f$, where t represents 6 points for each touchdown, e represents 1 point for the extra point after a touchdown, and f represents 3 points for each field goal.

3-63   (1) $5a + 9$ (2) $2n + 7$ (3) $2x^2 - xy - y^2$ (4) $a + 2$

3-64   1 and 4 are correct.   (2) Change 28 to $28x$.   (3) Change $-12ab$ to $+12ab$.

3-65   (1) $3a - 4$ (2) $-3b^2 + 2b + 1$ (3) $6st^2 - 7$ (4) $-3r^2s^2 + 5rs - 2$

3-66   (1) C   (2) B   (3) D   (4) A

3-67   (1) $x^2 + 5x + 6$ (2) $x^2 + 8x + 15$ (3) $x^2 + 6x + 9$ (4) $x^2 + 5x + 4$

3-68 $(4+6)^3 = 64 + 3 \cdot 16 \cdot 6 + 3 \cdot 4 \cdot 36 + 216 = 1{,}000$;
$(4-6)^3 = 64 - 3 \cdot 16 \cdot 6 + 3 \cdot 4 \cdot 36 - 216 = -8$;
$(a+b)(a^2 + 2ab + b^2) = a^3 + 3a^2b + 3ab^2 + b^3$;
$(a-b)(a^2 - 2ab + b^2) = a^3 - 3a^2b + 3ab^2 - b^3$

3-69 $9a^6 = (3a^3)^2$ and $25b^8 = (5b^4)^2$; $9a^6 - 25b^8 = (3a^3 - 5b^4)(3a^3 + 5b^4)$

3-70   (1) $a+4$ (2) $a-5$ (3) $7a-4$ (4) $6a^2 - b^3$

3-71   (1) $5, 1$ or $1, 5$ (2) $7, 6$ or $6, 7$ (3) $18, 3$ (4) $14x, 5$

3-72 $-9, (x-10)(x+1); 9, (x-1)(x+10); 3, (x-2)(x+5); -3, (x+2)(x-5)$

3-73   The length and width of the first rectangle are $(2x-1)$ and $(3x-2)$. Its perimeter is $10x-6$. The length and width of the other rectangle are $(5x+4)$ and $(x-1)$. Its perimeter is $12x+6$. The perimeter of the first rectangle is $2x+12$ less than the perimeter of the second rectangle.

3-74   (1) $(2-y)$ (2) $(1-a)$ (3) $(2-x), (-x+2), (2-x)$ (4) $(4y-1)$, $(4y-1), (4y-1)$

3-75   (1) $V = m^3 - 27$ (2) $B = z+1; h = z^2 - z + 1$ or $B = z^2 - z + 1; h = z + 1$
(3) $B = 2x - y; h = 4x^2 + 2xy + y^2$ or $B = 4x^2 + 2xy + y^2; h = 2x-y$

3-76   The equation and the vertex are provided for each problem.
(1) $y + 3 = (x-2)^2; (2, -3)$ (2) $y - 2.75 = (x-0.5)^2; (0.5, 2.75)$
(3) $y + 5 = (x+2)^2; (-2, -5)$

3-77   Term A is in sequences 1, 2, and 3. Term B is in sequences 1 and 2. Term C is in sequence 2. Term D is in sequences 1 and 3. Term E is in sequences 2 and 3.

3-78   (1) 165   (2) -15 (3) 1,023   (4) $18\dfrac{1}{3}$

3-79   Let $S_n = a_1 + ra_1 + r^2 a_1 + r^3 a_1 + \ldots + r^{n-1} a_1$. Then
$rS_n = ra_1 + r^2 a_1 + r^3 a_1 + \ldots + r^{n-1} a_1 + r^n a_1$. Next subtract:
$S_n - rS_n = a_1 - r^n a_1$, which implies $S_n = \dfrac{a_1(1-r^n)}{1-r}$. $S_{30} = \$1{,}073{,}741{,}823$

3-80   Explanations will vary. A possible explanation is that Roxanne knows the remainder theorem and the factor theorem and applied them correctly. Her error was in the division. Since $(x-5)$ is a factor of the polynomial, the remainder is 0, not 70, and $P(5) = 0$, which is consistent with the factor theorem.

3-81   (1) $-1, 1$ (2) 0   (3) $2, 3, -1$

3-82   Explanations will vary. Students should note that the coefficient of the term of the highest degree of the polynomial is positive. Therefore, the graph will rise on the left. Ella could also select a test point such as $(-2, -8)$ to determine that the graph will rise on the left.

3-83   Answers will vary. An example follows. $5^2 = 25, 12 + 13 = 25$, and the Pythagorean triple is 5, 12, 13. $5^2 + 12^2 = 13^2$.

3-84 $(x+y)^0 = 1; (x+y)^1 = x + y; (x+y)^2 = x^2 + 2xy + y^2$;
$(x+y)^3 = x^3 + 3x^2 y + 3xy^2 + y^3$
$(x+y)^n = \binom{n}{0} x^n + \binom{n}{1} x^{n-1} y + \binom{n}{2} x^{n-2} y^2 + \ldots + \binom{n}{n-1} xy^{n-1} + \binom{n}{n} y^n$

Note $\binom{n}{0} = 1$

$(x + y)^8 = x^8 + 8x^7y + 28x^6y^2 + 56x^5y^3 + 70x^4y^4 + 56x^3y^5 + 28x^2y^6 + 8xy^7 + y^8$

3-85   Answers will vary but should note that the numerator and denominator of a rational expression are polynomials. To rewrite a rational expression, divide the numerator by the denominator, which is the same as dividing polynomials. The division algorithm states: divide, multiply, subtract, compare, and bring down the next term. These steps should be repeated until there are no terms to bring down. If there is a remainder, the remainder should be written over the divisor.

3-86   (1) $x - 1 - \dfrac{1}{x + 4}$ (2) $x + 2 - \dfrac{18}{x + 3}$ (3) $2x + 5 + \dfrac{50}{x - 5}$
(4) $x + 2 - \dfrac{8}{2x - 1}$

3-87   1 and 4 are correct.   (2) $x - 7 + \dfrac{35}{x + 7}$ (3) $2(x^2 - x + 1) - \dfrac{1}{x + 1}$

3-88   (1) $\dfrac{x + 2}{x - 4}$ (2) $\dfrac{x - 5}{x - 3}$ (3) $\dfrac{2x + 1}{x + 2}$ (4) $\dfrac{x - 2}{x - 1}$

3-89   1 and 3 have the same answer; $x + 2$.   (2) $\dfrac{x - 1}{x + 3}$

3-90   Answers will vary. Students may explain to Noah how to factor the numerator of his answer by grouping, which is much more complicated than simply factoring $x^2 - 25$ in the original problem. The simplest way to solve the problem is to factor $x^2 - 25$ as $(x - 5)(x + 5)$. The correct answer is $\dfrac{(x - 1)(x - 5)}{x + 1}$ or $\dfrac{x^2 - 6x + 5}{x + 1}$.

3-91   3 and 4 are correct.   (1) $\dfrac{2x + 4}{x + 4}$ is the correct sum. $x + x$ was added incorrectly.   (2) $\dfrac{-2}{x + 2}$ is the correct difference. The quantity $(x + 3)$ was not subtracted.

3-92   (1) D   (2) B   (3) A and C

3-93   (1) Correct.   (2) Logan did not find the common denominator. The correct answer is $\dfrac{2x^2 + 2x + 3}{(x + 2)(x - 2)(x + 1)}$.   (3) Correct.

3-94   Audrey does not understand what a rational expression is. 1 is a rational expression. Problems will vary. Examples of correct problems include $\dfrac{5x + 1}{2x - 1} - \dfrac{3x + 2}{2x - 1} = 1$, $\dfrac{x - 3}{x + 3} \cdot \dfrac{x + 3}{x - 3} = 1$, and $\dfrac{x + 3}{x + 1} \div \dfrac{x + 3}{x + 1} = 1$.

3-95   (1) Distributive property   (2) Addition property of equality
(3) Division property of equality

3-96   Anthony is correct, but he could have solved the problem more efficiently. For example, he might have combined $\dfrac{1}{2}x$ and x on the left side of the equation and the numbers $8 - 1$ on the right to save a few steps.

3-97   Answers will vary. A possible answer is that Jodi did not multiply both sides of the equation by $5(x + 4)$. If she did, she would have found $x + 4 + 15 = 5x + 20$. The solution is $x = -\dfrac{1}{4}$, which checks when it is substituted into the original equation.

3-98   (1) $x = -1$ (2) No solution   (3) No solution

3-99   4 is incorrect. $\sqrt{54} = 3\sqrt{6}$

3-100 Explanations will vary but should note that numbers such as $\sqrt{-1}$, $\sqrt{-4}$, and $\sqrt{-9}$ will result in an error message, because the square root of a negative number is an imaginary number.

3-101 Answers will vary. A possible explanation follows. The grade of 60% was based on deducting 20 points for problem 2, and 10 points each for problems 3 and 4.

1 and 5 are correct.   (2) Incorrect, $\dfrac{\sqrt{15}}{4}$ (3) Partial credit, $\dfrac{9\sqrt{2}}{4}$

(4) Partial credit, $4\sqrt{3}$.

3-102 (1) $2\sqrt{17}$ (2) $3\sqrt{3}$ (3) $\sqrt{2}$ (4) $-47\sqrt{3}$

3-103 Explanations will vary, but should note that in both cases, the first term of the product is the square of the first terms in the binomial. The last term of the product is the square of the last terms in the binomial. The middle terms of the product are opposites, and their sum is zero. For example, $(2 + \sqrt{3})(2 - \sqrt{3}) = 4 - 2\sqrt{3} + 2\sqrt{3} - 3$. $(2 + 3)(2 - 3) = 4 - 6 + 6 - 9$

3-104 (1) A   (2) C   (3) D   (4) B

3-105 (1) $x = 39$ (2) $x = 0$ (3) $x = 49$

3-106 Explanations will vary. A possible explanation is that by isolating $\sqrt{3x}$, Jayden may have realized $\sqrt{3x} = -3$, which has no real solution. If he was to solve that equation by squaring both sides, he would find that $3x = 9$ or $x = 3$, which is an extraneous solution.

3-107 (1) Circumference of a circle; $r = \dfrac{C}{2\pi}$ (2) Volume of a cone or pyramid;

$h = \dfrac{3V}{B}$ (3) Converting from degrees Fahrenheit to degrees Celsius;

$F = \dfrac{9}{5}C + 32$ (4) Perimeter of a rectangle; $l = \dfrac{1}{2}P - w$

3-108 (1) $x = \dfrac{27}{A}, A \neq 0$ (2) $x = \dfrac{20}{B}, B \neq 0$ (3) $x = -\dfrac{5}{7C}, C \neq 0$

(4) $x = \dfrac{-2}{45 - D}, D \neq 45$

3-109 (1) $>, >, >$ (2) $<, <, >$ (3) $\geq, \geq, \leq$

3-110 In each case, the square of half of the coefficient of x and the perfect squares are equal.

3-111 (1) $18, -12$ (2) $12, 2$ (3) $3 + 5\sqrt{2}, 3 - 5\sqrt{2}$ (4) $3, 1$
(5) $11, 5$ (6) $4 + 7\sqrt{2}, 4 - 7\sqrt{2}$

3-112 (1) $1; 1 + \sqrt{21}, 1 - \sqrt{21}$ (2) $4; 2 + \sqrt{7},\ 2 - \sqrt{7}$ (3) $9;$
$-3 + 3\sqrt{2}, -3 - 3\sqrt{2}$

3-113 E, F, B, G, D, A, and C is the correct order.

3-114 2 and 4 are correct.   (1) $c = -4$ (3) $b = -7, c = 4$

3-115 (1) B   (2) D   (3) A   (4) C

3-116 Explanations will vary. Students should note that the only way the product of two or more numbers is zero is if at least one of the factors is zero. For example, $0 \cdot 8 = 0$ and $0 \cdot 0 = 0$. Another example includes the product of two binomials. $(x + 3)(x - 2) = 0$ implies $x + 3 = 0$ or $x - 2 = 0$ or both $x + 3$ and $x - 2$ are equal to zero.

3-117 2 and 4 are partially correct. (2) $x = 9, x = 4$ (4) $m = 0, m = 2, m = -2$

3-118 (1) $x = 7, x = -7$ (2) $x = \sqrt{7}, x = -\sqrt{7}$ (3) No real roots
(4) $x = 5, x = -5$

3-119 The sums of roots equal $\dfrac{-b}{a}$. The products of roots equal $\dfrac{c}{a}$.

3-120 Equations will vary and may include the following. (1) $x^2 + 1 = 0; x = i$ and $x = -i$ (2) $x^2 - 2x + 1 = 0; x = 1$ (3) $x^2 - 2x - 3 = 0; x = 3$ and $x = -1$

3-121 $x = -2, y = -1$ Answers will vary. A possible answer is that when these values are substituted into the original equation, both equations are true.

3-122 (1) $x = 1, y = 5; x = 0, y = 4$ (2) $x = \dfrac{1 + \sqrt{17}}{2} \approx 2.6, y \approx 6.6;$

$x = \dfrac{1 - \sqrt{17}}{2} \approx -1.6, y \approx 2.4$

3-123 (1) $\begin{bmatrix} 3 & -2 \\ 2 & 1 \end{bmatrix} \begin{bmatrix} x \\ y \end{bmatrix} = \begin{bmatrix} -9 \\ 8 \end{bmatrix}$ (2) $\begin{bmatrix} 1 & 1 \\ 2 & -5 \end{bmatrix} \begin{bmatrix} x \\ y \end{bmatrix} = \begin{bmatrix} 3 \\ -22 \end{bmatrix}$

(3) $\begin{bmatrix} 1 & -1 \\ 2 & -1 \end{bmatrix} \begin{bmatrix} x \\ y \end{bmatrix} = \begin{bmatrix} 4 \\ 12 \end{bmatrix}$

3-124

$A^{-1} = \dfrac{1}{19} \begin{bmatrix} 3 & 4 \\ -1 & 5 \end{bmatrix} = \begin{bmatrix} \frac{3}{19} & \frac{4}{19} \\ \frac{-1}{19} & \frac{5}{19} \end{bmatrix}; \begin{bmatrix} \frac{3}{19} & \frac{4}{19} \\ \frac{-1}{19} & \frac{5}{19} \end{bmatrix} \begin{bmatrix} 23 \\ -3 \end{bmatrix} = \begin{bmatrix} \frac{57}{19} \\ \frac{-38}{19} \end{bmatrix} = \begin{bmatrix} x \\ y \end{bmatrix};$

$x = \dfrac{57}{19} = 3; y = \dfrac{-38}{19} = -2$

3-125

$A^{-1} = \begin{bmatrix} 4 & -5 & 3 \\ 0 & 2 & 1 \\ 3 & -4 & 2 \end{bmatrix}; A^{-1} \begin{bmatrix} 29 \\ 11 \\ -20 \end{bmatrix} = \begin{bmatrix} x \\ y \\ z \end{bmatrix}$ The solution is $x = 1, y = 2$, and $z = 3$, which may have been what Luis meant by 1, 2, 3.

3-126 $(-2, -6)$ is not a solution to the equation. $(-2, -8)$ is a solution and it should have been on the graph Matt sketched.

3-127 (1) $(-4, 4)$ (2) $(0, -1)$ (3) $(0, 1)$ (4) $(0, 1)$

3-128 Inequalities will vary. A possible answer is $y > -2x + 9$ and $y < 5x + 0.5$.

3-129 (1) $(9 + 2x)(9 + 2x) < 100; x < 0.5$ The frame must be less than 0.5 inch on each side. (2) $x + \$376 = \$1,534; x = \$1,158$
(3) $x = \$500(1.04)^{10}; x \approx \$740.12$ (4) $86 \cdot 3 + 100n = 93(n + 3); n = 3$

3-130 Equations will vary. Possible equations include $x + y = -1, 2x - y = 10$, and $x - y = 7$. Graphs will vary, but all lines should contain the point $(3, -4)$.

3-131 Sam is correct. Answers will vary but note that the lengths of sides are always positive numbers. Because he used a quadratic equation, he found two solutions. But only one solution, $x = 2$, applies to the context of the problem.

3-132 Explanations will vary. A possible answer is that a basic understanding of algebra enables a person to solve complex mathematical and real-world problems.

Section 4: Functions

4-1   Explanations will vary. A possible explanation is that "exactly one" means that every member of the domain is paired with a member of the range, and every member of the domain is paired with only one member of the range. *Exactly* means "one and only one." The values in the following table represent a function.

Domain	1	2	3
Range	3	4	3

The values in the following table do not represent a function because 1 is paired with 1 and 3.

Domain	1	2	1
Range	1	4	3

4-2   Both graphs have the same y-intercept but different slopes.

4-3   The rates of change are arranged in ascending order:

(3) -1 (1) 1   (4) 1.5   (2) 2

4-4   1 and 3 represent linear functions. Explanations will vary. A possible explanation is that the rate of change in each of these functions is constant. 2 and 4 are not linear because the graphs of each of these functions are not a line.

4-5   1 and 4 represent linear functions.   (1) $y = 0.75x$ where x is the original cost of the item and y is the sale price.   (4) $y = 7x$ where x is the number of child tickets and y is the total cost.

4-6   It is true that $f(0) = 0$, but in the context of this problem, the domain (the values of x) must be larger than 0. Courtney is correct.

4-7   (1) C and E   (2) E   (3) B, C, D   (4) A

4-8   (1)   (2)

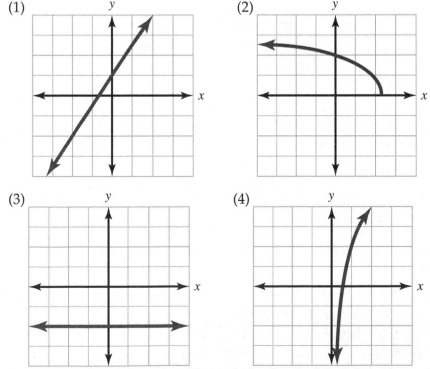

(3)   (4)

4-9   Answers will vary but should conclude that Andrew does not understand the concept of a function. Considering the points $(0, 0)$, $(1, 2)$, and $(3, 2)$, every element of the domain is paired with exactly one element of the range. It is not relevant that an element of the range is paired with two different elements of the domain.

4-10   (1) 9   (2) $\dfrac{1}{4}$ (3) 36   (4) 0.01

4-11   The next four terms in the Fibonacci sequence are 13, 21, 34, and 55. The next four terms in the Lucas sequence are 18, 29, 47, and 76. The sequences are similar in that the nth term in both sequences is found by adding the two terms preceding it. The sequences differ in their initial term.

4-12   The vertex is (5, 25), which means that when the length of a side is 5, the rectangle has a maximum area of 25. The axis of symmetry is $x = 5$. The domain is $0 < x < 10$, which means that the length of a side must be between 0 and 10. The x-intercepts are (0, 0) and (10, 0). The function is increasing in $(-\infty, 5)$ and the function is decreasing in $(5, \infty)$.

4-13   (1) $0 < x \le 10$ (2) All real numbers   (3) $s > 0$ (4) All real numbers

4-14   Because the information on this website is updated regularly, answers will vary.

4-15   (1) A, C, F   (2) B, D, E, G   (3) B, D

4-16

Cost of the Order	Shipping Cost
$0–$25	$7.00
$25.01–$50.00	$9.00
$50.01–$75.00	$11.00
$75.01–$100	$13.00
Over $100	$15.00

4-17   The zeros, axis of symmetry, and extreme values are listed in order.
(1) $(-3, 0), (1, 0), x = -1, (-1, -4)$ (2) $(17, 0), (-1, 0), x = 8, (8, -81)$
(3) $(3, 0), (4, 0), x = 3.5, (3.5, 1.25)$

4-18 $f(t) = \left(\dfrac{1}{2}\right)^t = \dfrac{1^t}{2^t} = \dfrac{1}{2^t} = 2^{-t}$ The function represents exponential decay.

4-19   Number 3 has the largest minimum. Number 4 has the smallest minimum. The minimums of the functions follow.   (1) $(0, 0)$ (2) $(0, -3)$ (3) $(0, 1)$
(4) $(2, -4)$

4-20 $T(x) = \$2.49x; P(x) = 50x; \left(\dfrac{T}{P}\right)(x) = \$0.0498$ This quotient represents the cost of one piece of candy.

4-21   1, 3, 6, 10, 15, 21, 28, 36, 45, 55; $f(1) = 1; f(n) = f(n-1) + n; f(n) = \dfrac{n^2 + n}{2};$
$f(100) = 5{,}005$

4-22   The graphs in 1–4 have the same size and shape as the graph of $f(x) = x^2$.
(1) The graph is translated up 3 units.
(2) The graph is translated down 3 units.
(3) The graph is translated 3 units to the right.
(4) The graph is translated 3 units to the left.
The graphs in 5–7 have the same shape (a "u") as the graph of $f(x) = x^2$.
(5) The graph is a vertical stretch of the graph of $f(x) = x^2$.

(6) The graph is a vertical stretch of $f(x) = x^2$ and is reflected in the x-axis.

(7) The graph is a vertical compression of the graph of $f(x) = x^2$.

4-23 Explanations will vary. A possible explanation follows: $f(x) = (2x)^2$ and $f(x) = (-2x)^2$ are even functions because $f(x) = (-2x)^2 = (2x)^2$. Therefore, the graphs coincide. $f(x) = (2x)^3$ and $f(x) = (-2x)^3$ are odd functions. Because $f(2x)^3 \neq f(-2x)^3$, the graphs are different.

4-24 $f^{-1}(x) = \dfrac{x - \$767}{\$87}$;

x	$767	$854	$941	$1,028	$1,115	$1,202	$1,289	$1,376
$f^{-1}(x)$	0	1	2	3	4	5	6	7

$f^{-1}(x)$ can be used to find the number of solar lights, given the total cost.

4-25 (1) C (2) B (3) D (4) E (5) A

4-26 (1) D; $x = 8$ (2) F; $b = 3$ (3) E; $y = -6$ (4) A; $x = 9$
(5) B; $b = 9$ (6) C; $y = -3$

4-27 Explanations will vary. A possible explanation is that had Jamie provided more values in the table, such as $f(3) = 6, g(3) = 8, f(4) = 8$, and $g(4) = 16$, she would have realized the functions are different. $f(x)$ is a linear function, $f(x + 1) = f(x) + 2$. $g(x)$ is an exponential function, $g(x + 1) = 2g(x)$.

4-28 (1) $f(x) = x + 3$ (2) $f(x) = 2^x$ (3) $f(x) = 5(2^x)$ (4) $f(x) = 5^x$ where $x \geq 0$ (5) $f(x) = 5x$ where $x \geq 0$

4-29 Explanations will vary, depending on the equations students entered. Exponential functions define quantities that will exceed the quantities defined by linear and polynomial functions.

4-30 (1) 5 (2) $\ln 5$ (3) $\ln 5$ (4) $\dfrac{\ln 5}{2}$ (5) 0.805

4-31 $P = \$10,000, r = 0.05$ or 5%, $n = 4$, and $t = 10$ years. $10,000 was invested for 10 years at an interest rate of 5%, compounded quarterly.

4-32 Explanations will vary but should note that if the measure of the central angle is 1 rad, the ratio of the arc length to the radius is 1.

4-33 Explanations will vary. Students should note that angles of different measures may have the same terminal side. These angles are called coterminal angles. To find coterminal angles, add integral multiples of 360 to the measure of the given angle. The trigonometric functions of an angle have the same values as the trigonometric functions of its coterminal angles.

4-34 $\sin \dfrac{\pi}{6} = \dfrac{1}{2}; \cos \dfrac{\pi}{6} = \dfrac{\sqrt{3}}{2}; \tan \dfrac{\pi}{6} = \dfrac{1}{\sqrt{3}} = \dfrac{\sqrt{3}}{3}; \sin \dfrac{\pi}{4} = \dfrac{1}{\sqrt{2}} = \dfrac{\sqrt{2}}{2};$

$\cos \dfrac{\pi}{4} = \dfrac{1}{\sqrt{2}} = \dfrac{\sqrt{2}}{2}; \tan \dfrac{\pi}{4} = 1; \sin \dfrac{\pi}{3} = \dfrac{\sqrt{3}}{2}; \cos \dfrac{\pi}{3} = \dfrac{1}{2}; \tan \dfrac{\pi}{3} = \sqrt{3}$

4-35 Explanations will vary. Possible answers follow.
(1) The cosine is even because the graph is symmetric to the y-axis.
(2) The sine and tangent are odd because their graphs are symmetric to the origin.
(3) The period of the sine and cosine is 2π. The period of the tangent is π.

4-36 (1) The graph represents the height of a seat from the ground during one counterclockwise rotation. (2) 4.5 meters (3) 2 meters

4-37   The domain must be restricted so that each function is one-to-one. The domain of the sine function is restricted to $\left[-\dfrac{\pi}{2}, \dfrac{\pi}{2}\right]$, the domain of the cosine function is restricted to $[0, \pi]$, and the domain of the tangent function is restricted to $\left(-\dfrac{\pi}{2}, \dfrac{\pi}{2}\right)$.

4-38 $\tan\theta = \dfrac{10}{30}; \theta \approx 18.4°$

4-39   Explanations will vary. A possible answer should note that since the unit circle is centered at the origin, both h and k equal 0. Because the radius of the unit circle is 1, the equation of the unit circle is $x^2 + y^2 = 1$. Because $\sin\theta$ and $\cos\theta$ are the y- and x-coordinates of a point on the unit circle, it follows by substitution that $(\cos\theta)^2 + (\sin\theta)^2 = 1$, which is the same as $\sin^2\theta + \cos^2\theta = 1$.

4-40   (1) D   (2) C   (3) B   (4) A

4-41   Explanations will vary but students should note that functions may be used to model a variety of real-world situations.

Section 5: Geometry

5-1   (1) Line segment, $\overline{CD}$, 2   (2) Line, $\overleftrightarrow{XY}$, 0   (3) Ray, $\overrightarrow{EF}$, 1
(4) Ray, $\overrightarrow{NM}$, 1

5-2   (1) $\overline{CB}$ (2) C   (3) Ø   (4) $\overleftrightarrow{AD}$ (5) $\overrightarrow{BD}$ (6) $\overline{AD}$

5-3   (1) $\angle DBC$ or $\angle DBE$ (2) $\overline{AE}$ (3) $\overrightarrow{AE}$ (4) $\overline{AE}$ (5) $\angle ABD$ or $\angle DBA$ (6) $\overleftrightarrow{AE}$

5-4   (1) $\angle ABC$, $\angle B$ (2) $\angle 1$ (3) $\angle b$ (4) $\angle BCA$, $\angle ACB$

5-5   (1) Acute   (2) Acute, right, or obtuse, depending on the angles
(3) Right   (4) Straight   (5) Obtuse   (6) Straight   (7) Obtuse
(8) Right

5-6   (1) Complementary, 15° and 75°; supplementary, 115° and 65°
(2) Complementary, 40° and 50°; supplementary, 60° and 120°
(3) Complementary, 70° and 20°; supplementary, 100° and 80°
(4) Complementary, 1° and 89°; supplementary, 90° and 90°

5-7   (1) Adjacent   (2) Adjacent, complementary
(3) Adjacent, supplementary   (4) Adjacent, supplementary
(5) Adjacent, supplementary   (6) Vertical.

5-8

5-9 $m\angle 1 = 95°$, $m\angle 2 = 85°$, $m\angle 3 = 85°$, $m\angle 4 = 95°$, $m\angle 6 = 85°$, $m\angle 7 = 85°$, $m\angle 8 = 95°$; $m\angle 1 = (180 - x)°$, $m\angle 3 = x°$, $m\angle 4 = (180 - x°)$, $m\angle 5 = (180 - x)°$, $m\angle 6 = x°$, $m\angle 7 = x°$, $m\angle 8 = (180 - x)°$

5-10   (1) The sum of $\angle 1$ and $\angle 2$; $\angle 3$; the sum of $\angle 4$ and $\angle 5$; $\angle 6$
(2) $m\angle 1 + m\angle 2 = 90°$ (3) $m\angle 1 + m\angle 2 + m\angle 6 = 180°$
(4) $m\angle 2 = 60°$; $m\angle 4 = 30°$

5-11   Students' sketches of polygons will vary; however, each polygon must have the required number of sides. When compared, sketches are likely to be different because a polygon is defined by the number of its sides, not its shape.

5-12   Quadrilateral, or more specifically a trapezoid; 8 units

5-13

The numbers in each row follow: $0, 2, 5, 9, \dfrac{n^2 - 3n}{2}$

5-14   Triangle, 3, 180°; quadrilateral, 4, 360°; pentagon, 5, 540°; hexagon, 6, 720°; heptagon, 7, 900°; octagon, 8, 1080°

5-15   (1) 3   (2) 6   (3) 4   (4) 7   (5) 8   (6) 5

5-16   Heptagon; $51\dfrac{3}{7}°$

5-17   Quadrilateral, 4, 90°, 360°; pentagon, 5, 72°, 360°; hexagon, 6, 60°, 360°; octagon, 8, 45°, 360°; decagon, 10, 36°, 360°; n-gon, n, $\dfrac{360}{n}°$, 360°. The sum of the measures of the exterior angles is equal to 360°.

5-18   (1) Equilateral   (2) Isosceles   (3) Isosceles   (4) Scalene

5-19   (1) Obtuse   (2) Equiangular   (3) Right   (4) Obtuse   (5) Right   (6) Acute

5-20   (1) False; $\angle E$ is included between $\overline{EF}$ and $\overline{ED}$.   (2) True   (3) True
(4) False; $\overline{AC}$ is included between $\angle A$ and $\angle C$.

5-21   (1) Longest side, $\overline{AC}$; shortest side, $\overline{BC}$ (2) Longest side, $\overline{FD}$; shortest side, $\overline{EF}$ (3) Longest side, $\overline{HG}$; shortest side, $\overline{HI}$

5-22 $m\angle 1 = 110°$; $m\angle 2 = 30°$; $m\angle 3 = 45°$; $m\angle 4 = 45°$; $m\angle 5 = 45°$; $m\angle 6 = 45°$; $m\angle 7 = 90°$; $m\angle 8 = 120°$; $m\angle 9 = 60°$; $m\angle 10 = 60°$

5-23   The second and fourth diagrams could be triangles. First diagram—the longest side should be between 9 and 13. Third diagram—the longest side should be less than 6.

5-24   (1) Three triangles—right isosceles, acute isosceles, obtuse isosceles
(2) One—obtuse isosceles   (3) Impossible   (4) One—acute isosceles
(5) One—obtuse scalene

5-25   (1) 5   (2) 15   (3) 13   (4) 17

5-26   Student explanations of the proof will vary but should support the essence of the proof that in a right triangle the square of the hypotenuse is equal to the sum of the squares of the legs.

5-27   (1) $\sqrt{13}$ (2) $2\sqrt{6}$ (3) $5\sqrt{3}$ (4) $2\sqrt{11}$

5-28   She is correct. She could have drawn another right triangle with the vertex $(-2, 1)$. Since this triangle is congruent to the first triangle, the length of the hypotenuse is also $\sqrt{34}$.

5-29   (1) Acute   (2) Acute   (3) Obtuse   (4) Obtuse

5-30   (1) $4\sqrt{2}$ (2) $2\sqrt{3}$ (3) 2   (4) 14

5-31   (1) B   (2) A   (3) F   (4) E

5-32   (1) 20   (2) 14   (3) 10   (4) 18   (5) 16   (6) 20

5-33   (1) 7.5, $7.5\sqrt{3}$ (2) 5, $5\sqrt{3}$ (3) 3, $3\sqrt{3}$ (4) 10, $10\sqrt{3}$

5-34   (1) $BC = 12\sqrt{2}, AC = 24$ (2) $DF = 24\sqrt{3}, EF = 36$ (3) $GH = 22$, $HI = 11$ (4) $JK = 1, KL = \sqrt{2}$

5-35   Explanations will vary but should note that accurate copying and pasting of rotations (turning), reflections (flipping), and translations (gliding) of figures does not affect the size or shape of the figures. Jamal's strategy is good.

5-36   (1) Reflection or translation (2) Rotation (3) Translation

5-37   Triangles 1, 3, and 4 are congruent. Triangles 2 and 6 are congruent.

5-38   (1) 4   (2) 2   (3) 3   (4) 5   (5) 5   (6) 1

5-39   (1) Perpendicular lines (2) Angle (3) Line segment (4) Circle (5) Parallel lines

5-40   (1) $A(2,7), B(2,1), C(-3,5)$; translation—two units up
(2) $A(-5,2), B(1,2), C(-3,-3)$; rotation—$90°$ counterclockwise about the origin
(3) $A(2,-5), B(2,1), C(-3,-3)$; reflection in the x-axis.
(4) $A(-2,-5), B(-2,1), C(3,-3)$; $180°$ rotation about the origin

5-41   Explanations will vary but should include that Andrew is correct when k is greater than 1. But if k is between 0 and 1, the polygons are smaller and similar to the original.

5-42   Agree. For example, an equilateral triangle has three lines of symmetry. A reflection in each will carry the triangle onto itself. A rotation of $120°$, which is $\dfrac{360°}{3}$ about the intersection of the three lines of symmetry, will also carry the triangle onto itself.

5-43   Answers will vary. A possible answer follows. For example, when $\overline{AB}$ is rotated $90°$ counterclockwise about the origin, the congruent segment has coordinates $(-1, 1)$ and $(-5, 3)$. When $\overline{AB}$ is reflected in the y-axis, the congruent line segment has coordinates $(1, 1)$ and $(-3, 5)$. When $\overline{AB}$ is translated 2 units down, the congruent line segment has coordinates $(-1, -1)$ and $(3, 3)$.

5-44 $1, 3, 2$

5-45   Molly translated vertex B incorrectly. B' should be $(2, 2)$. Then $\triangle A'B'C' \cong \triangle ABC$.

5-46 $\triangle ABC \cong \triangle FED$; $\angle A \cong \angle F, \angle B \cong \angle E, \angle C \cong \angle D$; $\overline{AB} \cong \overline{EF}, \overline{BC} \cong \overline{ED}, \overline{AC} \cong \overline{FD}$

5-47   (1) $\overline{ED}$ (2) $\overline{DC}$ (3) $\angle E$ (4) $\angle CDF$

5-48 $\triangle ABC \cong \triangle JLK, SSS$; $\triangle DEF \cong \triangle GIH, ASA$; $\triangle MQN \cong \triangle OQP, SAS$

5-49   It could be but it does not have to be.

5-50   (1) Definition of vertical angles.   (2) $\angle x$ and $\angle y$ form a linear pair and are supplementary.   (3) $\angle x$ and $\angle z$ form a linear pair and are supplementary.
(4) Substitution.   (5) Subtraction property of equality.   (6) Angles that have the same measure are congruent.

5-51   Explanations will vary but should note that Vinnie should construct $\overline{BD}$ to bisect $\angle B$.

$\overline{AB} \cong \overline{BC}$ (given); $\angle ABD \cong \angle CBD$ (definition of angle bisector); $\overline{BD} \cong \overline{BD}$ (reflexive property); $\triangle ABD \cong \triangle CBD$ (SAS); $\angle A \cong \angle C$ (corresponding parts of congruent triangles are congruent).

5-52   Explanations will vary but should note that Sasha must show $\overline{AE} \cong \overline{CE}$ and $\overline{DE} \cong \overline{BE}$. The proof follows. $\overline{AD}\|\overline{BC}$ (definition of a parallelogram). $\overline{AD} \cong \overline{CB}$ (opposite sides of a parallelogram are congruent). $\angle DAC \cong \angle BCA$ (alternate interior angles are congruent). $\angle AED \cong \angle CEB$ (vertical angles are congruent). $\triangle AED \cong \triangle CEB$ (AAS). $\overline{AE} \cong \overline{CE}$ and $\overline{DE} \cong \overline{BE}$ (corresponding parts of congruent triangles are congruent).

5-53   The radius or the lengths of the arcs were not long enough.

5-54   Following is an example of students' construction.

5-55   Rotation of $180°$ about the origin (2) Reflection in the x-axis (3) Translation of 3 units up, 1 unit right (4) Dilation of 2 with respect to the origin

5-56   1 and 4

5-57   Thomas is correct if the scale factor is a positive number. The length of the image is the product of the length of the preimage and the absolute value of the scale factor. The length of $\overline{C'D'}$ is $2CD$.

5-58   Explanations will vary. A possible explanation is that Michele realized that $\triangle DEF$ is the triangle that is formed when $\triangle ABC$ is dilated by a scale factor of 2 with respect to the origin. She knows that a dilation produces a similar figure.

5-59   Marcus is correct. Explanations will vary but should note that if two pairs of corresponding angles are congruent, the other pairs of angles are congruent and the triangles are similar.

5-60   (1) No similarity   (2) SAS   (3) AA   (4) SSS

5-61   (1) $\triangle ABC \sim \triangle EDF$, $2:3$.   (2) Several statements are possible. One is $\triangle GHI \sim \triangle JKL$, $5:3$.   (3) $\triangle MNO \sim \triangle RQP$, $1:1$ or $\triangle MNO \cong \triangle RQP$. (4) $\triangle STU \sim \triangle WXV$, $\sqrt{3}:3$.

5-62   She is correct to this point. The missing steps follow: $AD + DC = AC$, $BE + EC = BC$ (definition of between); $\dfrac{AD + DC}{DC} = \dfrac{BE + EC}{EC}$ (substitution); $\dfrac{AD + DC}{DC} = \dfrac{AD}{DC}$ and $\dfrac{BE + EC}{EC} = \dfrac{BE}{EC}$ (property of proportion); $\dfrac{AD}{DC} = \dfrac{BE}{EC}$ (substitution)

5-63   (1) $\dfrac{6}{15} = \dfrac{8}{y} = \dfrac{10}{x}$; $x = 25$; $y = 20$ (2) $\dfrac{3.5}{7} = \dfrac{1}{x} = \dfrac{y}{8}$; $x = 2$; $y = 4$
(3) $\dfrac{15}{10} = \dfrac{x}{12} = \dfrac{20}{y}$; $x = 18$; $y = 13\dfrac{1}{3}$

5-64 (1) 20 feet long by 16 feet wide   (2) 320 square feet   (3) 5 inches long by 4 inches wide   (4) 20 feet long by 16 feet wide   (5) They are the same.

5-65 30 square centimeters; 30 square centimeters; the area of each triangle is $\frac{1}{2}$ the area of the rectangle.

5-66 (1) 22.5 square inches (2) 20 square inches (3) 4 square inches (4) 600 square millimeters

5-67 The areas are the same. Explanations may vary. One is that the triangles have the same base and altitude.

5-68 Yes, the ratios are the same. Because corresponding sides of similar triangles are proportional and the $\sin\theta$, $\cos\theta$, and $\tan\theta$ are ratios, they are not affected by the length of the sides.

5-69 Eva selected $\angle A$ to write the ratio, and Chelsea selected $\angle B$ to write the ratio. Since $\angle A$ and $\angle B$ are complementary angles, $\sin\angle A = \cos\angle B$.

5-70 (1) About 32 feet   (2) About 43 feet (the third side is about 18 feet)

5-71 (1) $\sin C = \dfrac{b}{h}$ (2) $h = b\sin C$ (3) $h = \dfrac{2A}{a}$ (4) $A = \dfrac{1}{2}ab\sin C$

5-72 Natalie must write $\dfrac{1}{2}bc\sin A = \dfrac{1}{2}ac\sin B = \dfrac{1}{2}ab\sin C$ and multiply by $\dfrac{2}{abc}$ to

obtain $\dfrac{\sin A}{a} = \dfrac{\sin B}{b} = \dfrac{\sin C}{c}$.

5-73 170 feet

5-74 1.7 miles

5-75 (1) Parallelogram, rectangle; (2) Parallelogram, rhombus; (3) Trapezoid; (4) Parallelogram, rectangle, square, rhombus; (5) Parallelogram; (6) Trapezoid

5-76 (1) True.   (2) True.   (3) False; parallelograms that are rectangles have four right angles.   (4) False; no trapezoids are parallelograms. (5) True.   (6) False; rectangles that are squares have four congruent sides.

5-77 Explanations will vary but should note that the quadrilateral is a rectangle because it has four right angles.

5-78 Yes, a parallelogram is a kite if the parallelogram is a rhombus. No, a kite could be a parallelogram if all sides are congruent.

5-79 (1) All   (2) All   (3) All   (4) Square, rectangle   (5) Square, rhombus

5-80 (1) All   (2) Square, rectangle   (3) Square, rhombus   (4) Square, rhombus

5-81 (1) $y = 3x + 5$ (2) $y = -\dfrac{1}{3}x + \dfrac{5}{3}$ (3) $y = 3x$ (4) $y = -\dfrac{1}{3}x + \dfrac{5}{3}$

5-82 $(2, 1)$; $(4, 0)$

5-83 25 square centimeters

5-84 Statement 4 is false. The ratio of the area of a square to its perimeter is greater than or equal to 1 if the length of the side is greater than or equal to 4.

5-85 The area of bills printed prior to 1929 was about 23 square inches. The area of bills in circulation today is about 16 square inches. The area of the larger bills is about 1.4 times the area of the bills in circulation today.

5-86 10 squares

5-87   Celeste is correct. She realized that $\overline{BE}$ divides rectangle $ACDF$ in half. Because $\overline{BE}$ is a diagonal, it divides rectangle $ABEF$ in half. If the area of $\triangle ABF$ is 20 square centimeters, the area of $\triangle BEF$ must also be 20 square centimeters. Together the triangles make up half of the area of rectangle $ACDF$; therefore, the area of rectangle $ACDF$ is 80 square centimeters.

5-88   Smallest perimeter is 14 inches (a 3-inch × 4-inch rectangle). Largest perimeter is 26 inches (a 1-inch × 12-inch rectangle).

5-89   Peter could fold the paper along the diagonal and cut a $\frac{1}{2}$ inch by 12 inch rectangle on each side of the fold. The remaining area is 81.5 square inches.

5-90   Area of living room and kitchen, 525 square feet; area of family room, 300 square feet; area of deck, 144 square feet; total area, 969 square feet

5-91   Explanations will vary. A possible answer is that the height of a parallelogram is the perpendicular distance from a vertex to the base. In a rectangle, the height (or width) is perpendicular to the base. In both cases, the area is found by multiplying a perpendicular distance by the base.

5-92   Trapezoids 1, 2, and 5, 45 square units; trapezoids 4 and 6, 75 square units; trapezoid 3, 175 square units

5-93   The triangle has the largest perimeter ($P \approx 18.0$ units), followed by the rectangle ($P \approx 17.9$ units), followed by the pentagon ($P \approx 15.7$ units). The pentagon has the largest area ($A = 16$ square units), followed by the triangle and rectangle ($A = 15$ square units).

5-94   Answers will vary but may include recycling codes, peace sign, and various logos such as Mercedes Benz, Starbucks Coffee, General Electric, and Dell Computer. Explanations will vary but might note that circles imply infinity because a circle has no beginning or end.

5-95   10 units; 5 units. $\overline{AC}$ and $\overline{OB}$ are diagonals of rectangle $OABC$. Since the diagonals of a rectangle are congruent, $OB = 5$. $\overline{OB}$ is also a radius of the circle. Since the diameter of a circle is twice its radius, the diameter is 10 units.

5-96   (1) 62.8 inches (2) 47.1 inches (3) 56.52 millimeters (4) 6.28 centimeters

5-97   Explanations will vary. A possible answer is that the diameter of the rim is 18 inches and the diameter of a basketball is about 9.6 inches. This allows a skillful player to shoot the ball through the rim.

5-98   About 2,826 square miles; fog, mist, obstructions

5-99   The area of the smaller circle is about $\frac{1}{25}$ the area of the whole target.

5-100   The circle has the larger area. The area of the circle is about 78.5 square inches. The area of the square equals 61.6225 square inches.

5-101   Explanations will vary but should note that every circle can be dilated with respect to the center, producing a circle that is larger than the original circle if the scale factor is greater than 1, and producing a smaller circle if the scale factor is between 0 and 1.

5-102   Minor arcs: AB, AC, AD, AH, AG, AF, BC, BD, BE, BH, BG, CD, CE, CF, CH, DE, DF, DG, EF, EG, EH, FG, FH, GH. Semicircles: AE, BF, CG, DH. Major arcs: ABF, ABG, ABH, BCG, BCH, BCA, CDH, CDA, CDB, DEA, DEB, DEC, EFB, EFC, EFD, FGC, FGD, FGE, GHD, GHE, GHF, HAE, HAF, HAG.

5-103 $\angle AOD \cong \angle BOC$; $\angle DOC \cong \angle AOB$; $\angle ABD \cong \angle BAC \cong \angle ACD \cong \angle BDC$; $m\angle AOD = 60°$; $m\angle AOB = 120°$; $m\angle ABD = 30°$

5-104 $\triangle ABC$ is equilateral because $\angle C \cong \angle BAC \cong \angle ABC$. $\triangle AOB$ is isosceles because $m\angle AOB = 120°$ and $\overline{OA} \cong \overline{OB}$. (The radii of a circle are congruent.)

5-105 Diameter: $\overline{CD}$; radii: $\overline{OE}, \overline{OD}, \overline{OC}$; chords: $\overline{AB}, \overline{CD}, \overline{BE}$; secant: $\overleftrightarrow{BE}$; tangent $\overleftrightarrow{AF}$

5-106 (1) 180   (2) 200   (3) 100   (4) 120   (5) 80   (6) 60

5-107 For problems 1 and 3, the measure of the intercepted arc is $210°$. For problem 2, if the measure of one arc is $50°$, the measure of the other arc is $310°$. $\frac{1}{2}(310 - 50) \neq 80$.

5-108 No. Explanations will vary. A possible explanation is that a may equal d, but the quantities do not have to be equal. For example, if $a = 3, b = 6, d = 3$, and $c = 2$, then $ab = cd$ but $a \neq d$.

5-109 Explanations will vary. A possible explanation is that both cases involve finding the product of the secant and the segment of the secant that is outside the circle. In the case of the tangent segment, the square of the tangent segment is found.

5-110 (1) Definition of inscribed quadrilateral   (2) Definition of inscribed angles
(3) The measure of an inscribed angle is half its intercepted arc
(4) Multiplication property of equality and commutative property
(5) A circle contains $360°$ (6) Substitution   (7) Multiplication property of equality   (8) Definition of supplementary angles

5-111 The following is an example of students' constructions.

5-112 Explanations will vary but should note that because the arc lengths are different, they give the impression that they are from different circles. However, they are from the same circle.

5-113 The area of $\frac{1}{8}$ of the pizza is about 14.1 square inches. The area of $\frac{1}{6}$ of the pizza is about 18.8 square inches. The area of $\frac{1}{8}$ of the pizza is $\frac{3}{4}$ the area of $\frac{1}{6}$ of the pizza.

5-114 x represents the measure of the central angle (or the measure of the intercepted arc). Since there are $360°$ in a circle, $\frac{x}{360}$ represents the part of the circle that is in the sector. When the area of the circle is multiplied by $\frac{x}{360}$, the area of the sector is found.

5-115 The coordinates of the right angle are (x, k). The length of the legs are $(x - h)$ and $(y - k)$. Substituting these values into the Pythagorean theorem gives $(x - h)^2 + (y - k)^2 = c^2$. Since the radius of the circle is the hypotenuse of the triangle, $(x - h)^2 + (y - k)^2 = r^2$ by substitution.

5-116 The key steps are as follows: $PF = PD$; therefore $\sqrt{(x - 4)^2 + (y + 1)^2} = \sqrt{(x - x)^2 + (y + 3)^2}$. Squaring both sides shows that $(x - 4)^2 + (y + 1)^2 = (y - 3)^2$. Simplify this expression to find $(x - 4)^2 = -8(y - 1)$, and therefore $y - 1 = -\frac{1}{8}(x - 4)^2$, which is the equation of the parabola.

5-117 $a^2 = 25, b^2 = 16$

5-118 The following figures can be formed by slicing a cube: nonequilateral triangle, equilateral triangle, pentagon, square, hexagon, nonrectangular parallelogram, rectangle.

5-119 (1) Sphere   (2) Cone   (3) Cylinder   (4) None of the above
(5) None of the above   (6) Sphere   (7) Cylinder   (8) Cone

5-120 Answers will vary. Some objects include: coins (cylinders), basketball (spheres), bowl (hemisphere), garbage can (cylinder), ice cube (cube or rectangular prism).

5-121 (1) 7,776 cubic inches or 4.5 cubic feet   (2) 34.375 cubic feet
(3) 13,680 cubic meters   (4) 4.6875 cubic feet

5-122 Pete's reasoning is correct, but he forgot to multiply the number of cubes by the volume of each cube. $2,184 \times 0.125 = 273$ cubic inches, which is the same volume as given by the volume formula.

5-123 72 square units

5-124 The surface area of each box is 321 square inches. Because there are six boxes, Cheralyn will need 1,926 square inches. The total area of wrapping paper is 2,016 square inches. She has enough paper, but she will have to cut the paper carefully with very little waste.

5-125 18 square inches

5-126 $V = 91,636,272$ cubic feet; $SA = 1,496,880$ square feet

5-127 The dish with the 5-inch diameter. The volume of the dish with the 4-inch diameter is about 21 cubic inches. The volume of the dish with the 5-inch diameter is about 26 cubic inches.

5-128 The volume of the basketball is about 448.7 cubic inches. The volume of the soccer ball is about 371.1 cubic inches.

5-129 Students should agree. The volume of the cone is equal to the volume of the sphere if the height of the cone is $4r$, where r equals the radius of the cone and sphere.

5-130 The base of the parallelogram is $\frac{1}{2}C$ or $\frac{1}{2}(\pi 2r)$ or πr. The height of the parallelogram is the radius of the circle. Substituting these values into the formula for finding the area of a parallelogram, $A = bh$, gives $A = \pi r \cdot r$ or $A = \pi r^2$.

5-131 To apply the Pythagorean theorem, consider the sketch.

The area of the cross-section is πx^2 and by the Pythagorean theorem $x^2 = r^2 - y^2$. Therefore, the area of the cross-section is $\pi(r^2 - y^2)$.

5-132 New York City is more densely populated, with about 27,012 people per square mile. Tokyo's population density is about 15,456 people per square mile.

5-133 Answers will vary. A possible explanation is that the surface area of a cylinder that contains three tennis balls is less than the surface area of a rectangular prism that will contain three tennis balls.

5-134 Answers will vary. A possible answer is that geometric shapes and figures are found throughout nature and the human-made world. To Plato, an understanding of geometry was fundamental to learning. Student opinions will vary.

Section 6: Statistics, Probability, and Data Analysis

6-1 Questions will vary. Note that a statistical question anticipates a variety of answers, and a nonstatistical question has only one correct answer. An example of a statistical question: What is your favorite flavor of ice cream? An example of a nonstatistical question: What is the height of the tallest player on the school's basketball team?

6-2 Answers will vary, but note that there was no variability in the response, which means that the question was a nonstatistical question. If he had asked, "What did you spend for lunch the last time you went to a restaurant?" he probably would have received different responses. The different responses would have an average, range, and the graph would have a shape.

6-3 (1) 6   (2) 7

6-4 About $48.40

6-5 The letter T appears 8 times.

6-6 If there is an even number of data, then the data may not contain the median. For example, for $\{1, 3, 5, 10, 11, 15\}$, the median is 7.5.

6-7 1 has one factor; 4, 9, and 25 each have three factors; 16 has five factors. The median and mode each equal 3.

6-8 Mean = 120.9; median = 118; mode = 118

6-9 Answers will vary. A possible answer is that Carlo used a measure of center, the mode, while his mother used a measure of variation. The measure of variation that shows a range of prices indicates that the phone may in fact be affordable. Carlo might be able to purchase a low-end smart phone.

6-10
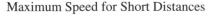
Rotation Rates of Planets

Rotation Rate	Tally	Frequency
9–23.9 hours	|||||	5
1–10 days			1
More than 10 days	||	2

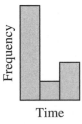

6-11
Maximum Speed for Short Distances

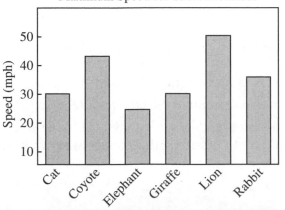

6-12

```
0 | 3
1 | 0   4
2 | 0   9
```

6-13

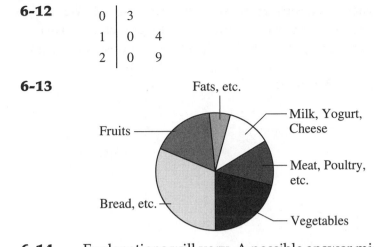

Fats, etc.

Milk, Yogurt, Cheese

Fruits

Meat, Poultry, etc.

Bread, etc.

Vegetables

6-14   Explanations will vary. A possible answer might be that Caitlyn's score is in the 80–84 range where most other students scored, so there is no need for concern. Another possible answer might be that because only a quarter of the class scored below her, there is a need for concern. In either case, Caitlyn should review her test and work harder.

6-15   Students should disagree. It is unlikely that Anthony found a sample that is representative of the population of vehicles that people in his town drove. For example, people who have children and drop their children off at school are more likely than the general population to be driving minivans or SUVs.

6-16   Students should agree. Answers will vary but should note that since printers' type was used to set the type on newspapers, books, magazines, and so on, it provided an excellent sample on which Morse could base his code.

6-17   The mean of the weights of the females is 62.5 pounds, and the absolute mean deviation is 1.1. The mean of the weights of the males is 73, and the absolute mean deviation is 1.6.

6-18   Explanations will vary but should note that jeans are less expensive at the outlet. Prices range from $89.99 to $29.99 at the store at the mall, compared to $49.99 to $9.99 at the outlet. The mode is $39.99 at the store, compared to $29.99 at the outlet.

6-19   No. Examples will vary. Three events that have a probability of 0: a one-year-old child will enroll in high school this year, a month will have 32 days, and time will stop. Three events that have a probability of 1: somewhere in the universe, a new star will form; under ordinary conditions, water will freeze at temperatures below 32°F; and green plants require light for photosynthesis.

6-20   (1) $\frac{8}{31}$ (2) $\frac{1}{31}$ (3) $\frac{11}{31}$ (4) $\frac{2}{31}$ (5) $\frac{4}{31}$ (6) $\frac{5}{31}$

6-21 $\frac{20}{200}$ or $\frac{1}{10}$ of the seventh-grade students won a prize at the dance. Based on the probability, $\frac{1}{10}$ of 20, 2 students would be expected to win a prize in Kirk's class. Explanations will vary. A possible explanation is that the students in Kirk's class who won were lucky because they beat the odds.

6-22 $0.50 off next purchase, 1,000; free soft drink, 200; free sandwich, 100; "sorry, try again," 700

6-23   Probability models will vary. A possible response is that the director could assign a random number to the name of each student of the glee club and ask a student to select a number ranging from 1 to 32. The student whose number was picked would sing the national anthem. The probability that Miguel Sanchez would be selected is 1 out of 32.

6-24

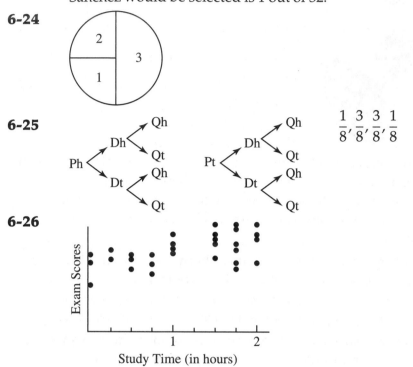

6-25 $\dfrac{1}{8}, \dfrac{3}{8}, \dfrac{3}{8}, \dfrac{1}{8}$

6-26

According to these data, there is no correlation between the amount of time students studied and their exam grades.

6-27   (1) B   (2) A   (3) C   Scatter plots B and C suggest a linear association.

6-28   (1) Positive   (2) Negative   (3) Positive   (4) Positive
(5) Positive   (6) No relationship

6-29   Explanations will vary. A possible response: The y-intercept is 40, which is the predicted temperature when no crickets chirp. The slope is 1, which means that each cricket chirp within a period of 14 seconds represents an increase of 1 degree Fahrenheit.

6-30   No, because 8 of 25 students own both smart phones and a laptop.

6-31   Note that the first quartile is $16.86, the second quartile (which is also the median) is $21.73, and the third quartile is $32.06.

6-32   The median selling price in Harmony Village is $317,500. The median selling price in Valley Town is $417,500. Answers will vary. Some answers include the following. The selling prices in Harmony Village range from $200,000 to $600,000. Selling prices in Valley Town range from $299,000 to $650,000.

6-33   Without the quiz grade of 40, the median is 90, the first quartile is 85, the third quartile is 94, and his average is 90. Answers about dropping the 40 will vary. Students might contend that the grade should not be dropped because it would be unfair to drop a grade for one student and not everyone else. Or they might contend that because the grade of 40 is obviously not indicative of James's general work, it should be dropped. Others might note that dropping the grade will depend on the teacher's (or school's) policy toward grades.

6-34 The mean is 46.5 and the standard deviation is about 12.7. $6.5 + 12.7 = 59.2$; $46.5 - 12.7 = 33.8$ Five running times $(45, 45, 40, 55,$ and $40)$ are within the range from 32.8 to 59.2.

6-35 Chloe is correct. She used the column frequency $\dfrac{60}{175} \approx \dfrac{1}{3}$ for the first statistic. She used the row frequency $\dfrac{60}{90} = \dfrac{2}{3}$ for the second statistic.

6-36 The relationship is a linear function. $f(x) = 2.3x - 16.8$, where x is the number attending and y is the amount collected for the raffle.

6-37 Explanations will vary. A possible explanation follows. The slope is -2, which means that for each $6.00 ticket that is sold, there are two fewer $3.00 tickets that are sold. The y-intercept is 210, which means that if no $6.00 tickets are sold, 210 $3.00 tickets are sold.

6-38 If r is close to 1, there is a strong positive correlation. Leon should have noticed that since r is close to -1, there is a strong negative correlation.

6-39 Students should disagree. Explanations will vary but should note that although exercise and weight loss are related, exercise is not necessarily a cause of weight loss. Exercise increases the likelihood of losing weight, but to say that exercise causes weight loss, students must show that exercising will always produce weight loss. For example, many people who exercise regularly do not lose weight. Many of these people have probably reached their ideal weights. For them, exercise and caloric intake are in balance.

6-40 Explanations will vary but should note that the most valid polls are based on truly random samples. For example, this poll should not be conducted only in areas that are known to have a specific population, including general political leanings, incomes, or age. (You can conduct a so-called random sample in a specific population, but in this case, your results will be skewed toward the general views of the population.) Likewise, the poll should not be conducted at times that might distort results.

6-41 Yes, the program is fair. Explanations will vary. A possible explanation is that if n students have handed their work in on time, Molly's chance of winning each week is 1 out of n. Since her friends each won twice, Molly can conclude that they are lucky.

6-42 (1) Observational study   (2) Sample survey   (3) Experimental study
(4) Statistical experiment

6-43 Carl's conclusions are not entirely valid. Explanations will vary but should note that while his sample survey can be used to estimate that Serena will win the election with a greater proportion of the student vote than Jacob (55% to 45%), his method of arriving at the margin of error is invalid. To calculate margin of error, Carl would need to know the population size, sample size, and standard deviation. Although he knew the population (100 students) and sample size (20 students), he did not know the standard deviation, which is the percentage of time respondents' answers were evenly split. Simply dividing assumed uncast votes between candidates does not result in the correct margin of error.

6-44 Steps E and D are out of order. The correct order is A, B, C, E, D, F, G.

6-45 Student answers will vary but should note that the report is probably accurate. The term "student–faculty ratio" is likely causing the confusion. The student–faculty ratio is found by dividing the total number of students by the total number of teachers in a school, which includes many teachers who typically teach small groups of students, for example, special education teachers, speech teachers, and other specialists.

6-46 (1) $(2,5),(2,7),(3,5),(3,7)$ (2) $(2,4),(2,6)$ (3) $(1,7),(2,6),(2,7),(3,5),$ $(3,6),(3,7)$ (4) $(1,4),(1,6),(2,5),(2,7),(3,4),(3,6)$

6-47 (1) $\dfrac{2}{9}$ (2) $\dfrac{1}{3}$ 3) $\dfrac{1}{18}$ (4) 0

6-48 Spinner A contains a scalene right triangle, an acute isosceles triangle, and an equilateral triangle. Spinner B contains a trapezoid that has no congruent sides, a rectangle, a square, and a rhombus.

6-49 $P(A|B) = \dfrac{1}{6}; P(A \text{ and } B) = \dfrac{1}{12}; P(B) = \dfrac{1}{2}; \dfrac{\frac{1}{6}}{\frac{1}{2}} = \dfrac{\frac{1}{12}}{\frac{1}{2}}$

6-50 (1) 50   (2) $\dfrac{7}{13}$ (3) $\dfrac{1}{4}$ (4) $\dfrac{1}{5}$

6-51 Explanations will vary but should note that an individual's chances of developing heart disease increase if he consumes a diet high in saturated fats. This is an example of conditional probability. In this case, event B (developing heart disease) occurs given that event A (consuming a diet high in saturated fats) has already occurred. However, if a person has heart disease, it does not necessarily follow that his chances for consuming a diet high in saturated fat increase. In this case, the events are independent of each other. (In fact, many people who are aware that they have heart disease reduce their consumption of foods high in saturated fat on the advice of their doctors.)

6-52 Paulo is correct. Explanations will vary but should note that $P(\text{heart}|\text{red}) = \dfrac{1}{2}$. The fraction of red cards that are also hearts is $\dfrac{13}{26} = \dfrac{1}{2}$.

6-53 $P(\text{ace or diamond}) = P(\text{ace}) + P(\text{diamond}) - P(\text{ace and diamond})$
$= \dfrac{4}{52} + \dfrac{13}{52} - \dfrac{1}{52} = \dfrac{16}{52} = \dfrac{4}{13}$

6-54 12.5%

6-55 21! or more than 5.1×10^{19} ways

6-56 (1) 6,720   (2) 504   (3) 604,800

6-57 (1) 20   (2) 58,905   (3) 792

6-58 The second column of the table is $\dfrac{1}{9}, \dfrac{2}{9}, \dfrac{1}{3}, \dfrac{2}{9}, \dfrac{1}{9}$.

6-59 151

6-60 Joshua's example is valid. His probabilities, random variables, and expected values are all correct.

6-61

x	Yes	No	Not Sure
$p(x)$	0.33	0.53	0.14

The question regarding smart phone ownership for the current year cannot be answered because the survey was taken in 2012, and more people have smart phones today. The number is impossible to determine based on the 2012 survey.

6-62   Answers will vary. Students may or may not agree with Deena, but they should note points such as the following. Although the cost of the policy is rather high, the policy protects against major flood damage. Based on the fact that there has been no major flood in the area for 50 years, with the prior major flood having occurred in 1915, a person could say that the probability of a major flood occurring in the area is about once every 50 years or so. Since the last major flood occurred 50 years ago, a major flood in the area may be likely. Although Deena's grandfather is correct in saying that he will save at least $20,000 in premiums over the next 10 years if he cancels his policy, a major flood is likely to cause more than $20,000 in damages. Also, it is unlikely that he will in fact save his premiums for a catastrophe that may not happen. (Although his intentions are to save, he would likely find it difficult to save for a flood he is sure will not occur.)

6-63   Answers will vary. Explanations might note that it seems unfair that students whose numbers are generated multiple times may then pick friends to go on the trip. Because the probabilities of having your number selected changes after every time another student's number is generated, it is not necessarily unfair to run the random number generator more than 48 times in the case of multiple numbers being selected. For example, prior to any numbers being generated, the probability of being selected for the trip is $\frac{48}{94}$ or $\frac{24}{47}$ or about 51%. After a student is selected, the probability of being selected changes. For example, after 20 students have been selected, the probability for being selected is $\frac{28}{74}$ or $\frac{14}{37}$ or about 38%.

6-64   Answers will vary but note the following. For the Panthers, kicking the extra point is likely to be successful, and the game will be tied. Should the Panthers' defense hold the Lions, the game will go into overtime with each team having an equal chance of victory. At 45%, the chances for making a two-point conversion are less than 50–50. Failure to convert would likely ensure the loss. Assuming that the Panthers either tie the game or go ahead, the Lions will receive the following kickoff. Assuming that they receive the ball at their 10-yard line and run it back 25 yards to their own 35-yard line, they will need to move the ball 45 yards to the Panthers' 20-yard line to give their field goal kicker a 50% chance of kicking a winning field goal. They will have 120 seconds to move the ball that far. If it takes them about 22 seconds to huddle and run a play, they can expect to run 5 plays. Based on their average of 4 yards per play from scrimmage, they will likely move the ball only 20 yards or so. They will need to rush their offense or gain more than their average yardage. Even if they get to the Panthers' 20-yard line, their kicker has a 50–50 chance of making the winning kick. It would seem that the probabilities favor Coach Smith's choosing to kick the extra point and try to win in overtime because the Lions are unlikely to score in the final two minutes, but the Panthers' failure to make the two-point conversion will surely result in a loss.

6-65   Explanations will vary. A possible explanation is that some people accept statistics without considering how those statistics were generated. For example, some statistics may be presented out of context. In such cases, the data may lead to faulty conclusions because the individual did not take the time to educate himself or herself about the topic addressed by the data.

Section 7: Number and Quantity

7-1 $9^{\frac{1}{2}} = \left(\sqrt[2]{9}\right)^{1}$ and $\sqrt[2]{9^{1}}$

7-2 (1) $\dfrac{1}{4}$ (2) 2   (3) $\dfrac{1}{4}$ (4) 8   (5) $\dfrac{1}{5}$ (6) 2

1 and 3 are equivalent.

2 and 6 are equivalent.

7-3 Explanations will vary. One explanation is that if you are adding a fraction with a number that cannot be expressed as a fraction, it is impossible that the sum can be expressed as a fraction. If you think of multiplication as repeated addition, it follows from the explanation above that the product of a nonzero rational number and an irrational number is irrational.

7-4 A joule is a unit of energy that is equal to $\dfrac{1kg \cdot m^2}{sec^2}$.

7-5 Answers will vary. A possible explanation is that Maria would need a cylindrical container to catch the falling rain. She would also need a measuring tool, for example, a centimeter ruler, to measure the amount of rain that falls during a specific period of time.

7-6 Answers will vary. A possible answer is that Roland's brother would point out that using a yardstick to measure the dimensions of the flowerbed is likely to yield inaccurate measurements. Even though the measurements might be accurate to within an inch or less, they would still be inaccurate. Also, the longer the distance that is measured with the yardstick, the greater the inaccuracy is likely to be.

7-7 (1) $3i\sqrt{2}$ (2) $-3i$ (3) -9 (4) -7

7-8 $1, -1, i, -i$

7-9 (1) $(1 - 2i) + (3 + 4i)$ (2) $(5 + 6i) - (3 + 4i)$ (3) $(3 + 4i)(1 - 2i)$
(4) $(5 + 2i)(1 - 2i)$

7-10 (1) $\dfrac{15 + 8i}{17}$ (2) $\dfrac{9 - 20i}{13}$ (3) $\dfrac{19 + 2i}{5}$

7-11 Radical sign

7-12 (1) $3 - 2i, (3, -2)$ (2) $-2 - i, (-2, -1)$ (3) $-1 - 4i, (-1, -4)$
(4) $2 - i, (2, -1)$

7-13 Melanie is correct. Caryn should have found
$|1 + 4i - 9 - 10i| = |-8 - 6i| = \sqrt{64 + 36} = \sqrt{100} = 10$

7-14 (1) Two imaginary roots, $x = \dfrac{7 \pm i\sqrt{11}}{6}$ (2) Two real roots, $x = \dfrac{3 \pm \sqrt{13}}{2}$
(3) Two imaginary roots, $x = 2 \pm i$

7-15 $x^2 + 16 = (x + 4i)(x - 4i); (x + 4i)(x - 4i) = x^2 - 4ix + 4ix - 16i^2 = x^2 - 16i^2$
Since $i^2 = -1, x^2 - 16i^2 = x^2 + 16.$

7-16 Fernando is correct. Explanations will vary. A possible explanation is that the quadratic formula can be used to find the solutions to quadratic equations of the form $ax^2 + bx + c = 0$. Because $x = \dfrac{-b \pm \sqrt{b^2 - 4ac}}{2a}$, there are two solutions: $\dfrac{-b + \sqrt{b^2 - 4ac}}{2a}$ and $\dfrac{-b - \sqrt{b^2 - 4ac}}{2a}$. If $\sqrt{b^2 - 4ac} > 0$, there are two real roots. If $\sqrt{b^2 - 4ac} < 0$, there are two complex roots. If $\sqrt{b^2 - 4ac} = 0$, there is a double root.

7-17 (1) $5\sqrt{2}$ (2) $5\sqrt{2}$ (3) The vectors have the same magnitude but opposite directions.

7-18 (1) $(4, 4)$ (2) $(4, 4)$ (3) $(-6, 6)$ (4) $(-4, 4)$

7-19 About 166 mph; about $157.5°$

7-20 The two vectors are perpendicular vectors, which are also called orthogonal vectors.

7-21 Students should agree. Explanations will vary but should note that when the absolute value of a scalar is larger than 1, the length of the vector increases. This is similar to a vertical stretch of a function. When the absolute value of the scalar is between 0 and 1, the length of the vector decreases, which is similar to a vertical compression of a function. If the scalar is a negative number, the direction of the vector is reversed, which is similar to a reflection of a function.

7-22 $\begin{bmatrix} 18 & 12 & 20 \\ 18 & 18 & 12 \\ 10 & 20 & 18 \end{bmatrix}$ Rows 1, 2, and 3 represent team 1, team 2, and team 3, respectively. Columns 1, 2, and 3 represent the obstacle course, the relay race, and the bean bag toss, respectively.

7-23 (1) $\begin{bmatrix} 153 & 216 & 144 & 225 \\ 192 & 213 & 186 & 150 \end{bmatrix}$ (2) $\begin{bmatrix} 224 & 317 & 211 & 330 \\ 282 & 312 & 273 & 220 \end{bmatrix}$

7-24 (1) $x = 3, y = 7, z = 9$ (2) $x = 11, y = -4, z = -1$ (3) $x = 2, y = 6, z = 8$

7-25 (1) $\begin{bmatrix} 12 & 16 & 9 \end{bmatrix}$ (2) $\begin{bmatrix} 1 & 9 \\ 24 & -8 \end{bmatrix}$ (3) The matrices cannot be multiplied. (4) $\begin{bmatrix} 6 & -3 \\ -3 & 5 \end{bmatrix}$

7-26 Answers will vary. A possible answer is that Tony showed that corresponding elements in the product of $(AB)C$ and $A(BC)$ have the same value. To prove the distributive property, he would use the three matrices $A, B,$ and C and show $A\begin{bmatrix} e+i & f+g \\ g+k & h+i \end{bmatrix} = AB + BC$.

7-27 Explanations will vary but should note the following major points. The sum of any matrix and the zero matrix is equal to the original matrix. The sum of a matrix and its opposite is equal to the zero matrix. The product of any matrix and the identity matrix is equal to the original matrix. The product of any matrix and its inverse is equal to the identity matrix.

7-28 $(-2, 6)$ and $(-1, 9)$

7-29 $(3, -5), (2, -8),$ and $(0, -5)$

7-30 $\begin{bmatrix} 3 & 0 \\ 0 & 3 \end{bmatrix}$ It is 9 times larger.

7-31 $\frac{1}{2}\begin{vmatrix} 2 & -1 \\ 5 & 2 \end{vmatrix} = \frac{1}{2} \cdot 9 = 4.5$

7-32   Answers will vary. A possible answer is that understanding and applying mathematics is not limited to any country, culture, or ethnicity.

Section 8: Potpourri

8-1   Answers will vary. Other than 13 and 31: 11, 17, 37, 71, 73, 79, and 97.

8-2   (3) 41   (4) 50

8-3   (2) 28

8-4   48 is the number. $1 + 2 + 3 + 4 + 6 + 8 + 12 + 16 + 24 = 76$

8-5   28 is perfect. 20, 24, and 30 are abundant. The others are deficient.

8-6   2,000 strides. It is inaccurate because strides vary.

8-7   His arm is 23 feet. His leg is 15 feet. His ear is 1 foot. The distance around his chest is 60 feet. His nose is 2 feet. His height is 50 feet.

8-8   The compsognathus is 60 centimeters in length. The brachiosaur is 2,600 centimeters in length. The brachiosaur is about 43 times as long as the compsognathus.

8-9   About 210 feet by 410 feet

8-10   16 digits

8-11   10 feet

8-12   Explanations will vary. A possible answer is that if a person does not try to do the best she can, she will never know how well she could have done.

8-13   1 pound; 1.25 pounds; 1 pound 5 ounces; 1.5 pounds; 32 ounces; 200 pounds; 0.75 tons; 30,000 ounces; 2,000 pounds

8-14   About 3,100 kilograms

8-15   1, 2, 3, 4, 5, 6, 7, 8 (in grams)

8-16   3 quarts; 7.5%

8-17   (1) 0.0036 kiloliters   (2) 0.00013 liters   (3) 0.4 kiloliters
(4) 23,000 milliliters   (5) 0.006 liters   (6) 7,300,000 milliliters

8-18   16 hours, 21 minutes

8-19   Explanations will vary. A possible answer is that in real life, Sam would probably not be able to keep up a consistent pace for the 6.5 laps.

8-20   The letter *m*

8-21   B, E, A, C, D, F, G

8-22   (1) 104°F   (2) 80°C   (3) 12.2°F   (4) about 0.6°C

8-23   About 4.253 light-years

8-24   Explanations will vary. A possible explanation is that there are 3,600 seconds in an hour, which is 10 times the number of degrees in a circle.

8-25   The missing number in each row follows: row 1: 6, row 2: 8, row 3: 8, row 4: 30, row 5: 12.

8-26   Total is 204. 64 1×1 squares; 49 2×2 squares; 36 3×3 squares; 25 4×4 squares; 16 5×5 squares; 9 6×6 squares; 4 7×7 squares; 1 8×8 square

8-27   36

$1 \times 1, 1 \times 2, 1 \times 3, 1 \times 4, 1 \times 5, 1 \times 6, 1 \times 7, 1 \times 8$

$2 \times 2, 2 \times 3, 2 \times 4, 2 \times 5, 2 \times 6, 2 \times 7, 2 \times 8$

$3 \times 3, 3 \times 4, 3 \times 5, 3 \times 6, 3 \times 7, 3 \times 8$

$4 \times 4, 4 \times 5, 4 \times 6, 4 \times 7, 4 \times 8$

$5 \times 5, 5 \times 6, 5 \times 7, 5 \times 8$

$6 \times 6, 6 \times 7, 6 \times 8$

$7 \times 7, 7 \times 8$

8×8

8-28   400 square feet

8-29   4,840 square yards

8-30   39.69 square units

8-31   About 78.57 square inches; about 78.5 square inches. Explanations will vary but should note that the formula $A = \pi r^2$ uses π, which has an approximate value.

8-32   Examples will vary. Example: $11 + 22 = 33$; $33 - 22 = 11$. No. $313 + 404 = 717$. The sum of these two palindromes is a palindrome, but $404 - 313 = 91$ is not.

8-33   Answers will vary. Examples: $11 \times 44 = 484$; $11 \times 22 = 242$; $22 \times 22 = 484$; $33 \times 121 = 3,993$; $11 \times 424 = 4,664$

8-34   Answers will vary. One solution is $O = 2$, $N = 1$, $E = 6$, $T = 4$, and $W = 3$.

8-35   "Two is the only even prime."

8-36   Messages will vary.

8-37   "One is a perfect square."

8-38   Problems will vary.

8-39   Explanations will vary but should note that the infinity sign was mistaken for the number 8 turned on its side.

8-40   (1)   (2)   (3)   (4)

8-41   1,024

8-42   81

8-43   100; perfect squares

8-44   (1) Odd   (2) Odd   (3) First, second, odd   (4) The seventh square number is 49, and it is the sum of the first, second, third, fourth, fifth, sixth, and seventh odd number.

8-45   Sketches will vary. Note that sketches should have at least two rows and two columns.

8-46   There are four ways: $2 \times 9, 9 \times 2, 3 \times 6, 6 \times 3$. Yes. Prime numbers are not rectangular.

8-47   (1) 32, 64, 128; multiply by 2   (2) 36, 49, 64; perfect squares
(3) 6.25, 3.125, 1.5625; divide by 2   (4) 8, 7, 10; subtract 1, then add 3

8-48   Patterns will vary.

8-49   I, E, Y, M, and T. Examples will vary and may include mom, 11, and 88.

8-50

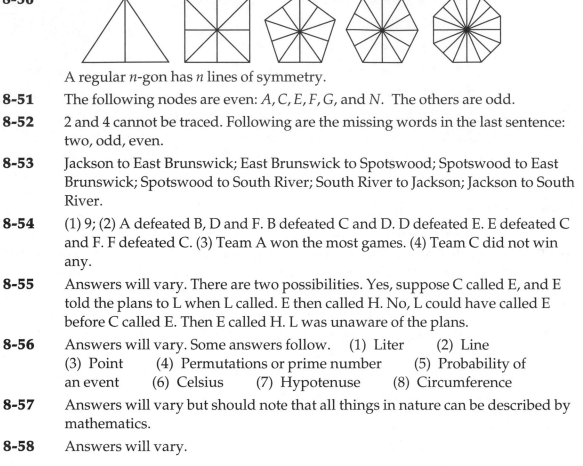

A regular *n*-gon has *n* lines of symmetry.

8-51   The following nodes are even: A, C, E, F, G, and N. The others are odd.

8-52   2 and 4 cannot be traced. Following are the missing words in the last sentence: two, odd, even.

8-53   Jackson to East Brunswick; East Brunswick to Spotswood; Spotswood to East Brunswick; Spotswood to South River; South River to Jackson; Jackson to South River.

8-54   (1) 9; (2) A defeated B, D and F. B defeated C and D. D defeated E. E defeated C and F. F defeated C. (3) Team A won the most games. (4) Team C did not win any.

8-55   Answers will vary. There are two possibilities. Yes, suppose C called E, and E told the plans to L when L called. E then called H. No, L could have called E before C called E. Then E called H. L was unaware of the plans.

8-56   Answers will vary. Some answers follow.   (1) Liter   (2) Line
(3) Point   (4) Permutations or prime number   (5) Probability of an event   (6) Celsius   (7) Hypotenuse   (8) Circumference

8-57   Answers will vary but should note that all things in nature can be described by mathematics.

8-58   Answers will vary.

Jossey-Bass Teacher

Jossey-Bass Teacher provides educators with practical knowledge and tools to create a positive and lifelong impact on student learning. We offer classroom-tested and research-based teaching resources for a variety of grade levels and subject areas. Whether you are an aspiring, new, or veteran teacher, we want to help you make every teaching day your best.

From ready-to-use classroom activities to the latest teaching framework, our value-packed books provide insightful, practical, and comprehensive materials on the topics that matter most to K–12 teachers. We hope to become your trusted source for the best ideas from the most experienced and respected experts in the field.

For more information about our resources, authors, and events please visit us at: www.josseybasseducation.com.

You may also find us on Facebook, Twitter, and Pinterest.

Jossey-Bass K-12 Education

jbeducation

Pinterest jbeducation